The Longest Trail

Roni McFadden

THE BISCUIT PRESS

The Longest Trail

A True Story

Copyright © 2012, 2015 by Roni McFadden

The Longest Trail is a work of creative non-fiction. The Author has taken the liberty of changing the names of some of the people, places, and incidents to protect the privacy of those who may have been involved.

No part of this book may be reproduced or transmitted in any form or by any means without the written permission of the author, except where permitted by law.

All Rights Reserved.

Contents

Dedication

First and foremost, this book is dedicated to John Slaughter. None of this would have happened to me if he had not taken me under his wing, and then when the time was right, set me free.

To my husband, John, who has always let me be myself and never tried to change me.

And, to my children: Randi, Jaime, Shane, and Corey, and my step-daughter Kim. I hope by reading this book they understand my trials, triumphs, lessons learned, and how I lived before I was their Mother.

"A horse is the projection of people's dreams about themselves – strong, powerful, beautiful – and it has the capability of giving us escape from our mundane existence" -Pam Brown

Prologue

I am not a ghost. But I'm sitting here on this rock looking down on a desert *filled* with many of them.

The corrals and bunkhouse were over to the right, along the edge of the small canyon coming down from the rough-n-tumble hills dotted with sagebrush, all climbing to meet the steeper tree-covered peaks of the Eastern Sierra. Across the road was the cabin where meals were prepared and served before we all headed out to saddle up, pack up, and head up that long steep winding trail to the high country.

Now, thirty years later, I've returned, hungry for those adventurous days of my youth. But all that remains is an old, cracked concrete pad where the cabin sat, and one very scraggly old juniper tree. It's the only tree for miles and appears to stand as a sentinel guarding this almost sacred place. Nature, seeing that the land was no longer being used or abused, simply reclaimed it.

I can barely make out where the corrals were. Nothing is left but the memories of all those who lived and worked here, and visions of the horses, the very core of my existence.

What brings me back here to this dry, hot, and sometimes miserable place after so many years away?

I think it's the spirits of those ancient people who lived here before me. *They* are the real reason I'm pulled back. I hope those spirits are walking with me, feeling my joy and elation at being back in this primitive world.

I have brought my family to show them the land that had such an impact on me, though I fear they are too hurried and rushed in their daily routines to slow down enough to even hear the quiet that is around us.

"What are you looking at, Gramma?" asks the young boy next to me, jarring me from my daydream.

"I'm trying to remember this place as it was the last time I saw it, Kenny. So much has changed here, yet it still seems the same." I pull him closer to me as we sit on the rock.

"Why do you look so sad, Gramma?"

"I'm trying to hear them and I can't."

"Who's 'them,' Gramma?"

"The ancient people who used to live here. They were friends during my lonely days."

"Were they ghosts, Gramma?"

"Not really, Kenny. Not in the way you think."

Sitting on that rock looking down at this peaceful place, I'm suddenly overwhelmed by the presence of the spirits I long for after all this time away. Ah, they're still here after all. Of course! Why wouldn't they be?

How can I begin to impart my feelings about this place to this boy whose sole desire right now is to chase lizards and throw rocks at anything that moves?

"Gramma, would you tell me about them? I'm not afraid of ghosts. I like 'em!" he says seriously.

My other grandchildren motion for us to come down to the newly ignited campfire. I feel the friends of my past surround me, empowering me to tell their stories.

"You really want to hear about them?" I asked.

He nods, his face beaming, as he gets up and runs down the hill toward his cousins.

Excitedly, he yells at them, "Hey, you guys, Gramma's gonna tell us about the ghosts here when she was really, really young like a hundred years ago!" I chuckle to myself as I rise and make my way down to join them.

While the children settle in around me by the campfire to listen to my tales, I'm mesmerized by the flames and feel an instant connection with *my* past. My mind takes me back to my very last night in the high country, thirty-five years earlier.

John had lost his lease on the pack station and we were loading all of our supplies and equipment onto the horses to take home. I felt sad that the Forest Service wanted to burn down all the cabins and turn that beautiful country back into a wilderness area. Lost forever would be the history written on the walls of those very old log structures as well as shelter for those suddenly caught by bad weather.

But mostly I felt sad for John. His whole way of life in those mountains was coming to an end.

John, the man who turned my life around. John, the man who means everything to me.

Chapter One

John Slaughter

He was in his 40s when I first met him, this rugged horseman who would change my life.

I wasn't quite sure where to start my story with these children. They all knew about John, but they didn't know about my past and how I got to that oh-so-low point in my life. The part where I was just watching life go slowly by, hoping for something wonderful to happen to me because it seemed like nothing ever did. I hated school, I hated my teachers, I hated most of the kids at school, I hated men, sometimes I hated my mom, and most of all I hated my life!

My friend, Doug, had decided that I should meet this guy down the street from me who had a bunch of horses and a riding club. Doug was my closest friend and confidant, one of the few people I didn't hate. We rode horses together and he probably knew me better than anyone else on Earth. He knew I had been sinking lower and lower into a world where I shouldn't be. A world of self-loathing and degradation. A world where it was becoming easier for me to see it without me being in it.

I was fourteen years old and my mom had just gotten a divorce from my stepdad of four years. My real dad had been killed in a racing accident when I was a baby, so I'd never had a real father figure in my life. Then, when I was ten, she thought things had finally changed. When she married my stepdad, she was sure we would finally be the family she had always hoped for. Those four years had been rough for both of us, and they finally divorced.

I felt guilty about my part in their divorce. I had finally told her about what happened at night when she went to work. How, from the time I was twelve, as soon as she left, he came into my room. Looking back, I think my mom knew what was going on long before I told her.

Through it all, I let my mind wander and I was saved from this torment by racing the wind on the back of a horse.

From my earliest memories, horses seemed to live in my soul. My make believe world was gleefully overrun with them. They were all I dreamed about. In real life, a horse was all I ever wanted. My mom and stepfather kept saying "No." Horses were too expensive. But that didn't hold me back. Someday, somehow, I was going to have a horse of my own.

Trying to take my mind off horses, they bought me a swimming pool, a new bedroom set, and lots of stuff they (he) thought I wanted. But the one thing I really wanted, they wouldn't budge on.

Undeterred, I saved every cent I earned from babysitting. Mom would ask, "What are you saving up for?" She was always surprised when I wouldn't spend any of my money on special things.

"Horse, of course!" I would answer. She would just smile, amused at me, and go on with her business. But I was serious. And when at long last that moment came, and she finally saw how important it was to me, she agreed to pay for his board if I had enough to buy him. All of the money I had earned over two years paid for my first horse. I was twelve years old, and he was my life. It seems funny that my first horse came into my life when I needed him the most.

Sparol was his name. I never really knew what it meant. Most people called him "Sparrow," like the bird. But it was really Sparol. I paid $125.00 for him in 1963. That was a fortune to a twelve year old in those days.

On horseback the bad feelings and confusion I had about life stayed at the gate of my driveway as I rode my horse down into the canyon and away from reality. In my imagination, we would ride over prairies chasing buffalo, or along rushing rivers where no cities existed. I could ride off into never-never land and leave my sad, miserable, real life behind.

After Mom got her divorce, she bought a house where I could keep my horse. The lot was about a quarter of an acre with a cute little two-bedroom house at the front of the lot and lots of orange and grapefruit trees in the back. The whole area had once been an orchard before they subdivided. Now it was filled with small houses and many people had horses in the back of their houses. We were going to build a barn and I was so excited. Mom knew that actually having him at our house where I could care for him meant everything to me. I think she felt this was a small way to make up for what I had been through all of those years. But the damage had been done. Nothing would bring back my innocence or my trust in humans.

While mom continued to work to support us, I took up with some less than desirable people and started to experiment with marijuana and other drugs. Sex, drugs, and rock and roll! It was the 1960s; free love and all that came with it!

Sparol saved me every time we rode off down the canyon. He thought I was special. Only my little horse could see past the surface of my "tough girl" persona. Sparol and I connected on a level that only those who have loved a horse can understand.

No, I don't need to share all that with these children. We will start with John.

ᔓ

Doug took me over to John Slaughter's place one day after school. His place was about two blocks away from mine, with corrals in the back that he leased from the owner.

As he introduced us, I was instantly drawn to the man. He had an easy, down-home manner about him. Relaxed and cheerful, with a rugged look. It was evident that he had spent most of his life outside. He had a "cowboy" attitude and a way with horses that came straight out of the Old West. I was told there wasn't a horse he couldn't handle and there was no horse he didn't respect. Doug told me that respect was mutual. John's horses loved him and did most anything for him.

When he spoke to me, I immediately felt he knew me down to my very soul. He talked like he was my oldest, closest friend. His voice was like a well-worn pair of old jeans. It fit just right and felt perfect.

"Well, hello, young lady," he said. "Doug tells me you've got a horse and might be interested in helping me with some of mine."

I gave Doug a dirty look for butting into my business. "Well, I don't know about that. I've got school and my own corral to keep clean. But if I did, what would you want me to do?"

"Oh, there's always lots to do. Brushin', cleanin', shovelin'. But if you don't think you'll have time, suit yourself," he said as he turned back to repair a post that had been knocked down.

"Well, when would I *maybe* do all this?" I asked.

He turned back to me with a great big grin and said, "Just as soon as you think you're ready to change your life."

"What do *you* know about my life?" I glared once more at Doug.

"Enough to know you are in trouble at school and in trouble with some of your so-called friends at school, too. Listen, Doug cares about you and doesn't want you to get hurt by that crowd you're with. That's why he came to me and told me about you. If you want to, you can start working for me and helping with the horses. And I promise you that if you stick with me, you won't be sorry. Your life absolutely *will* change."

Unsure of why, I was at his stable the very next afternoon. I didn't know what he could do to make my life not suck anymore, but I guess I wanted to find out.

"Well, I didn't expect you back here quite this soon," John said as he came out of a stall.

"Is it okay? I mean that I'm here? Or was that stuff yesterday just all for Doug because you knew I was mad at him?" I sat down on a bale of hay, watching him.

He put a halter on a gorgeous palomino horse, led him out of the corral, and tied him up next to where I was sitting. Then he handed me a brush and motioned towards the horse. "Might as well make yerself useful."

I got the hint and started brushing the horse. "What's his name?" I asked, brushing down the sleek, shiny, golden neck. He was the most amazing color I had even seen.

"This is Zorro. He's a mustang. Best horse I've ever had. Flies when I let him. See his wings?" he chuckled at his own joke.

I could see the love for this animal radiating out of John. I could tell he was an honest, caring person by the way he touched his horse. His fingers caressed Zorro's neck like they were touching it for the first time. Slow, soft, sure strokes that spoke to the horse with every movement and told him that no one on this planet loved him more than John.

I was mesmerized at the connection between man and beast. Could a man really be that sensitive and in tune with an animal? I had never known anyone like that.

"I think I like him. I've never seen a mustang before." I said as I continued to curry him, still mesmerized by the shimmering golden color of his coat.

He was staring straight into my eyes as he asked, "What else do you like?"

I sensed he was trying to learn more about me, but I was resistant. I tended to withdraw into myself and as he asked me that question I could feel the wall starting to build up that I used to protect myself from people, especially grown men. But John seemed different somehow. His eyes told me I could trust him, that he was really interested in helping me. I decided to give him a chance.

"I like to ride. That's about it. Nothing else matters if I'm on my horse. I'm not worried about what my mom wants. I don't think about school. I just feel out of sorts anywhere else. Riding is all I ever think about." I moved around to the other side of Zorro.

John looked at the horses in the corral, then back to me. "I s'pose there's a few here you could ride. They all could use a bit more attention. I don't have the time and they need to stay in good shape for weekend rides and pack trips."

"What trips?" I asked.

"Pack trips. I take hunters up to a pack station in the High Sierra Mountains. We load them and their gear up on the horses and pack them in eighteen miles into the high country to hunt deer, fish, or just get out of the city and camp. It's hard work for these horses. They tend to get pretty soft during the winter months. Think you might like to come along on one?" he asked as he brought Zorro's saddle over and tacked him up.

"You mean to the High Sierras? Really?" I suddenly sat back down on the hay, instantly disappointed. I knew that it didn't matter how exciting something sounded, it would never happen.

"What's wrong?" he asked as he tightened up Zorro's cinch. He then absentmindedly patted the horse's rump as he walked back around to where I was sitting.

"My mom will never let me," I answered, picking out a piece of hay and twiddling it with my fingers. I avoided looking up at him. Somehow, I didn't want him to see the disappointment in my face, to know how much I would have enjoyed the adventure he had just offered me. It was as if my mind had jumped ahead and was ready to run with the idea and I had suddenly fallen back hard on reality. I felt almost as if I was going to cry and I certainly didn't want him to see that.

"She doesn't let me do stuff like that. My grades aren't good and she said if they don't pick up I'll be grounded from my horse. She doesn't like any of my friends. Except Doug. She says they're a bad influence on me. She thinks they're all druggies."

"Are they?" he asked, as he brushed his hand lovingly across Zorro's neck, petting him for no other reason I could think of than to communicate his respect to the big horse.

"Some of them," I replied. He looked doubtful. "Well, okay most of them. It's just that since we moved nothing seems to be going right for me. I can't ever please her. She's always suspicious of everything I do. The only peace I get is when I go riding."

He mounted up and said, "Tell you what, you come and clean stalls and brush horses every day after school and I'll talk to your mom. She'll let you go. You have to prove to her she can trust you."

"That'll be the day," I said. "But okay. I guess I could come over here after I clean my corral."

ꟹ

Within a week I was officially "working" for John. I'd go over after school and clean corrals. I was in heaven with all that horse poop, horse hair, and horse smell!

At school, I'd sit in my last class of the day and watch the clock stand still, willing the second hand to move, which it seemed to refuse to do. I would start to squirm just as the bell rang and off I'd go. Home to change, clean my corral, and hop on Sparol for the short ride to John's stable. My thoughts about school and the people there were being pushed further and further to the back of my head. From the time I woke up all I could think of was how long the day would be until I could be with the horses. They called to me in my head all day long. It was maddening! The quiet in my mind was only achieved once I opened the gate and got on Sparol's back. Then, finally peace!

John was soon helping my mom's friend finish the barn in my backyard. Always on the lookout for new places to keep horses, I'm sure his eyes fell out of their sockets the first time he came to my house and saw that big backyard and all the room it had for *lots* of horses. It wasn't long before a few of his horses were at my house.

My house sat on a dead end street in Altadena overlooking the Arroyo Seco Canyon north of the greater Los Angeles area. I could ride two blocks away from home to the trailhead at the end of Altadena Drive and within minutes be alone in the mountains.

I met his son, Jim, a few weeks after that first meeting while riding in the canyon. I went down by the Rose Bowl Riders arena, which was a sort of gathering place for the horse people of Altadena, and I saw him riding one of John's horses. I hollered at him to wait up and he did.

"That's 'Big' isn't it?" I asked. Then I saw the resemblance to John and realized who I was talking to. "Oh, are you, I mean, you must be Jim. Sorry. I thought someone stole John's horse." I felt foolish. He looked at me and smiled.

"Well, YOU must be the new girl. What's your name? Don't tell me, it's a guy's name, right? Toni? No. Jonnie? No, that's not right. Bobbi? No?" I made a face at him and he laughed. "Roni! That's it."

He then turned his horse around and kept going in his original direction. I just sat there on my horse until he stopped, looked over his shoulder and said, "You coming or not?"

I trotted on up to him and we rode side-by-side for the longest time without saying a word. I felt that same sense of comfort with him that I felt with his dad. This was all brand new for me. Finally, he asked me if I liked my new job.

"Yeah, but it isn't really a job to me. It's more of an escape," I answered.

"Escape from what?"

"Basically from life. The only time I'm at peace is around the horses. My mom is always on my case about my friends. And some of those friends, I'm finding out now, aren't really friends at all. I'm in a lot of trouble at school. My mom doesn't understand me at all. So I take off on the back of this guy and escape! Or, I go to your dad's place and escape. Either way, I'm gone!"

He looked at me as if he understood everything about me. "You can 'escape' with me anytime you want or need to. Ever been to the waterfall up the canyon?"

"No" I said, "I've never ridden that far."

"No time like the present. Let's go."

He urged his horse into a trot, and before I could decide for myself, Sparol had decided we were going. We trotted side-by-side, then loped a little, then settled into a nice rhythmic walk.

We talked a little about mundane things. Once in a while he asked questions about me and how I felt about things. I had never known a guy who cared about my opinions. They usually just wanted to cut to the chase. This guy was different. And I liked him.

We got to the end of the trail, and Jim said, "We have to tie them up and hike a short distance. Does your little horse tie up okay?"

"Yes, he'll be fine." I said as I dismounted and walked him over to the tree next to where Jim was tying Big.

Jim started walking up a small trail that had fallen logs and boulders in the way. I ran and caught up with him. We rounded a bend and there it was. A beautiful waterfall and a pool of crystal clear mountain water.

He walked over to a massive rock and sat down. I followed him and we both sat there staring at the tumbling water.

"Do you ever dream about living in another time and place?" he asked, breaking the silence.

"Sure, all the time. I've always believed I was born too late. I should've lived a hundred years ago. I would have fit in much better," I answered.

"I have dreams like that too. They're sometimes so real I wake up totally confused that I am here and not there." he said. "I wonder what it all means."

"I don't know," I answered. "But most of the time I'd rather be *there* than here. That's for sure!"

We talked for over an hour as I watched the waterfall. Its beauty seemed to fill my soul. I felt happy as I watched the spray glisten in the sunlight and listened to this boy who seemed to know so much about life.

"We'd better get back. It'll be dark soon. I don't want to get you into trouble." He stood, reached his hand out and helped me up.

We stood for a second face-to-face, his eyes searing into mine. I tried to look away but couldn't. It was as if there were things we both wanted to say, but couldn't, things we just didn't have the words or the power to speak. I felt I had looked into those eyes a hundred times before.

He broke it off and led me down the trail. I tried to breathe.

"I won't get in trouble ya know. It's not a school night. How old are you anyway?" I asked as we neared the horses.

I studied him a bit closer. He had a lean build and a long stride. But it was his eyes that drew me in. They seemed like ancient eyes that looked right past my soul into all of those hurt places in my walled off heart, yet I didn't sense it as an invasion. There was just something about them, sort of like the touch I'd seen his father give the horses, a genuine caring that radiated from his soul. I was *very* curious about him.

"How old do you think I am?" he asked.

"I'm not sure." I wasn't good at guessing.

"Eighteen. How 'bout you?" he asked as we both mounted up.

"Wow, you are younger than I thought. I'm fifteen." I replied. "Well, almost. Like in about four months or so." I added honestly.

"Wow, you are younger than *I* thought!" he grinned.

We turned the horses homeward and off we went down the canyon making small talk all the way. I was extremely attracted to him. There were feelings bubbling to the surface that I had forced down long ago. But still I had doubts as to whether any boy would ever find me attractive. Especially one who seemed as sophisticated and confident as Jim.

When we got to the top of the trailhead we said our goodbyes since we were going in different directions. He turned and said, "Hey, let's do it again."

"Anytime. Maybe I'll see you at the stable."

"Count on it!"

He rode off towards his corral, and I rode off towards mine.

I was smiling the rest of the evening. I know my mom must have wondered about the grin on my face, but she didn't ask. There seemed to be a sort of peaceful connection growing between us. Something that had been missing in my life and yet it seemed familiar, as if it had been a there a long time ago. Sometimes at night I tried really hard to remember how our life had been. Just her and me all those years ago before my nightmare began.

I saw Jim every few days at the stable when I went to clean stalls. I got very excited thinking about seeing him. There were feelings stirring in me every time he looked at me that I had never known before. He would be working John's young stallion, Jade. I loved to watch. He had a way with horses similar to his father. Gentle, kind, and knowledgeable.

Sometimes Jim would even let me help. He would let me curry Jade and saddle him up. Then he would mount up and work him a little. Jade was an extremely calm stallion and if his lesson had gone well, Jim would let me sit on him. I was thrilled when he let me do that. Just think, I was sitting on a stallion! Who would have thought I would ever have a chance to do that?

After Jim was done, we would rub Jade down and put him away. Then we would sit until almost dark, just talking about things. He made me think about the issues of the day and challenged me to really think about this world and my place in it. The mid-1960s were a tumultuous time, and I had never really thought about the world around me until he made me see it.

We talked a lot about our dreams. Oddly enough, our dreams were very similar. Mine, that I would find peace and happiness somehow in my messed up life. And his, that his life would have meaning in this messed up world and that the world would find peace. I felt closer to him than I had *ever* felt with a guy before.

For the first time in my sort of grown up life I was happy. Around these people I now felt I had true friends and a purpose in life, even if it seemed to be no more than shoveling horse poop for John.

I was even starting to tolerate school and tried to avoid all those people that I'd thought I couldn't live without. Trouble was, they weren't done with me. It's not always easy to turn your back on your past, and they kept after me. "Try this one." "Come on, just one time?" "Hey, we're gettin' some good stuff tonight. You coming?" I ignored them. Or at least I tried to.

Now, it seemed I didn't fit in anywhere at school. The popular kids always had their noses in the air and the ones that I had hung out with moved on. I was a loner now, who just wanted to be left alone to go be with the horses. School was dragging me down into the gutters where I felt I had been steadily climbing out of.

Then a group of girls got mad at me one day for something I didn't do. They retaliated by getting me busted at school. Someone planted a bag of pot in my locker and told the principal. He got me out of class, then called the police, who then led me off to jail. I was promptly expelled from the Pasadena Unified School system. Today, it would have been a slap on the wrist.

After that I spent almost every waking moment with John and his horses. Right after we met he moved his horses to a new place. A stable on the east side of the Arroyo Seco Canyon at the foot of the mountains in Altadena called "The Meadows." The place consisted of old barns and decrepit corrals. Everything was falling down around itself. There were boards wired together with rusty baling wire that looked like they would fall if you were to breathe on them too hard. But it was down a steep trail away from people and traffic and was just perfect.

We jumped right in and started fixing it up. We replaced rusty wire with new wire. It was just amazing to see what a person could do with baling wire. Especially John! We moved the horses up and I had a real job! My first! Except, of course, for babysitting. I was still too young to drive, so when John didn't pick me up, I would ride a horse up from my house. There were always a few in the backyard now to keep Sparol company.

The trailhead at the end of Altadena Drive, around the block from my house, went down the part of the canyon where the famous Jet Propulsion Laboratory (JPL) is, and then took off to the north of their parking lot. About a half mile up, another trail split off and went directly to the stable. It took me about twenty minutes to get there. I spent every afternoon at the stable.

John had a small riding club. Several kids leased horses from him. A few had their own and boarded them there. On weekends he took city kids out on rides to experience, some for the very first time, what it was like to be free on the back of a horse. I started helping with some of those groups, and became a "regular" with the stable gang.

It wasn't long before I was one of the leaders. I never asked to be in charge. I was always a follower. But John gave me more and more responsibility. One of the best things he did was to believe in me. When I got into trouble at school, he wasn't disappointed in me. Or at least he didn't let it show if he was. My mom was certainly upset about it. But John just put me to work.

My responsibility was to get my butt out of bed every single morning at 7AM and ride up to the stables and feed the horses. Rain or shine, sick or whatever. Stayed up too late? It didn't matter. Horses had to be fed. So I would saddle up and ride there every morning, feed, clean, then ride back home and do the cleaning at MY barn and corrals. Then come 4:30PM I would have to do it all over again. If John wasn't working, he would come and pick me up in the afternoons, but it was still my job! And I couldn't let John down.

I started riding every horse he told me to ride. All of his horses were used to many different types of riders, but I had only ridden a few different horses. So it became a learning experience for me as I rode and exercised each horse and learned about his or her personalities and quirks.

Soon, I was riding most of them and riding them well. I was not afraid of any horse he had, and that newfound confidence spilled over into my daily life. I felt more able to deal with people I met, as well as take charge of the kids we would take on rides.

I got to know all of his horses very well. Their personality differences, their likes and dislikes. I knew who could be with whom and who had to be by themselves. Sometimes the ones we left by themselves would be found somewhere else with a friend the next morning. It was always an adventure going to the stable every morning. I was never sure what exactly I would find.

ᔓ

"So are you going?" Jim asked me as soon as I got to the stable one afternoon a couple of months after I started working there.

"Going where?" I replied.

"On the pack trip! Dad has one planned next week. I can't go, but he said you were going." He broke open a bale of hay and started to feed the horses.

"I am?" I was surprised. No one had mentioned any pack trip to me. "Well, I don't know. I mean..."

"Just the person I was looking for!" John said as he came around the corner of the barn.

"Here's a list of things you'll need to bring. We'll leave Sparol home for your first trip. You can ride Big Brown."

"But, I haven't asked..."

"Don't you worry your little head over that. I'll talk to your mother. She'll let you go," he said that as if he'd read my mind.

"Well, if you're sure. Where exactly are we going?"

"I've been going to this old pack station up in the Owens Valley for years now. Like I told you, we pack in hunters and campers. We ride up this skinny trail where no vehicles are allowed. It goes up into the high country on the east side of the Sierras. Then we descend down into a canyon with the South Fork of the Kern River running through it. You ever been outta the city with horses? You're going to love it! Now get in the truck and I'll take you home and speak with your mom." His enthusiasm was catching.

I hopped in, barely able to contain my excitement. Was I really going on a trip with horses? Was I dreaming?

Chapter Two

First Pack Trip

I was so excited to be going on a pack trip. I had never ridden horses anywhere but in my own mountains. This was going to be such an adventure. Little did I know how that first pack trip was going to impact me and be the start of the best years of my life.

John had no problem talking my mom into letting me go with him. She was almost relieved that she wouldn't have to worry about me for a few days.

The night we left for the pack station was electric for me. Sparol was staying home and I was going to be riding Big Brown. He was one of the few horses I hadn't ridden yet. He was a great big bay Morgan gelding, one of the tallest horses John had. He was very stout and heavy muscled, as Morgans are, with a long, black mane flowing every which way. I wasn't used to such a large horse after my little Sparol, but I wasn't scared because John had an uncanny way of fitting riders with his horses. They always seemed to be the perfect match, so I knew that Big Brown and I would get along just fine.

This late October trip was the last weekend of hunting season and I knew one of the men going along. He was a neighbor who

I had ridden with a few times. Herb was a quiet man, an accomplished hunter, and a good horseman who loved the outdoors. I'd known him for a couple of years and it felt good to be going with someone I knew besides John. I didn't know what to expect being the only girl on the trip. I was very disappointed that Jim wouldn't be on that first trip. Our relationship was definitely blossoming into something special.

Herb picked me up and we drove to the stables. There was a flurry of activity, with John stuffing gear into the truck. He told me to start bringing up horses. "They're all tied up, ready to go!"

"You look nervous," Herb said.

"No, just uncertain what I'm getting myself into. Excited too," I told him as we made our way down the trail to the stable to bring the horses up to the Big Rig.

The "Big Rig" was John's "horse haulin' truck."

Basically, it was an old nursery van attached to a Dodge two-ton truck. It looked like a big silver box. He had it rigged up to haul eight to ten horses depending on if the bunk was in or not. The "bunk" was a partition up at the front of the "box" that would provide space to carry supplies and feed. On top of the partition, he would place a sheet of plywood and sometimes a mattress, and more stuff could be loaded there. Most times, when the bunk was in, kids were riding on it. On hunting trips it was filled with supplies.

The back of this converted truck consisted of a tailgate that doubled as a loading ramp. It was made out of heavy wood, and hinged with a second piece that would open to the ground at a slant. When being closed, it would fold in half then be raised against the back of the truck where chains would be pulled through the hinges on the sides at the back. The sounds of those chains being pulled, metal against metal, always vibrated through my whole body like fingernails on a chalkboard. The chains would then be hooked up and the tailgate would be secure, covering up half of the opening, leaving the top open. This way there was lots of air for the horses and they were not in a completely closed up van.

The first horse in was faced sideways in one direction, then a cable hooked beside him, and the next horse brought in was tied the opposite way with a cable between him and the next one. By the time they were all in, half faced one way and half the other. All of this usually went very smoothly. That is until it came time for the last horse to be loaded. There wasn't very much space left. And when that last horse did get up there, he had to turn and sort of step up sideways, and then *stay* there while the tailgate was closed.

So many trips were delayed because of loading that last horse. But after years of doing it, John knew which ones could be there and which ones shouldn't. For instance, Charlie spent almost two hours one night letting us know that he did NOT belong there.

Often, we would have to unload and start over in a different order to get them all in. It was sometimes the most difficult part of the whole trip. Oddly, there wasn't usually a problem loading them to come home!

As I watched all of this activity for the very first time, I felt just a bit anxious, but not enough to back out. Finally, around 7 PM, all was ready and we pulled out of Altadena, bound for the upper Mojave Desert.

I rode with Herb, and we followed the Big Rig. There was a light inside the back of the truck so you could see the horses. You could tell if any had trouble keeping their feet under them around corners. Herb and I chatted about the horses a little but mostly we drove in silence. I was mesmerized just watching the horses swaying with the rhythm of the road.

It seemed to take forever to reach our destination. What was only a three-hour drive in a car became much longer when driving a truck full of horses. They would shift and sway and the driver had to constantly be on alert or he would find himself pulled off the road by the weight of the shifting horses in the back.

John had his special stops on the way to the pack station to break up the trip and rest a little. Handling that rig with all those horses could really wear him out and he would stop to get a cup of coffee and check on the horses.

The first stop was in the tiny town of Mojave at White's Café. As we walked in I saw that it was an old-fashioned café with the small jukebox machines on the tabletops. The usual fare was coffee and apple pie. I was still mostly in denial that this was even happening. I never went anywhere. My first diner! The next one was a lonely little hole in the wall on the side of Highway 395 called Brady's Café. They made the best coffee and chocolate pie around. I also loved their burgers and I became great friends with them. It was just about an hour south of the pack station.

After what seemed an eternity, we finally arrived at our destination close to midnight. When we turned off of Highway 395 my heart skipped a beat in its excitement to see where we were going. There was a sign at the beginning of that dirt road that said "Sam Lewis Pack Station." Oh my, we were really there!

The dirt road from the highway to the pack station at the foot of the hills was about three miles long. It could be very rough, bouncy, and filled with rain gullies. Sometimes it had been graded, but more often it wasn't. So it was very slow going up that dusty dirt road with that heavy truck full of antsy horses. It took forever!

When we finally reached the top, we pulled up below the corrals and parked the rig there so as not to interfere with the operations of those who owned (leased) the pack station.

"How come you park down here?" I asked John as he opened his door and hopped down, stretching his back.

"Well, there's a little bad blood between me and them," he said, nodding his head toward the cabin. "We just don't see eye to eye on who can use God's country. They seem to think they have the sole right to use these trails which are on public lands. I've been coming here for years and they haven't stopped me yet. Even when they let the air outta my tires."

"Wow," I said. "Do they really do stupid stuff like that?"

"Oh yeah, and worse. One time they tried to steal some of my horses. But I caught them. I got the sheriff out here and he told them to knock it off. So there has been a sort of uneasy truce for the last year or so."

About year or so after my first trip, the lease became available and John leased it. We then renamed it the Sierra Lady Pack Station.

We unloaded all the horses. The cables that had been used to separate the horses inside became their picket line outside. He snapped the ends together and stretched them alongside the outside of the truck. The horses were then tied to them loose enough so they could reach to eat the hay piled on the ground. We went around the truck feeding and watering all of them. Then we found a soft spot on the ground to get some shuteye before the sun came up.

As I lay there looking at the millions of stars in the sky, I felt it was all a dream. I had never in my life seen so many stars. They were so crisp and clear that I felt I could touch them. They seemed that close. The crickets and other nighttime insects provided just enough music to sing me off to sleep.

"We're burning daylight! Rise and shine!" John hollered, as he gently kicked my foot to wake me up.

Groggily, I sat up and for a moment forgot where I was, my sweet dreams disturbed by all that shouting. "Oh yeah, now I remember!" I bounced out of my sleeping bag eager to see what the place looked like.

There was a small house-like building with an outhouse in the back. A large juniper tree stood in front of it for shade. The road ran between the cabin and the corrals, which were made from thick logs and were as solid as could be. There was one large corral and four smaller ones. The large corral had several large triangular feeders constructed of railroad ties. It also had an old bathtub with a spring piped to it for fresh running water. Next to the corral was an old, long wooden shed. This wasn't really a barn, but more a bunk-house-type quarters. Now it was filled with an accumulation of junk from days gone by. At one end of this building there was a tin room added onto the original building. Maybe it was for more sleeping quarters or a tack room. There was also what looked like an old hay shed standing separate from the longer building.

Looking around I felt shivers through my body, as if I knew this place. I could picture in my mind all of the activity that must have taken place here. But of course that was silly. I'd never been here before. I'd never been anywhere!

While the horses finished up their breakfast, the last hay they would have for several days, John started getting them ready for the trip in.

There were eight horses on this trip. Enough for the six hunters and me. John would pack the eighth horse and walk in. In all the years I packed in with John, I can count on one hand the number of times he actually RODE. He felt more comfortable on the ground because he was better able to get to a horse in trouble than if he had been on horseback. And he stayed in great shape, too.

I suddenly felt I wasn't earning my keep. "What do you want me to do?" I asked, as I followed him around.

"Well you can start getting horses saddled. I've laid their tack out by them," he answered.

"Okay, no problem. Should I brush them first?"

"If they need it, like on their backs. This ain't no beauty contest," John said as he moved off to saddle up another horse.

I moved in the opposite direction and soon we had them all saddled up.

The packs came next. John didn't have traditional panniers and pack saddles. He usually only had one packhorse. So, on each horse with a rider, the saddle was equipped with a custom-made saddle pack.

"I had these made special," John explained to the hunters and me. "See, they're sewn out of canvas and fit right behind the saddle. Each pocket is deep and square enough for a five-gallon plastic trashcan. The way we work it is if you folks got a bunch of stuff, you got room for ten gallons worth. You got more than that, you can leave some here at the station and pick it up when you leave. Means you brought too much, you won't need all of it." The hunters laughed and glanced at one of their troop, whose name I learned was Mitch.

Mitch flushed, and then he joined the laughter. "They've been kidding me all the way up here about how much stuff I've brought," he admitted. "I kept thinking of stuff we might need, then couldn't decide what to bring and what to leave behind. So I just brought it all."

"Don't worry, we'll get it sorted out," John told him, his eyes twinkling. "I'm with you, it's better to be safe than sorry. Any of you have extra room and we'll tuck in things being packed in for camp. I usually put grain in the bottom half of the packs, then add the lighter things on top. Just make piles of your stuff, and then we can see where we're at."

We all made individual piles of our things, and John grinned when he saw the extra clothing Mitch had brought along, but he didn't comment.

"Food for camp or pots and pans we distribute among all the packs," John said, adding items to the piles as he spoke. "Once we get this done, we put your bedrolls on top of the pack behind the saddle, and tie 'em securely. That's what these leather strings on the saddle are for. There are also straps from the bottom of each pack that attach to the cinch rings on the side of the saddle, to keep them from flapping around when the horse walks. We also need to be very careful to make sure each pack's weight is evenly distributed. If it's not, we'll be stopping constantly on the trail to adjust things. Suppose you folks go ahead and load 'em up and then I'll help you unload and show you how it shoulda been done."

We all laughed appreciatively and went to work. I noticed that when John inspected our handiwork, he found something to praise about the job each one of us had done, even if he did have to give us a bit of help with some repacking. John was a kind man.

The packhorse would get whatever was left over. There was sometimes a lot, and other times not so much. We hardly ever packed in hay, but we always had bags of grain for the hard-working horses. Any fishing poles and other odd sized equipment went on the packhorse. Almost all of John's horses could be used for pack-horses. Well, except for maybe Brownie and Big Daddy. But those stories come later.

ꟹ

"Well, I think that's enough stories for now," I told my grand-children. "Why don't you run and see if you can find some really nice rocks, just little ones, so we can take them home and then we'll have a part of this place with us in the city. I'll tell you more stories later."

"Ok, Gramma," said Kenny. "I'm gonna find you some nice arrowheads too."

"Me too. Gramma," said Terry. "You can have the best ones I find!"

The boys ran off to look for arrowheads, and the girls, Kacee and Lindsey, wandered off on some mission of their own and left me to think about my memories. I could feel my beloved friends from the past surrounding me with their love, and I needed just a bit of time to myself to remember and let the memories flow through me.

"Will you tell us some more about the good old days, Gramma?" asked Terry as we gathered around the campfire that evening.

"Yeah, what happened next when you went on that pack trip?" asked Lindsey, as she scooted over to me.

"Well, after what seemed like hours, we were finally ready to go," I told them.

ᔕ

"Let's get a move on!" shouted John as he got the hunters all mounted on their horses.

I mounted the big, brown gelding and felt on top of the world. John tightened everything up for me, and then checked all the other cinches, grabbed the lead rope to the packhorse, and up the trail we went.

The pack station sat right at the mouth of the Haiwee (Hayway) Canyon about 90 miles south of Bishop. The trail wound its way along the canyon floor, crossed the stream many times. After a few miles it then started to climb. It soon became very steep, narrow, full of switchbacks and loose, unstable, rocky shale. Then, it climbed higher still into fir trees, thin air, and unspeakable beauty.

"Wait till you get to the summit," John told the hunters. He shook his head. "There just aren't words to describe it, or if there are, I sure don't know any of them. It usually takes four or five hours to ride in. It just depends on many things, such as rider experience, heat, the horses, and trail conditions."

At the summit, you can look down on the desert and see the reservoir across the highway. On the other side of the summit, it flattens out onto gently rolling mountaintops before reaching the canyon through which the South Fork of the Kern River flows. A few more switchbacks down the cliff face to the river, and there we were, at our campsite by the river. After John leased the pack station, we would cross the river and go another mile or so to the log cabins that were built in the early 1900s. But for now, primitive campsites by the water were all there were.

We all dismounted, some a bit more slowly than others. I was still in a dream, not believing that I was really here, away from all of my problems at home.

Once again John snapped me back to reality. "Young lady, we got horses that need unpacking, unsaddling, and watering. You gonna look like a tourist all day, or ya gonna help me?" I looked over at him and he had the biggest smile. How could I think he was mad at me for loafing?

I unsaddled Brown and led him to the water down from the campsites, where Herb was watering his horse.

"Hey, how'd you like the ride?" he asked me.

"Incredible," I replied. "I never ever thought in my wildest dreams that I would be on a ride like this. I feel like I'm at home here. It's the oddest feeling."

"And a very common one to those of us who come here regularly. It gets in your blood." Herb said as he led his horse back to camp.

A picket line was strung for the horses between two very sturdy trees. A small pile of grain was put out for each horse and they were tied up and left to eat and rest.

After the horses were settled, we all went about our business of setting up sleeping bags, starting campfires, and getting supper ready. John unpacked all the food supplies and cookware and set a pot of water on the rocks in the fire pit to boil.

"Can I help do anything?" I asked. I wanted to be sure I was earning my keep, so to speak, but wasn't quite sure what I should be doing.

"Naw, you just sit there and enjoy the scenery. There will be plenty of chores for you to do tomorrow." John said.

We slept under the millions of stars lighting the high mountain sky. The Kern River was rushing by right next to us. I had never camped like this when I was a Girl Scout! It was magical. I lay awake for quite some time listening to all the sounds of the night in that primitive wilderness. I wondered how many people had lain right there at that campsite looking at those same stars that felt so much closer than on the desert. I felt at peace with the universe for quite possibly the first time in my young life.

The next day, I tagged along with Herb while he hunted. We went out on foot and I had no idea what I was doing. I remember there was climbing involved.

"You gotta be quiet," Herb kept telling me. "We don't want to scare away the game." Yet the sounds of me gasping for air at the top of a hill seemed to echo through the air.

I lost my brand new Buck knife, bought special for this trip. And by the end of the day when we came dragging back to camp (me anyway) we had not seen a single deer. I'm sure it was because they heard me making all that noise. Herb acted like it was just another stroll in the hills, while I was exhausted but fulfilled. The country was just so rugged and pristine.

On the second night, after having checked my sleeping bag for stray rattlesnakes, I drifted off to easy slumber to dream of the trails yet to explore.

All of a sudden, I was rudely awakened by the most blood-curdling scream. I sat bolt upright trying to figure out what I had heard. It came again, from up on the side of the cliff above us. The horses were shifting restlessly and pawing at the ground. The hunters and John were all sitting bolt upright as well.

"What is it?" I asked, my voice shaking.

The scream echoed across the canyon once more.

"It's a mountain lion." John said calmly.

"Yeah, they can be downright spooky sounding," Herb said. "I've heard them sound like a woman screaming as well as a baby crying. Depending on their mood." This was definitely the woman screaming technique.

As all of us were sitting up listening to this freaky serenade from on high, when one horse in our string, Little Oats, decided the cat must be serenading *her*. She started answering the cougar, scream for scream. The first time she let one out, it sounded so real that we all jumped straight up in the air thinking there was a lion in *camp*! This mutual admiration vocal display went on for several minutes before we were all too spooked out by it and started yelling at the mare. The other horses were even more spooked than us.

"Okay boys and girls, it's okay." I could hear John talking soothingly to the horses as he went up and down the picket line, calming them. Soon there was silence up on the cliff and we all settled back down. But for me, and I suspect a few others, it was a rather sleepless, jumpy night.

On the third night I had dreams of the mountain. Images blurred with other images. People I could not make out. Voices that I could not understand. They would get louder, then stop, and all was quiet. I opened my eyes and looked into the ebony sky dotted with millions of stars. The faint voices returned as I was staring into the great abyss of the universe. Who were they? What were they saying? And why were they in my head? Soon they seemed to settle into a soft pulsating tempo that lulled me back to sleep.

The next morning I all but forgot about the images and voices as I hurried to get dressed and eat. I didn't want to miss anything in camp. That usually meant you got up before the sun, and were gone from camp to hunt well before normal people ate breakfast.

The rest of the trip was spent wandering up and down trails and getting the feel of the country.

"Well, what do you think of your first trip?" John asked as we were packing up to leave.

I hesitated, not sure how to put what I was feeling into words. "I feel such a connection to this place," I told him. "I can't explain it. Even though this is my first time here, I feel like this land has been waiting for me. I feel like I've come home. Does that even make sense?"

John nodded. I could see satisfaction on his face. He and I knew I would be back. Nothing would keep me away from these mountains.

Chapter Three

The Horse Nobody Wanted

"So did you get to go on those backpack trips a lot of times, Gramma?" asked Kacee.

I chuckled at her use of words. "They weren't backpack trips, Kacee, they were *horse* pack trips. The horses carried everything just like your backpack carries everything you need.

"See? I told you, Kacee!" chimed in Lindsey, poking fun at her cousin.

Kacee glared at her, then turned back to me and asked, "Okay, so Gramma, did you go on lots of *horsepack* trips?" satisfied she had saved face with her cousin.

"Oh, yes, lots and lots," I told her. "But unfortunately, my first pack trip was the last trip of the year, so I had to wait until the next summer to go again. But I had plenty to do to keep me busy. John never let me sit idle while the world passed by. He kept me busy with the horses. And truthfully, there was nowhere in the world I would rather have been."

ᔓ

Most mornings I couldn't wait to get up there and just be alone with all of those horses. John usually had ten to fifteen horses there waiting to be fed. I would zip through the barn and throw hay over fences and talk to everyone as I went. Once in a while, John brought horses in from other places, so I would sometimes get to meet new ones that I didn't know about until I went to feed.

One day after throwing out the hay, I realized that the stall at the end of the barn was shut up with a horse inside. I didn't know why he was shut up inside, and wasn't sure exactly what I was supposed to do with him. Just as I sat down staring at the stall door and thinking about what to do, John came down the trail. "Hey, be careful of that one," he hollered.

"Why? What's going on with that horse?" I asked.

"His name is Brownie, and he's pretty mean tempered right now," answered John. He opened the top part of the door and jumped back quickly, as the horse started towards him threateningly with his ears laid back. He pursed his lips together thoughtfully as he watched the horse.

"He used to be one of the gentlest horses you could ever ask for," he told me. "I leased him out to a girl over in Flintridge about a year ago. A few months back he got kicked in the knee by another horse and she didn't want him anymore, so he's just been locked up in a stall ever since. They never even had a vet come take a look at him and the knee just kept getting bigger and harder and more painful. Then he started getting mean and nasty, so they called me to come and get him." John sighed deeply. "Poor fella, poor old fella." He closed the upper stall door and latched it securely.

"Sounds to me like they were the ones who were mean and nasty," I told him. "How could anybody have a horse get hurt like that and never do anything to help him? So what are you going to do with him?"

"Not sure yet," answered John. "It's a darn shame. He used to be a good horse. Good disposition, kind and even-tempered. I really don't know what will happen to him. If he stays like this, I'll have to take him to the auction. I can't have a horse here that could hurt someone."

"Well, how should I deal with him?" I questioned.

"Make sure you stay out of his reach when you open the top door to throw the hay in. He'll try to lash out at you. Just be careful. And under no circumstances do you go in with him or take him out. I've got to think on this one!" he told me as he headed back up the trail.

I stood there in front of the stall for a few minutes with a flake of hay. Suddenly, there was pounding against the door from the other side.

"Oh, are you hungry or something?" I said as I gingerly slid open the latch on the top stall door. I swung it wide and jumped back expecting a raging, crazy horse.

Slowly he moved out of the shadows and into view. He didn't seem like a "killer" horse to me. He snorted and pinned his ears back. Yet the threat seemed empty. It was his eyes that I noticed. Eyes that no longer trusted. Eyes filled with pain. Lonely eyes.

I stood back and stared at the big brown horse, wishing there was some way I could let him know that he was among people that cared now.

"Hey, Brownie," I said calmly. "You want your breakfast now?"

As I stepped closer, he pinned his ears back and made his move, trying to scare me away. I dodged back. He snorted.

"That's no way to treat the person holding your food, ya know." I tossed the hay in through the open door and then left it open while I went about the rest of the chores. When I was done, I went back and sat outside his stall. He was still munching away. I just sat there and listened to him. Every now and then he would raise his head and look out at me, snort, and go back to his food.

"Well, goodbye, Brownie," I told him after about an hour. "I'll be back and see you tomorrow." I closed the stall door and left.

Each day I would repeat the process. I'd open his door first. He would give me nasty looks. I would ignore his nasty looks, toss his hay in, and come back after my chores to just sit there with him.

"You're such a beautiful fellow," I would tell him. "Just such a nice, beautiful fellow."

Relaxing on a bale of straw outside of his stall, I would carry on a running conversation with him. I'd talk about the weather; I would talk about the other horses, or him or me. Just anything at all to keep him aware of my presence. His ears would twitch back and forth as he listened to my incessant noise and his head would pop up over the door with a mouthful of hay. He would duck back down, grab another mouthful, and pop up again.

After doing this for a couple of weeks, one morning I was greeted with a *nicker* as I opened the stall door. Had I really heard what I thought I'd heard?

I didn't throw the hay in and run. This time I stood there as he poked his head out. With the hay still in my hand, he started nuzzling it, grabbed a big bite, chewed it and came back for more. I pulled some off and hand fed it to him. I stood there and fed him that whole flake of hay. I never tried to touch him. I decided it would have to be his idea. And after he was done with his hay, he made his move.

I was leaning against the stall door. He put his head over it and rubbed his nose on my shirt. He got green stuff all over me. But it was a beautiful green to me. I had made a breakthrough.

After that day, I would throw his hay in and go clean stalls and return to his stall about an hour later to play with him.

"You're a good boy, aren't ya?" I'd say to him, and soon he was allowing me to rub his nose and scratch his ears. Total trust had been achieved. He didn't charge the stall door anymore, and he seemed most eager for my touch.

After about a month, I told John what I had accomplished and he met me at the stable one morning to watch.

As I whistled at Brownie, he nickered in reply. John's face lit up as I opened the top door and the horse nickered again. To a horse lover, there is no sound on earth as heartwarming as a horse making that special sound just for you.

"Well kiddo, he certainly knows you." John said, as he watched Brownie put his head over the door and rub his nose on my shoulder. "Let's get him out and see what he does."

Brownie let me put a halter on him and lead him out of his prison. He was a little nervous, and so was I.

"Come on boy, it's okay," I spoke soothingly to him. I tried not to let my nervousness show as we walked out into the corral.

It was then that I took in his whole being for the very first time. His knee was huge, but the rest of him was beautiful. He was an American Saddlebred, all sleek and delicate looking. Standing about sixteen hands (a hand is 4 inches) tall, dark bay in color, with a white star on his forehead and a snip of white on his nose. Added to that was a thin, short, scraggly, black mane and forelock that looked like it belonged on a totally different animal, and a tail that was in need of a good combing. But it was his attitude and almost regal demeanor that was unique and made you sit up and take notice.

John looked at him, appraising his condition. I trotted him out a little bit and noticed the slight head bob that told us of his lameness in that front leg.

Then John said something to me that would change my life forever.

"I thought you two might understand each other. Seems like you both have a lot in common. If you can get that knee down and get him sound enough to ride, you can have him!"

Did I hear that right? I could *have* him? "Are you kidding me? This is a joke right?" I asked.

John replied, "Nope, I'm dead serious. This horse loves you. Sometimes horses just choose who they belong to, there's no getting around it. It's obvious he needs you. And I think you need him. Get him so you can ride him, he's yours! Deal?"

"DEAL!" was all I could say.

I didn't waste any time. I started rubbing his knee with liniment before wrapping it, and exercising him every day to try to loosen it up. Soon, he was lunging and moving well with barely a limp at all.

Within a couple of months I was riding him. He'd been hurt badly, and I don't mean by the horse that kicked him. The people that had leased him had betrayed his trust and now that he'd started trusting me, I wanted to make sure he felt safe and secure. I didn't want to push him, I wanted him to feel good about everything as we went along.

I started by just getting on him bareback while he was eating and playing with him. Soon, I had a bridle on him, still bareback, riding him around the corral.

"You're a good boy, Brownie," I'd tell him. "A really good boy. I love you."

After that, we went out on the trail and soon we were saddled up and riding to my house and all over. I loved him so much.

Being a Saddlebred, he had a spring to his step like his cousins in the show ring. However, he was not gaited like them. He could walk very fast when he was in the lead, but if behind other horses his temper flared and he would start to jig in place making his forward progress that much slower.

"Come on, fella, easy, easy does it," I'd tell him, but no matter what I did I could never convince him that by just *walking* he would get places much faster. He would get so hyped up that soon he would be cantering in place. The up side of this was that on trail rides I was almost always in the lead and not eating dust in the back.

The other thing that was fun about Brownie was how easy it was to show off on him. All I had to do to get him jigging and side-stepping was to nudge his sides a bit with my heel, and make a little click-click sound. Then he would be *on*! Head and neck all arched, lifting those front legs almost in slow motion while swinging his rear end from side to side. He was just beautiful when he did that.

The down side was that he never really settled back down after such a show, and in those days with a lot of us girls going braless, it was always a challenge taking Brownie on an all-day ride!

"I'm a little leery taking him to the high country," I told John as we readied for the next pack trip that fall.

"I really don't think you need to be," he told me. "That horse just plain flat out loves you, so I don't expect you'll have any trouble. Long as he knows you think something is all right, I think he'll go along with it just fine. He really trusts you. But I'll be right there to help if you need me."

Actually, I needn't have worried. After slightly objecting to the packs behind the saddle, he was all business on that trail. He was too busy just trying to climb the steep trail to think about any funny business.

That is unless he encountered wild animals. He had a real problem with anything that moved if it wasn't equine, canine, feline, or humanoid! Even a mouse set him off one day and if he saw deer he would completely jump out of his skin. A rider could never totally relax on Brownie, because if something as small as a mouse crossed your path, you were very likely to be on the ground before you knew what happened.

This was all made clear to me one day the following summer up in the high country on a pack trip. We were becoming a well-seasoned team. Or at least I thought so.

We were riding alone down a narrow trail to our favorite swimming hole at the river. My beagle Sheridi was with us. We came around a sharp corner and I heard the sound that always sent chills down my spine. The unmistakable hissing of a rattlesnake, the first one I ever encountered up in the high country. Unfortunately, as the sound was registering in my brain, it had already zipped through Brownie's and I was sitting in a cloud of dust in the middle of the trail not six feet away from the snake. Luckily, I still had hold of one rein, but was now faced with a problem. My stupid dog had never seen a snake before and thought she should bark and charge at it to protect me. So I had one scared horse behind me, and one overly brave dog in front of me who would not listen to me calling her off. Anyone who has ever owned a Beagle knows that once they are "locked" on something, the rest of the world ceases to exist. Someone upstairs must have heard my plea, because all of a sudden the snake realized *he* might be in danger with these three noisy intruders and decided to slink off into the underbrush.

I finally got Sheridi under control and hooked the lead rope to her collar to keep her from running in after it.

Brownie decided this was all too much and we needed to get back to the safety of camp. Try as I might, he would *not* let me get back on him on that skinny trail. So we turned around and headed back.

I was soon being more or less trampled by him in his eagerness to get back to his friends. Not that he actually stepped on me, but with his shoving at me to get me to move faster, it felt like it. So I put him in front of me and I tailed him most of the way back to camp.

As we got closer to the cabin, he walked much too fast for me and I let go. He reached camp a few minutes before I did.

A crowd was assembling as I got there. "We were just wondering if a search party was needed," one of the men told me when I came huffing and puffing up the trail with Sheridi happily trotting beside me.

"Come on, boys," Joe said, after hearing my story. "Let's go find us that snake."

"Yeah, good luck with that!" I said while several of the boys tore off down the trail and I went inside to nurse my wounded pride.

ග

"Wow, Gramma, that must have been really scary," said Kenny.

"Yes, it was," I told him. "It's kinda funny remembering it now, but not so funny then."

"Brownie sounds like a nice horse," said Lindsey. "Will you tell us some more about him?"

"Oh, I'll tell you lots of stories about him," I told her. "But right now, we've got other things to do. There were other very special horses, as well as some very special adventures. Let's get cleaned up for dinner and I'll tell you more tonight at the campfire."

So we all got busy tending to things that need to be done on a camping trip, like getting the fire going, and I thought ahead to what story I would tell my grandchildren next.

I was so very glad they enjoyed hearing about "the old days." It felt so right sharing these memories with them. So very, very right.

Chapter Four

Blaze

As the children gathered around me the second night of our campout, I remembered back to what it had been like all those years ago.

Terry asked, "So Gramma, do you have some more good stories tonight?"

"Well, as a matter of fact, I do," I answered as I sat down on a log in the middle of them as they jostled for position next to "Gramma."

ෆ

While I settled into my day-in-day out routine with John and the horses, my life became one of meaning to me. The horses took over my life and were all that were important to me. I was either in my own backyard brushing my horses and shoveling poop, or up at the stable caring for John's horses, or up at the pack station in heaven.

It seemed my whole life now revolved around when the next pack trip was. Waiting a whole winter became almost excruciating to me. My soul went through such withdrawals having to come back to the unbearable crowds and noise of the city.

Once in a while, John took pack trips to places other than the old Sam Lewis place. I was on two of those trips, but one was very memorable.

We were taking a group to go wild pig hunting into the National Forest near Big Sur on the coast of central California. I was the only girl on this trip and was so excited to be going because this was so much farther away than I'd ever been before with the horses. It felt like we were going to another country.

It was a long, tiring drive for both the horses and us. It took us around ten hours to drive with that load of horses before we got to where we were headed. We made several stops for food and bathroom breaks; however, the poor horses didn't get to be unloaded at all. Fortunately the weather was mild and they were very good horses, so it was okay.

There were twelve horses on this trip. Ten of them were in the Big Rig and behind it we had two more in a horse trailer. My horse, Brownie, and Doug's horse, Drifter, were chosen to ride in the trailer. John and Jim were in the cab of the truck, and with the back full of horses, Doug and I rode in a camper belonging to one of the hunters following behind.

Lying on the bunk inside the cab-over-camper, we had a good view of the road. We were on the last leg of this long drive and were getting excited. The rugged coast highway was extremely steep and winding as we watched our horses in the trailer swaying back and forth on that very curvy road.

"I'm sure glad it's John driving and not Jim," Doug told me. "I mean, Jim's a good guy and all, but he doesn't have the experience his dad has."

"Yeah, a winding road like this, with moving cargo, needs an experienced driver," I told him.

When we pulled over at what looked like just a wide spot in the road, imagine our surprise when Jim got out of the driver's door with a big smile on his face.

Doug and I just looked at each other and said, "Wow!" We were very impressed. He was indeed his father's son. From that moment on he could drive *my* horses anywhere! Of course he already had my heart.

"This is it," John said as he climbed down from the cab.

I looked around and saw nothing but vibrant green hills rising almost straight up, and on the other side of the highway, a rocky cliff plummeting straight down to the ocean. The coastline was very wild there. The sea was a brilliant blue green and violent waves crashed against those rocky cliffs below.

"Wow this is beautiful," I said to Doug. "But where is the trail? I don't see one."

"Me neither," he answered. "But John said they've been up here before, so I guess we'll be finding out."

While I just stood there taking in the gorgeous scenery, John and Jim started unloading horses. As they were unloaded, they were tied to the side of the truck and fed some hay.

"Hey, you gonna earn your keep or be a sightseer all afternoon?" John hollered.

I didn't say what I wanted to say, and instead went over and started unloading gear from another pickup with the group that carried all the tack and supplies.

About an hour later we were saddled up and ready to go. I was still unsure of where we were going until one of the hunters, who had been here before, motioned toward the hill. There was a faint trail heading up from the parking area. We got into a single line with Jim leading the way, me in the middle, Doug a little further back, John bringing up the rear, and off we went.

The grassy trail started climbing and climbing. It was all switchbacks as we rode up the face of that mountain. I didn't have a camera with me and wished I did. The scenery was absolutely astounding. As we neared the top, you could look down and not see anything but the ocean. The highway, our trucks, and the cliffs had all but disappeared and it looked like you could throw a rock straight into the ocean. What a powerful feeling it was up there on the side of that mountain.

At the top of the trail, the landscape turned into thick, heavy forest. It was wild beautiful country.

When we left the grassy hillside and rode into the trees, the hunters thought it would be fun to "scare the girl."

"Better be watching out for those wild pigs," the one named Calvin told me.

"That's right," chimed in Vince. "One of those pigs could snap a horse's legs clean in two. And, if they catch you on the ground they'll run their tusks clean through you."

Since I was on Brownie, my "nervous Nellie," I was a tad uncomfortable with these wildlife lessons. The trail we were on went through some very dense trees and undergrowth, and was only wide enough for one rider, so we were all stretched out in a long line.

I was deep in thought about what I would do if a boar came charging out of the brush when a rider in the rear started making pig sounds that sounded like they were coming from the bushes behind me. Brownie was no help because he was scared anyway, regardless of the fake sounds. He was snorting and fussing, acting normal for him. I didn't appreciate his jigging on this unkempt trail either. When I finally was able to ignore them and settle him back down, the teasing wasn't fun for them anymore.

We were moving along at a pretty good pace when the trail got very rocky and unstable. Suddenly, Jim hopped off his horse. "Everyone, *stop* your horses and dismount," he told us.

The trail was crumbling away in places. Jim then checked the trail and determined we could walk the horses slowly over the bad part. One by one we got off and slowly led our horses over the disintegrating trail, as loose rocks tumbled down the side of the mountain.

There always seemed be one know-it-all in every group. This one was riding Blaze. He didn't get off and just kept riding onto that bad spot.

"Hey! STOP! Get off!" Jim hollered at him, but it was too late.

As Blaze started across, the added weight of the man caused the big horse to lose his footing as the trail began to give way beneath him. By that time we were *all* yelling at the rider to jump off.

As the quiet brown gelding struggled to get his footing, he started to slip off the trail. Because of being off balance with the rider on his back, he was soon tumbling end over end down the side of that mountain. They dropped out of sight leaving all of us staring helplessly down into the ravine.

"Oh my God!" said Ed, echoing my thoughts exactly.

All we could see was a rising cloud of dust, but we could still hear the horse crashing down the side of the mountain. We heard trees breaking and rocks falling, and then, nothing but dead silence. It seemed to last forever. Everyone stood there helplessly not believing what we had just seen. All the horses had their ears pricked up staring down into the nothingness with startled eyes.

John broke the eerie silence. "Roni, you and Doug watch the other horses. Jim get your rifle and come with me. If that fall hasn't killed Blaze, I'm sure we'll have to put him down. I'm pretty sure he probably didn't live through that."

The injured rider was found about thirty yards down with a long cut on his scalp. It looked like someone had drawn a line from the nape of his neck to his forehead with a razor blade. It was bleeding very profusely, as head wounds tend to do. His buddies helped him back up to the trail.

Doug and I were watching over all the horses, who seemed to be waiting with us for the gunshot that was sure to come. The silence was deafening. It seemed like the whole forest was holding its breath waiting for the verdict on Blaze. We tried to yell down at them, but the drop off was too steep for them to hear us.

After what seemed like an eternity, we heard faint noises reaching up to us. Getting louder, they were soon mixed with voices and hooves scrambling over loose rocks. And then, unbelievably, up out of the depths of the still unsettled dust came two men and one very beat up horse.

The horses on the trail heard the commotion, and whinnied to Blaze and he bravely answered them as he struggled back up that hillside to reach his friends.

John and Jim looked relieved and happy. They reached the other side of the bad part of the trail and everyone sat to catch their breath.

Once the adrenalin settled down, we were able to look Blaze over and assess his injuries. He was pretty banged up. No big cuts, nothing was broken. He had a pretty nasty scrape wound over his hipbone, but we didn't have a vet available in the middle of nowhere, so we made the best of it. It could have been so much worse.

"When I got down to him, he was sitting on his haunches like a dog with his front feet out in front and sort of leaning against a tree," John told us. "Right in front of him was a sheer drop and certain death," John shook his head. "I don't know how he ever managed to keep from slipping any further. It was like he was saying, 'I'm not ready to die and I ain't goin' any further!'"

We relaxed a bit to let Blaze regain his composure and then headed up the trail to find a place to camp. The injured rider needed some attention and we were still far from our intended camping spot.

The joking and fooling around had gone by the wayside and all the hunters were thinking more about how to make their buddy more comfortable. I wasn't glad he got hurt or anything like that, but every time I looked at poor Blaze and thought about how he got hurt I didn't feel as sorry for that guy as I might have.

About an hour later, we came upon a small cabin that was marked with a U.S. Forest Service sign. It was padlocked.

"Okay, well, we'll do what we gotta do," John said. He busted the lock off the door. "It's getting dark and we're in need. Blaze has gone about as far as he can; his beat up body is getting stiffer and sorer by the minute. He needs rest and so does our patient, so we'll set up camp here."

Doug and I took care of all the horses and then tended to Blaze.

"Poor fella. He's so reluctant to move now. I think that all we can do is to try to make him as comfortable as possible," I told Doug.

"We've got this tarp that we can turn into a makeshift blanket for him," Doug said.

We put it over him and tied a couple lead ropes together to secure it around him. Then we cleaned his wounds and put grain and water in front of him for the night. "I guess that's about all we can do," said Doug.

We patted him, fed him some extra grain and went inside to see how things were going with our hunter. He was starting to feel very sore as well. The cut on his head had finally quit bleeding and he didn't appear to have any other injuries except to his pride for being so stupid.

"That was a darn fool thing to do," he admitted.

"Yes it was," John told him sternly. "You pay for us to lead you on these trips and then you don't pay attention to what we tell you. My son may be young, but he knows trails, he knows the dangers with horses, and he knows what he's doing. What you did today could well have cost you your life as well as the life of one of my best horses. To say nothing of the pain that poor animal is going through right now because of it. If there's anything more like that, anything at all, one of us will be taking you back. We can't afford to be taking risks like that." John held the man's gaze for several seconds. Then the man nodded wordlessly and looked away.

"Here's dinner," said John, as he passed around the plates. His attitude was one of having said all he was going to say on the subject and that it was over. We all ate in silence, each of us distinctly aware of what had almost happened that day.

"I'm going back out to check on Blaze and make sure everyone is okay for the night," I said. "Doug, want to come?"

"Sure," said Doug, hopping up and following me.

"I'm kinda scared of wild pigs in the brush," I told him. "I'll feel better with two of us out there."

One of the hunters made a choking sound which he quickly turned into a cough. I guess none of them figured that right then would be a good time to admit that the antics of wild pigs had been a product of wild imaginations.

"Oink, oink," said Doug after we had gotten outside. I gave him a good shove. It may not have helped anything, but it did get rid of a bit of frustration.

The horses whinnied at us for more grain. We watered them and then went over to where Blaze was standing.

"You poor horse," I told him rubbing his scrapped up face. "Poor old Blaze, getting hurt like that." I put my head against his nose and he nuzzled my cheek. He was shifting his weight back and forth, in obvious discomfort.

"Doug, don't we have some Bute in the saddle bag? I think he could use some."

"Yeah, I'm pretty sure I saw some in here." Doug said, picking up the leather bags to look.

We gave him a dose of the painkiller, and redressed his wounds. He ate his grain right up which was a good sign since a horse in a lot of pain won't eat.

He now had a swollen knee to add to his other injuries. The Bute would help with that as well. He wasn't sweating now and seemed warm enough, but we left the blanket on him for the night just in case he got cold.

The next morning it was decided that Jim would take the hunters back out so they could get their buddy to a doctor. His head was very swollen and he was in a lot of pain.

"I'm no doctor and he's probably fine, but it won't do any harm to be sure," John told them.

"I think it's the right thing to do too," said Calvin. "We really shouldn't take any chances with a head injury."

The injured man protested that he would be all right and didn't want to ruin their big adventure, but they all overrode him.

The men all opted to walk out, with Jim leading their buddy on horseback. It was an easy hike since it was all downhill, and once they got to the highway Jim got them on their way. He then rode back in and we planned to stay another day or so. It all hinged on Blaze and how fast he got over his ordeal.

Before we were able to leave, the Forest Rangers came through and cited us for breaking into their cabin.

"It was an emergency situation," John told them, recounting what had happened. "We had an injured rider with a head wound. We needed to get him inside out of the cold damp air. We couldn't tell how seriously he was injured."

They didn't believe John even when he showed them Blaze with his obvious injuries. They thought it wasn't true and they didn't much care what we had to say.

"Well, he obviously wasn't hurt so bad, since you folks didn't send someone down for help," the head Ranger told John. "We have to draw the line somewhere and I don't think this qualifies as an emergency."

We slept outside that last night and headed back down the mountain the next morning.

"I don't like those rangers very much," I said to Jim. "I mean isn't that U.S. property???? Why can't U.S. citizens use U.S. property in an emergency?"

The ride down the mountain was slow with us having to lead all the horses out. They weren't used to being led in a string without riders. Leading one horse was far different than leading two. The horse in back would tend to crowd the one in front of him and if it hadn't been for the narrow trail it could have been messy. We were moving much, much slower than normal because of Blaze.

When we reached the bad section of the trail, we all got off. Jim crossed and then John walked each horse over separately. None of them refused to cross that spot. Not even Blaze.

After we got to the truck, we tied them all up and fed them the rest of the grain. One of the hunters had left his pickup there so we could haul all of the saddles and gear home. We packed everything up and were loading the horses into the truck when a Ranger came by.

"Here's the date you should show up at court. You can explain everything then. Just bring all your proof with you as to what happened, and have that fellow bring in paperwork from his doctor. We'll see what the judge says. Have a nice day."

The trip home was uneventful, and we were so tired. John drove the Big Rig, Jim drove the pickup, and because of all the extra things we had to haul, Doug and I had to ride the whole way home in the back with the horses. It wasn't so bad though, because we loved being with them and I think they liked having us with them as well.

A few months later, John had to appear in court and he was fined for breaking into the cabin. We never went back there again.

೮೨

"Wow, was Blaze all right, Gramma?" asked Kenny. "Did he get okay?"

"Yes, he was lame and had a big swollen hip for a while. But after his bruises healed, he was as good as new."

"What about the hurt man?" asked Terry. "I mean, it was his own fault and all, but was he okay?"

I smiled, glad to see that the kids did care about what happened to the man rather than just feeling he got what he deserved.

"Yes, like Blaze, he was lame for a time. But soon, he too was as good as new," I told them. "I'll have another story for you later."

"Okay, Gramma," they chorused and ran off together while I sat, surrounded by my ancient friends, remembering.

Chapter Five

Poppin'

When I turned sixteen years old John gave me my first rifle. "I figure you're old enough now to have enough common sense to handle one of these," he told me. It was a .22 caliber magnum. I did target practice, but never killed anything with it. All the boys would fight over it on pack trips and *they* would certainly kill things! Not my cup of tea, but I did enjoy target practice.

"Good thing to have in case of wild pigs," Doug told me, teasingly. I had an idea that was one joke I was going to be the victim of for a long, long time.

John also taught me to drive in his old blue Studebaker pickup truck that happened to be a stick shift. I had driven my mom's station wagon a few times and wasn't intimidated by that. But his truck, that was another story. I vividly remember coming around the corner to my house and John telling me to downshift and me running right into a car that was stopped at a stop sign. By the time he was through with me I was driving on the Pasadena Freeway in the mornings, going with him to his job and back. He taught me to drive everything in sight.

At sixteen-and-a-half I had my first truck. A 1955 lemon yellow Chevy pickup! It was a three-speed automatic. It didn't have a radio and the heater didn't work. Like all vehicles from that time period, to cool off it had "wind wings" that you could open all the way to get a cross wind going. Oh, how I loved to drive that old truck, but it always seemed that John's vehicles would break down and he would need mine!

John taught me how to drive his Big Rig, too! He would have me drive it when we were going to get hay on back roads. But I never drove it with horses. That was a whole other story. Hay didn't move around inside.

"I'm telling you this, so I can tell you the story of Hellzapoppin'," I told the children gathered around for yet another story.

"Gramma!" gasped one of them.

I laughed. "No, I'm not using a bad word," I told them, smiling. "Hellzapoppin' is the name of a horse, a very special horse." I leaned back and let my mind wander to that long ago time as I continued with my story.

ꕥ

Hellzapoppin' came to us by chance. The daughter of my mom's realtor owned him and had to sell him. She knew that I had fallen in love with him and that we had a new home with room for him in that big backyard. He came to live with us in 1966 at the age of four. His name, from a Broadway play, was the basis for a lot of conversation among the kids and adults around me. The adults called him Poppin' which sounded much more prim and proper. The kids relished the fact that they could say "Hell" and get away with it. As the years went by he simply became Poppin' to us all. Hellzapoppin' if I was particularly annoyed with him.

He was absolutely, unequivocally *the* best horse I have ever come in contact with in my whole life. He was a beautiful leopard appaloosa and built like a stocky quarter horse, with a thick neck and bulging chest and butt muscles. He had a large head that was nicely shaped and not out of proportion with the rest of his body. He had a long flowing white tail that somehow made him look more like a show horse than a backyard pet.

His temperament was his most amazing quality. He would outsmart you whenever he had the chance. He could open gates that were escape proof, buck to unseat you when he knew you weren't paying attention, give his all when riding up a steep hill, jump over most obstacles, and be the fastest in the keyhole event. Yet, he could be as gentle as an old broken-down nag with a young child on his back. He always knew the ability of his rider, so I was never afraid to let anyone ride him. He would take care of them.

The very first pack trip Poppin' went on he established himself as herd leader. We were camped in the Big Rig below the corrals. This was still before we leased the pack station, but no one else was around, so we put the horses in the corrals for the night. There were several other teenagers on this trip with us, kids who I rode with on a regular basis at the stables.

After sweeping out the horse poop, we all rolled out our sleeping bags in the back of the Big Rig and settled in for the night.

I put a red blanket on Poppin' because he had been blanketed all his life and was not used to "roughing it" just yet.

"Here ya go, fella," I told him. "Nice and comfy now."

A slight commotion woke us up at dawn and we peered out of the back of the truck just in time to see the horses escaping from the corral. There was Poppin' in all his glory, his red blanket so askew he looked as if he was a mighty warrior doffing his cloak for battle, leading the charge of horses out of the open gate and to the freedom of the open desert. We all jumped from our sleeping bags and charged out to head them off.

"Poppin', no!" I yelled. "Get back here!"

Poppin', stealthy as a cat, slipped back past us into the corral and was standing by a feeder eating when I reached the gate. He looked up at me as if to say, "Well, what took you so long? I tried to talk them out of it, but they wouldn't listen. I told them they would get caught!" Then he went back to eating his hay. His red blanket was now wrapped around him in a most unkingly like fashion. I couldn't stop laughing. He was just so "human"!

It was always entertaining and fun to ride him into the high country. There was nothing he wouldn't do. He was up for any challenge on the trail. He liked to be in front, but you could place him anywhere along the string and he would do great.

On rides out, if we were with experienced riders, we would cut straight down ravines and take shortcuts down the shale hills instead of using the switchbacks. I always trusted him completely, and was never worried that he would lose his footing. Sometimes if we were going too slowly for his liking, he would get so bored he would yawn incessantly. And once we got to the switchbacks, he would throw his head in the direction we were turning as if he had turn signals to warn the riders behind him. He did it all the time, every trip.

However, Hellzapoppin's most memorable ride in the high country was one without me.

It was the end of hunting season and the last group of five hunters were packed up and ready to be taken out. I had Brownie saddled up to lead them out while John stayed behind and stowed things for the winter.

"If you don't mind, I'll keep Poppin' here for me to ride and I'll pack up Sandpiper. Be nice to actually ride out for once," John told me.

"Sounds good to me," I told him. I knew John didn't really care for Brownie's bouncy gait. He had the big palomino gelding, Sandpiper, for his packhorse. Piper was very dependable as a packhorse and could carry quite a load. He stood about 16 hands and weighed a good 1200 pounds.

I reached the desert in the early afternoon, unpacked all the horses, and sent the hunters on their way. After feeding the horses, I settled in to wait for John, who had planned to be about an hour behind me.

I was alone on the desert with just the horses for company. The always-present sounds of the desert lulled me off for a short catnap. When I woke, it was nearing dusk. I looked around and saw no sign of John.

"Where is he?" I thought to myself. Trying not to panic, yet imagining all sorts of scenarios, I saddled Brownie to start back up the trail to look for him.

About that time, I glanced up and saw horse heads snapping up out of feeders with their ears pricked forward all looking towards the trailhead. I followed their gaze and sure enough, there came a rider and two horses moving very slowly.

As he got nearer, I saw that there was blood on his face and hands and he looked dazed. The horses didn't look all that much better. "John!" I yelled. "What happened?"

I ran to him and he slid down out of the saddle, barely able to stand. We managed to get to the tailgate of the truck and I sat him down while still trying to figure out what had happened to them.

He wasn't very coherent, so I ran and got a bucket of ice-cold water from the trough. His shirt was torn and his pants were ripped and the bone of his little finger was shoved back and sticking out of the back of his hand. I washed his face, noting that there were just scratches and bruising but no serious lacerations. I stuck his hand in the bucket of water and took off his shirt to check his torso for damage. His chest and arms were covered with bruises. He looked like he had been in a prizefight and came out on the losing end.

After fully assessing John's condition, I decided he needed to lie down. "Here, come on," I told him. "Let's see if we can't get you at least a little bit comfortable." I got him situated on the tailgate, used my jacket for a pillow and covered him up with my sleeping bag. I then turned my attention to the horses.

They were both standing exactly where they had stopped as John slid off, seemingly unable to move any further. Looking them over, it finally registered in my mind what had happened. The saddles were all scuffed up and Sandpiper's pack was all but non-existent. They both had scratches, scrapes, and cuts all over their legs. Sandpiper had hide missing from a hipbone, and Poppin' had a gash over one eye. Suddenly, it was clear to me that they looked pretty good for a couple of horses that appeared to have just fallen off a mountain!

When he came to, John was able to piece together what happened. "Well, as you know, one of the first things I teach you, is to never, ever, put the lead rope of the animal you are leading over the saddle horn," he told me. I saw a faint flicker of a grin, even though John was obviously hurting. This was something he had impressed on me emphatically a number of times.

"I was riding down from the summit on that part of the trail that narrows and has the big boulder jutting out into it, that place where we always have to sort of tuck our leg in as we go by the rock. I was getting warm, and we were moving down the trail at a pretty good clip. I decided to take my coat off, so I put the lead rope over the saddle horn just for a second as I took it off. At that exact moment, Sandpiper was passing by that boulder on the trail. The pack bumped into that boulder with such force that it knocked Sandpiper completely off the trail."

"Oh no!" I gasped.

"Oh yes," he assured me. "With the lead rope over the saddle horn, my leg was completely trapped by the tight rope. I couldn't bail out so I was hoping that Poppin' would be able to keep his footing and pull that big guy back up onto the trail. But the sudden backwards motion on the steep hillside caused Poppin' to lose his footing and he started to slip. As Sandpiper slipped further down the hillside, Poppin' tried to stay upright. But as the hillside crumbled beneath us, soon he was being pulled over backwards. As soon as he flipped over, the lead rope popped loose, and I was able to jump free of him. I'm tellin' ya, there was nothing but dust and dirt and rocks flying everywhere as the three of us went head over heels, end over end down through the sagebrush and trees to the very bottom of that ravine. The content of that packsaddle was being thrown every which way as Sandpiper went tumbling down. I was rolling after him, and every time I looked up, Poppin' was coming down right on top of me. I bet I've got Poppin's hoof prints in several places on my body." John started to shake his head, then grimaced as he thought better of it.

"After what seemed like the longest end of forever, the noise stopped. I stayed still, dazed, but somehow alive. I looked at the horses who had taken this little side trip with me. They were also dazed, but alive. The three of us just sat there for the longest time. I think none of us wanted to move for fear that something would really hurt. I finally got my wits about me and started to try to figure a few things out. Like, am I hurt? And, if so, how bad? Are the horses hurt and how bad? And how in the heck am I going to get out of here?"

"I looked at my hand and realized I had a compound fracture of this finger and a couple dislocated fingers next to it. It was hard to breathe, so I supposed I had a couple of broken ribs and there was a nice horseshoe imprint on my groin. I knew I couldn't stay there all night. It would be cold and the horses would need feed and water."

"Soon the horses were moving about, testing their muscles and acting like they didn't want to stay there either, so I started gathering what was left of the supplies that were within reach. I took the saddles off and looked for any serious wounds on the horses. Finding none I re-saddled them. I repacked what I could on Sandpiper and decided to leave what wasn't necessary behind. With my hand and my ribs hurting, it seemed to take forever to re-saddle those two. I realized I couldn't go up the way I came down, so I started searching for a way back to the trail. We couldn't go down the ravine because it became too steep. So, we started walking *up* the ravine. I knew that the trail crossed it farther up."

"It took about an hour for us to make our way back up to the trail. It was steep going and with no sort of trail to follow we had to pick our footing carefully. Once we were back on the trail we rested for a bit." John was silent for a few seconds, then continued. "It was fortunate that I had those two particular horses with me. Any others and it might have been a real disaster. Because Sandpiper is such a gentle, quiet, and calm fella, and Poppin' is just the smartest horse ever, they trusted me completely and, well, I completely trusted them." John took a sip of water before he continued. "Finally, it was time to get moving. The longer we stood, the stiffer we'd get. I tightened the cinch on Poppin' and with muscles that screamed at every movement, I somehow, slowly pulled myself up into that saddle and off we went down the trail as if nothing had ever happened."

"Man, I tell ya once we got to 'the rock,' I was pretty nervous. I know I tensed up pretty good. Not just because I was mentally reliving my E ticket ride down the mountain, but because I didn't think the horses would go by it."

"Yeah, that's one thing about horses," I told him. "Once they have a bad experience, they don't like a repeat."

"So I just started talking to them," John said. "I said things like, 'What do ya say?' 'Think we can get by this ol' rock this time boys?' 'It will be a whole lot easier if you can manage to stay on the trail this time. And I know for a fact yer gettin' hungry. There's hay and oats awaitin' for ya.' 'You just gotta get us by this one tiny little rock and its home free. Heck ya done it before. You've done it lots of times. And I think you're gonna do it this time too!' And they did. They didn't snort. They didn't shy away. They barely slowed down as they strode right by that rock like it was just any other trip. I was elated because I had no idea what I would do if they refused to pass by that rock."

Once I got the horses unsaddled, rubbed down, fed, watered, and put away, I went back to see about John. He had a bottle of whiskey, which I opened, gave him a swig and then took a bigger swig for myself. Then I poured some over the wounds on his broken hand.

As I examined his fingers, I stretched them out and quickly pulled on the two that were distorted. That brought the bone that was sticking out more in line with the others. I got them into a somewhat normal looking position and taped them up. I thanked God for the first aid kit that was in the truck and for my basic Girl Scout First Aid training. I dressed and treated his other wounds and wrapped his hand up so the fingers would stay put. Then I got him into his sleeping bag. I don't think he was even aware of anything I was doing. The whiskey had done its job well. I finished it off.

We spent that night huddled up in the truck trying to stay warm. We should have been home long ago, but there was no way John could drive that rig. I had nightmares trying to figure out how we were going to get all those horses and *us* back to Altadena.

The next morning dawned and John was barely able to move. "You're going to have to drive the rig," he told me.

"You're kidding right? I've never driven it with horses before, John! And never on a busy highway! You've only had me drive it on back roads when we were getting hay. And I have always been apprehensive about driving it with horses in it because of all the scary stories you've told me." He was always regaling me with stories of how hard it was to handle with horses in it moving back and forth.

The most memorable one was when he was run off the road and the whole truck tipped over and skidded on its side with horses hanging upside down and trampling each other. As he started to climb into the back to get his horses out, someone thinking of his safety grabbed the back of his belt and he just whirled around swinging. The CHP officer hit the ground dazed, and watched as John climbed back up and whistled loudly. The horses calmed immediately knowing that John was there to help them. They trusted him completely as he started undoing lead ropes and kicking them out the back. A carload of teens had stopped and helped catch and hold horses until the tow truck came to right the rig and John could load them all back in. And every single horse *did* get back in. Such was the relationship he had with his horses.

Yeah, I had heard all those stories, and he expected *me* to drive that truck? "You'll do just fine!" he told me.

I got the horses all loaded with no problems. They were always anxious to get in the rig, knowing they were headed home. Life was much easier for them in Altadena. John gamely climbed up into the passenger seat and told me, "Get a move on, day's a wastin'!"

Reluctantly, I slowly got up into the driver's seat. I don't think I had ever in my whole life been this nervous. There were eight horses in this rig that I was responsible for. Oh, how was I going to be able to do this? It was a four-hour trip with horses. Sometimes, even longer. How would I be able to keep it together that long? I was scared to death!

My fingers turned the key in the ignition and the old truck roared to life. John didn't seem nervous at all. "You're fine. You can do it!" he told me. It was pretty easy driving the truck down the three-mile long dirt road. It was all in low gear and I didn't have to think about anything really. I could feel the horses leaning and swaying every time we went around a bend in the road. But I never heard any scrambling like they had lost their footing. My confidence grew as we plodded along at ten or fifteen miles an hour.

As we finally approached the highway, my stomach started doing little flip-flops again. Here was the moment of truth. Could I actually pull this big truck out onto busy Highway 395, not freak out, keep it running straight, fast enough not to annoy other drivers, *and* try to figure out how to shift it and not stall out all at the same time?

I waited for the longest time before there was no traffic then swallowed the lump in my throat, let out on the clutch, and off we went. It was slow going for the first several miles. I decided that I didn't care what people called me as they went around the slow moving truck. And there were a few who thought I had never seen that silly finger gesture before. I was building up my confidence and they could take a flying leap! By the time we got to Mohave, I was getting pretty good.

John kept coaching me on when to shift and when to push that mysterious red button on the gearshift that gave you more power. It was getting smoother and easier. The next big fear I had was encountering traffic as we got closer to L.A., but by that time, it seemed the truck was handling *me* just fine! The horses were barely noticeable and it was smooth sailing the rest of the way.

We went to the stables first and unloaded all the horses. I made John stay in the truck since he was barely able to move, so I had to do everything that it usually took both of us to do. I fed and watered all of them, and got them settled in for the night.

Next, we went to my house and parked the rig there and I took John home in the car. "Good night, young lady. You did a helluva job."

I felt such a sense of pride. I had conquered a monster!

"Ouch!" I said as I got out of bed the next day. "Man, I'm so stiff and sore I feel like it was me that went down off the mountain. I must have been so tense while driving that truck that I lamed up every muscle in my upper body," I said to my mom. I drug myself out of bed, aches and pains and all, because I had to go feed the horses at the stables.

When I got there, Poppin' and Sandpiper were very reluctant to move. I had squelched my pain with a handful of Excedrin, but

I couldn't do the same for them. I did have some old Bute (horse aspirin) lying around and gave them each a dose. Their scrapes and cuts were well scabbed over and I was reluctant to do anything more to them. They just stood in the same spot all day. Way too sore to move. But that was nothing compared to how John felt.

He went to the doctor the next day and got a good once over. He had a couple of broken ribs, multiple contusions, bruises, hoof prints in his groin area and on his back, and one hand with two broken fingers, one of which had been a compound fracture. As far as treatment, they didn't really do anything. Time would heal his wounds. The doctor was surprised while examining his hand "Who set your finger so well?" he asked John.

"Oh, just a sixteen year old girl with a Girl Scout Merit Badge and training in first aid. That's who!" John beamed.

∽

"So, that was Poppin's most memorable trip," I told my grandchildren. "And it was an important trip for me as well. It brought out the 'can do' in me that I hadn't known even existed before. I had a new attitude after that trip, and very rarely felt inadequate again."

Chapter Six

Closet Cleaning

It didn't take long to settle into my new life without school by working for John at the stables and by going on every single pack trip that came along. He had acquired the lease on the station right after the fall with Poppin', so we went all the time.

This meant that we had an actual cabin on the desert to use with all the corrals and outbuildings. Plus, three log cabins in the high country were ours to use as well. No more camping at the river! Hooray!

We had a beautiful new sign made for the entrance down at the highway. It was now called "The Sierra Lady Pack Station." Sierra Lady! What a beautiful image that conjured up. And it *was* beautiful in a dry, hot, dusty sort of way.

ʚɞ

I was sixteen when John left me alone at the pack station for the first time.

"You've got the dogs here for protection," he told me. "You'll do absolutely fine."

It was the first of spring and the first trip back since Poppin's fall and my ordeal driving the Big Rig. I mean, if I could handle that, this would be easy. It was just for overnight while he went back for a second load of horses. I would be there for several weeks getting trails and cabins ready for trips in. I wasn't scared. After all, I had my brave dogs with me!

After I rustled up some dinner for us, we headed out to make sure all the horses were settled in for the night. "Okay, I'll see you tomorrow evening," John told me. He jumped in the truck and off he went.

I called the dogs in and locked the door. I had just a small fleeting moment where I realized I was absolutely alone here. No phones and no way to contact anyone at all, but it really didn't seem like a big deal. I mean, I had the dogs, and John would be back tomorrow; all was fine. Plopping down in the chair by the wood-stove, I decided to read for a while. Then I got up, said goodnight to my little white beagle-sized Frosty, and the scruffy, Airedale-type mutt, Hobie, my trusty guardians; stoked the fire; put out the lantern; and went to bed.

For some reason I couldn't sleep. I tossed and turned for an hour or so before getting up to find something to do. I didn't feel like reading anymore. The cabin was relatively clean, but there was this energy in me that needed releasing.

Finally, I remembered the closet in the back of my little room at the rear of the cabin. "Perfect. I'll clean that out," I said to the dogs as I jumped out of bed. They responded by yawning their disapproval of me relighting the lantern.

I grabbed a couple of bags from under the sink, went to the closet, and opened the door. We hadn't bothered to look in that closet after we took possession and I told John that the back bedroom was going to be mine. He didn't see a problem with it. It would give me some privacy when others were there.

"But you'll have to clean it!" he told me with a grin.

Inside I found several shelves with what looked like old clothes and newspapers. There had been plenty of rats in there and I was hoping that I didn't surprise one right then. But when I saw Frosty's curiosity peaked as he came into the back room from his spot in front of the wood-stove, I knew there would be no problem with rats! "Good boy," I told him. "You can stay right here and be my protector!"

I started pulling things off the shelves and semi-sorting through them. All the clothes were old and non-usable, and all went into the trash. I was a little more careful looking through the papers and several old, musty boxes. However, there wasn't really anything to save. It just looked like papers and junk that meant nothing to any of us who were now involved with the pack station.

As I reached for the last box on the very top self, the dust rolled off the lid of the old shoebox and nearly suffocated me. I coughed and sneezed and went to the sink to wash it off. I grabbed a rag and went back to wipe the box clean. When I raised the lid, inside was an old leather-bound book and several pictures. There were also old letters and a ledger book. Carefully I lifted the book out. I opened it and found to my surprise that it was a journal of some kind. I slowly opened the cover I saw it belonged to Sam Lewis, the very man whose name had been on the old sign at the highway. "Wow! How could it be that this wasn't discovered long ago?" I said out loud.

Looking at the pictures, I recognized many of them as the same places I had come to love. Only these were in black and white and from what appeared to be the 1920s and '30s. There were pictures of Sam and his horses strung out along the trail to the summit, pictures of Sam and his children standing in front of the cabin at Dutch John Flat, pictures of the cabin on Deer Mountain, of hunters with their kills, of Sam's homestead and him riding across the desert, of Sam and his horses standing in the river at the very same crossing *we* used. Timeless pictures of the man who built this place.

I grabbed the journal and crawled back into bed and started reading. I hadn't gotten past the first page before I yawned, put out the lantern, fell into a deep sleep, and dreamed about this man I would never know, but somehow did.

The pictures I had seen floated around in my brain. Old images were overlapping the newer ones of my life in this spot.

ꕥ

I am packing in with Sam. His horses are packed the conventional way. Something I am not used to, as John does things differently. Up the trail we go. The man who built this place and the girl from the city who feels she has lived here all her life. Sam talks the whole way up the mountain telling me all about how he came to be here. He tells me how he built the cabins, and how once he had his family, they helped him run his pack station. We ride and talk. I listen and soak up every word this simple, uncomplicated man of the land has to tell me.

ꕥ

Sunshine on my face let me know that morning had snuck up on me, and the horses were probably lined up at the fence waiting for me to feed them. I stretched and remembered my dream. It had seemed so real. I got up and the journal fell to the floor. I gently picked it up and ran my fingers across the cover as tenderly as if it were the Holy Bible.

"I'll be reading more of you tonight!" I said, placing it under my pillow.

ɕɔ

With a grunt, I pulled on my boots and the dogs and I stepped out into the bright, crisp, early spring morning. I made a stop at the outhouse, then headed for the corral.

The horses were trying to outdo each other for my attention, and by the time I reached the hay shed they were in a frenzy. When feeding a bunch of hungry horses, it is important to keep your eyes on them, because when horses are hungry, they have absolutely *no* brains. Nada!

So, what I usually did was throw a big armful of hay over the fence. Then, while they were all fighting and sorting that out, I went around inside the corral and put hay in all the feeders. By that time the lower ones on the totem pole were looking in other places for something to eat. By the time I was done, there were usually four to six groups of horses eating quietly.

While they were eating, I went back in and tidied up the place a bit, fed the dogs, and grabbed a bowl of cereal and a glass of milk. John wasn't due back until evening, so I had the day all to myself. I just wasn't sure how to spend it.

I went outside and sat on a rock to eat while enjoying the busy sounds of the desert. In the early morning it was very noisy as all of God's creatures were getting on with their day. I closed my eyes and turned my face to the sun, absorbing the peacefulness of this place. My mind, body, and spirit seemed to soak up the essence of the desert. I had never been in such a peaceful state of mind.

When I gathered my dishes and went back inside, the dogs came racing in to show me the latest deer bone they had found. I laughed at little Frosty being drug around by the larger dog as they each had an end of it in their mouths.

For some reason I didn't feel like riding today. That was unusual since I always needed to be on the back of a horse. So I decided to go for a walk.

"Come on fellas, wanna go for a walk?"

The dogs were excited the minute they heard me say "walk," and even more so as we stepped out of the cabin.

This time I headed away from the cabin instead of across to the horses. They felt an adventure was in store as I made my way over to the edge of the canyon and started walking.

Both dogs were bounding in front of me, sniffing the ground and the air at the same time. One would get a scent and off he'd go with the other one hot on his heels. They were having so much fun chasing lizards and an occasional rabbit. Hobie was getting covered with burrs in his long silky coat that would take forever to comb out. They were having a grand time.

I was so busy watching the dogs that I almost missed it. The brush halfway covered the large flat rock that lay there along the canyon rim. It was the size of a large desk. It had eleven very deep round holes in it as well as two very shallow ones. This was the most amazing rock I had ever seen. I cleared some of the brush away from it so I could have a better look. Most of its holes were six to eight inches deep. It was obvious to me that this was a grinding stone that must have been used for centuries.

When I sat down next to it and put my hand on it, at first it just felt cold. But soon, I felt an odd warmth that seemed to emanate from the stone right up my arm and into the depths of my soul.

"This is unbelievable." I said out loud. I can't explain how that stone made me feel. My whole being was calm and relaxed. My mind was not in the present, but in some distant faraway time. There was that familiar jumble of noises in my head that were usually reserved for my dreams. Only I was wide awake in broad daylight this time. At least I thought I was.

The soft noises in my head turned to distinct voices. Women's voices. There was also the sound of stone rubbing against stone. I closed my eyes and saw them. Shadows seemed to be sitting there before me grinding their nuts into fine powder. The voices were happy and seemed so carefree. I was hypnotized by the light sing-song tone of their voices.

I sat there for quite some time until I was jarred from my trance by the sounds of two happy but worn out dogs crashing through the sagebrush. They jumped all over me before I had a chance to stand up. Licking me on the face, their breath smelled foul like they had caught up with "something." I didn't want to know what!

I stood by that rock a few more minutes, trying to remember a story I had heard about people crossing into another time and place. There was a term for such objects. "Oh, what is it? Think girl. Port something! That's it!" I said to myself. The story I had read about time travel that used that term. "Portal," I said as I reverently backed away from the stone.

The dogs and I then walked a little further down along the edge of the canyon. There were so many obsidian chips everywhere. We were always on the lookout for a real arrowhead. My head was still somewhat in a daze from the encounter on the stone that I almost missed it.

It was laying right smack dab in front of my foot. If I hadn't been looking down at that *exact* second, I would have walked right over it. *It* was a perfect, shiny black arrowhead. My very first one. I reached down for it and was struck by that same warmth in this tiny object as the grinding stone had. I turned it over and over in my hands marveling at the craftsmanship. What it must have taken to create these tools. I looked up to the bright blue, cloudless sky and whispered a silent thank you to no one in particular for allowing me to find this arrowhead.

As I put it in my pocket, I whistled for the dogs. "Come on, let's go," I called. We all raced each other back to the cabin. I went out and checked the horses and then decided a nap was in order. It had been hard work all morning keeping track of those dogs and daydreaming by that rock. I was exhausted!

I fixed a sandwich and settled down in the chair with Sam's journal. This time I read several pages before falling asleep.

ൾ

"I was born July 31, 1893 in Galesburg, Illinois, to Charles William Lewis and Estella Turner Lewis. My father worked for the Santa Fe Railroad and we followed it to New Mexico when I was two years old. We lived in the town of Eddy, which was renamed Carlsbad in 1899. It was a primitive life with no electricity, no telephones, and no running water. A water tank wagon came around and sold water by the bucket. Livestock grazed the open range and everyone fenced their gardens to keep the animals out.

"When I was five years old I started school and rode my horse two miles. My teacher had to help me on to ride home. I don't ever remember falling off. Both my brother, Charles, and my sister, Isabel, were born in Carlsbad.

"My father worked many jobs after the railroad was done. One of them was Deputy Sheriff. It was a pretty rough place with saloons and gambling. Fights and shootings were common. He quit after my mother nearly had a nervous breakdown. I started working various jobs when I was a young teen. Anything from tending sheep to hauling goods by wagon to helping my dad run the power house to working in a sawmill.

"Then Dad decided to go to California to work in the oilfields, and I went too. The work was hard and the days were long. I had dreams of finding a place of my own in the mountains to homestead. Southern California had way too many people to suit me, and it offered me no chance to get the home I dreamed of. So I quit, bought me a couple of horses--one to ride and the other to pack my bed--and headed north to get away from the crowded conditions of the Los Angeles area. That was July 1914."

 က

The hot afternoon sun on my face woke me from my nap. I heard the droning of a truck engine and realized that John was probably returning with the load of horses.

I jumped up, ran to the sink, splashed some cold water on my sleepy face, and ran outside to wait for the truck. The dogs had been napping in the afternoon sun as well and now stood and stretched with their ears perked looking down the road. I always loved watching that big rig inch its way up the road from the highway. Most of the time you could just barely see the top of the truck. Then it would disappear and all you could follow was the dust cloud it was raising. Soon, it would reappear closer.

Then the horses in the corral heard it and they all trotted to the fence looking toward the dust trail. Closer and closer it came, until finally the whole truck came into view. John laid on the horn and suddenly the horses all started whinnying and trotting around the corral. Equally excited whinnies were coming from inside the truck. Hobi and Frosty wiggled with excitement thinking that finally something fun was happening. It had been pretty darn boring for them around here last night!

The truck passed by me as he drove it up around by the gate. I ran up to help him unload the new arrivals. The horses in the corral were going crazy by that time.

"Well, how was your night?" John asked as he climbed down from the cab.

"It was interesting," I answered. "I sat out and stared at stars for quite a while. Then tried to go to sleep and couldn't. So I cleaned out the closet."

"Your mom sent some clothes up for you and says she loves you," he said, as he started to lower the tailgate.

I didn't say anything. "Don't be so hard on her, kiddo. She loves you. She's worried about you. I promised her you would be okay here. But you can't cut off all communication from her. She'll make you go back home."

"All right, I'll write her a note," I said. "She can't make me leave here. She wouldn't, would she?" I asked, defiantly trying to think of all the reasons I needed to stay here and the thousands of reasons why I couldn't go back.

The horses in the truck thought John was taking too long and were getting very impatient. One started pawing and that set several more off. John let out a loud whistle and a second later all was quiet.

"That's what I love about you, John," I said as I grabbed the first horse and led him down the ramp. "Your horses love you! They listen better than most kids listen to their folks!"

We unloaded them, put them into the smaller corral and threw out hay for everyone. "We'll keep the two groups separate until after they eat," John told me. "They're too wound up to mingle with each other for a while."

Then we went down to the cabin with the boxes of supplies he had brought with him and unpacked everything and put it all away.

As I heated up some chili for dinner, I told him about the journal I found.

"Well I'll be," he said. "I didn't think there was anything of his left around here. That's some piece of history you've got there."

After we finished eating I washed the dishes while John played with the dogs. They loved him. All animals loved him. And most people did, too!

"How's Jim?" I asked as I finished cleaning up. He always seemed to be on my mind and was the *only* person I missed when away at the pack station.

"Don't you go getting' stuck on him, you hear? He's not good for you," John snapped. It took me by surprise. Little did I know that they had a strained relationship, probably brought on by the fact that they were so alike.

After John helped put the dishes away, we went out and opened the gates to let the new bunch of horses in with the old. They all trotted up to each other snorting and squealing and kicking as horses do. "Even though they all know each other it's like they have to re-establish their pecking order," John laughed. "You would think they would know the routine by now. They'll quiet down in a little bit." He was right, by dusk all was quiet in the corral.

John built a fire in the woodstove. "I know its early spring and the days are getting' warm, but these nights still seem to have a touch of that winter chill reluctant to let go," he said. Soon it was toasty warm inside and the dogs settled down to sleep curled up in front of the stove, and in no time at all they were running and yipping in their dreams.

"Well, I'm afraid I'm not much company tonight. Been up since before the sun, and this ol' body wants some sleep," John said as he tried to stifle a yawn. "I'll see you in the morning bright and early. We've got a family arriving tomorrow to take in. Get some sleep." He spread his sleeping bag out on the couch, climbed in and was fast asleep before I closed the door to my room.

I lit my lantern and climbed into bed with Sam's journal, eager to read more about this pioneer of the desert and mountains I loved so much.

My eyes didn't get through very many pages before they got blurry. I shut down the lantern, rolled over, and faded fast to dreamland.

ഗ

I am following a string of horses up a dust-choked trail. Up ahead is a man on an Appaloosa horse. He turns around and smiles at me. His face seems familiar.

"It's about time you caught up. Thought I'd lost you!" the cowboy says.

I look around and realize I am on the trail to the high country. Ah, now it's becoming clearer.

"You were wantin' to know more about how I came here," he says, seeing the confusion on my face.

"Oh, right," I reply. I listen with rapt attention. I am no longer confused about my whereabouts, because it doesn't really matter. I am with Sam Lewis. And he is telling me his story.

He starts to speak, "I followed the road here to Owens Valley where they were building the Los Angeles Aqueduct to bring water to that thirsty city. I knew nothing about the country I was going into. When I got to Little Lake in Inyo County, I ran into a man who gave me a job breaking horses. Then, after a few more odd jobs, I took a job working for John Calloway, a cattleman whose ranch was on the east side of the valley where China Lake Naval Ordinance Base is now.

"I liked Rose Spring Valley. There was a place against the Sierra Nevada Mountains where a small spring came out and formed a meadow that looked good to me. It was held by an old man who, I felt sure, would give up before long. I offered to buy his relinquishment, and he took me up on the offer. Then I realized what I had done. I had no money and no idea how I could make any. So I borrowed some. Enough to fence my place and buy some cows, and I put up a tent until I could build a home. That was in 1916 and we were headed for war. So I joined the Navy."

We stop at the summit and dismount. The string of packhorses also stops to rest. They seem to know that this is a usual stop on the trek in. Sam loosens his cinch a bit and comes over to check mine. He has a handsome face, wrinkles finely chiseled around his eyes by the years of living outdoors.

"I've been watching you," he says to me. "You don't seem like no city girl I ever met. You sit a horse real good, and don't seem afraid of these rough mountains."

I look at him and try to envision where and when he has been watching me. "This is the first place I have ever felt truly at home." I tell him.

"Yep, me too," he says with a wink.

"Tell me more," I say.

"Well, after the war I came back to the 'High Lonesome,' that's what I call my place, and that's what I was, lonesome! So I married a gal named Olive Truax on December 22, 1918, and we took up life on the homestead. I worked at any job I could find, from County road work to teamwork for mine claims, to riding for cattlemen and doing farm work or fence building and packing. After several drought years and the depression years, it became evident I couldn't make it with cattle. But I saw I could make it with horses. I could work with horses by packing people to the mountains for fishing and hunting and camping through the summertime, so I sold the cattle and bought some horses and set up my packing business.

"I used to take off from the High Lonesome and head up into the mountains to what is now called Kennedy Meadows. I would drop groups of people all over these mountains. Then I got hold of the land at Haiwee Canyon and built the pack station. I built some of these cabins up here in the high country too.

"My wife and I had six children. Lucille was born in 1920; Estella in 1921; Sam Jr. in 1924: Helen in 1926; Richard in 1933; and Barbara in 1935. All were perfect, healthy, and beautiful, and each was worth their weight in gold. They all helped me with the packing business. Olive cooked all the meals that would be needed in the high country. The kids, as they got old enough, would help with the horses. If they were still too young to ride, I would put them in a pack box and they would ride in that way. They sometimes stayed in the mountains all summer. They were such a big help to me."

"People around here say you did things different than most other packers," I say to him. I am so fascinated by his way of doing things.

"Yes, I s'pose that's true," he answers. "Fer instance, I didn't string my pack animals all out behind me on the trail. I trained them to drive ahead of me up the trail. That way there were no stragglers and I had everyone in front of me so I could see 'em! They got so used to this way of going that once they were packed and the gate was open, they took off up the trail. My horses loved their jobs and loved to be up in the high country.

"Sometimes I wouldn't see them again until I reached the first cabin. In fact there was one time that a very well-off gentleman came to be packed in for a week of fishing. He brought along his Chinese cook. I got the cook mounted up on his horse and he looked a little scared. I asked him if he could ride. In his broken English he said, 'Yes, I ride!' as he gripped the saddle horn with both hands until his knuckles turned white. About that time someone opened the gate before we were all ready and the packhorses took off up the trail. Well, that horse with the cook on it wasn't about to be left behind, so he took off, too. That cook was hanging on for dear life. Well, I knew we wouldn't see those horses again for hours so we finished mounting everyone else up and made our way up the trail. We kept thinking we would come across the cook in a pile of dust on the trail, but there was no sign of him. Five hours later when we arrived at the cabin, there standing at the hitching post with all the other packhorses was the cook's horse with the cook still firmly planted in the saddle. He was as white as a sheet as I rode up to him and he looked at me with a smile on his face and said, 'See? I told you I ride!'

"My memories are full of all the fine people I packed into these mountains. People from all walks of life. Professional people, teachers, lawyers, doctors, politicians. People who were successful and not out to haggle over costs, who wanted to enjoy this beautiful country. I had parties of people all over these mountains. Some seasons I packed in over one hundred and fifty people. In my fifty-five years of packing, many

people came back year after year for twenty-five or thirty years. And I always tried to leave things as natural as possible. I respected those who lived here before me."

A wave of sadness seems to come over his face. "Sad to think it is all over. Those were such good times I had. The wonderful people I met. The adventures. All of it better than I ever dreamed all those years ago when I left Los Angeles looking for a simpler life. But it is time to turn it over now. I'm getting too old to keep doing this. My body has been punished enough. It is time for me to move on."

ഗ

"Move on…" the words became an echo in my mind. "But Sam, how can you give all this up? Sam? Where'd you go?" I sat up looking around for Sam. But Sam wasn't there. Only Frosty was there snoring at the foot of my bed.

I got up and let the dogs out. The desert was already alive with the springtime aromas of another beautiful morning as I got ready for another wonderful day in God's country.

Chapter Seven

The Deer Hunters

"There was no end to the entertainment we had by observing the deer hunters that we packed in," I told the grandchildren as they cuddled up around me. "You could usually tell after the first day who was a real hunter and who was just there to party. The majority of them had no interest in hunting, they just wanted to blow off some testosterone and brag about how they roughed it in the mountains on a hunting trip."

"In all the years that I went in with hunters, I can count on one hand the number of deer taken. Good statistics for the deer population! Oh, it wasn't that the deer weren't there. They were plentiful. It was the ineptitude of the hunters that was the problem." The grandchildren gathered in closer, all ready for another story of what they called "the olden days."

ᔓᔕ

One of my best friends was a girl named Tonette. She was a no nonsense girl, a little over a year older than me, with long, bright red hair. She had been hunting deer with her father since almost before she could walk. She came on a pack trip with me in 1967 that was one of the best trips I remember. We had six hunters in the high country, and she and I would cook for them, get their horses ready, and then have the whole day free to ride and explore.

It was her first time in so I was excited to show her every trail there. She rode my horse Brownie since her horse, Larry, was not in good enough shape to make the trek. I rode my Hellzapoppin' and we spent just about every waking moment in the saddle.

This group of hunters had to be the worst I ever took in. One hunter blew out the end of his scabbard when his rifle fired while removing his gun from said scabbard. Luckily, it wasn't on a horse at the time.

Another hunter took six shots at a deer that was standing perfectly still by a tree one hundred feet away. It didn't move until he was done firing, and then it casually ambled away. He hadn't even hit the tree.

These were the kind of "one weekend a year" warriors we dealt with every fall. To me, they were the most dangerous kind.

After about four days, these hunters wanted to extend their stay for a few more days.

"That's fine and dandy," I told them, "but food will be running low and we will be out of meat. So, if one of you mighty hunters could bring in some camp meat that would be outstanding." I knew there was little chance of that happening.

The next two days, Tonette and I would be sitting out in front of the cabin when the hunters returned to camp. We would ask in unison, "Where's your meat?" All we got in return were dirty looks.

On the third day, we decided to take matters into our own hands and set out on Brownie and Poppin'. We hadn't gotten more than a mile from camp when Tonette grabbed her rifle, aimed and fired one shot, then calmly said. "Let's go get it." Heck, I hadn't even seen it!

Brownie was a bit unnerved at this point. I had fired guns from his back before with mixed results. This time he pretty much fell apart.

Luckily, Tonette was used to him and his tantrums and didn't let it bother her. She calmed him and then led us straight to the deer. I was amazed. One shot, through the heart, from the back of a squirrelly horse. I had always heard about how good she was. Now I had seen firsthand. Wow!

We got off our horses and decided we would put the deer on Brownie to carry back to camp. As we started walking towards him, he got a look in his eye that seemed to say, "Are you serious?"

What made me think that my horse that spooks at his own shadow was going to let us put a dead animal up on his back?

"I don't think so!" the snorting animal seemed to be saying as he sidestepped and spun away from us every time we lifted the deer towards him. He seemed to be almost near self-destruction when we realized it was never going to happen, so we laid the deer down and sat to take a breather. We were as tired as he was.

As we sat there catching our breath and watching Brownie eye the deer and us nervously, I had to laugh. What was I thinking? Trying to put that carcass on the back of the most skittish, spook easy, scared silly horse I had ever had the pleasure of knowing.

Finally after five minutes or so, we stood up, grabbed the deer and threw it up over Poppin's saddle, where it landed with a thud. *He* barely moved a muscle as we scooted it up to the center of his back.

After a few minor adjustments we were on our way. I was out in front leading Poppin', and Tonette was leading Brownie.

I heard Tonette giggling.

"What's so funny?" I asked as we trudged down the trail.

"I'm laughing at your stupid horse. He's freaked out because the deer's head is flopping back and forth with every step we take. I think he's sure that deer is going to jump off that saddle and come gobble him up!" We both laughed.

We got back to camp and Tonette took the deer over to the main cabin. There were two trees in front that were spaced just perfectly for hanging a deer for skinning. She commenced to dressing out the deer and I took our two noble steeds (well one noble and one nutty), unsaddled, brushed them, and turned them out in the pasture. Brownie never looked back as he ran off, happy to be out of sight of the devil deer at last.

I watched Tonette gut and clean the deer and was positive I had never seen it done as fast and efficiently as she did it. Soon, she had it all quartered and we stuffed it into burlap bags and strung it up high in a tree to keep the varmints from getting it. It wasn't even lunchtime yet!

There wasn't much else to do and we just lazed around the rest of the afternoon, eager for the hunters to return so we could heckle them about our deer. We didn't hear any other gunshots so we were pretty confident that the hunters would be coming back empty-handed.

The sun was casting long shadows as it sank into the early evening hours. The air was crisp but not too cold. It had been a very pleasant autumn day. I had started cooking dinner.

"Fresh deer liver fried with onions and blackberry brandy tonight," I told Tonette. "It's a camp ritual when a deer is bagged."

We heard the hunters coming up the trail and being the smart-alecky teenage girls that we were, decided to toy with them.

"So where's your meat? We're hungry." I yelled as they rode past me to the hitching post. They were not very amused and one of them turned around and angrily yelled, "Well, where the hell is yours?"

That was all we needed. Tonette stood straight as an arrow and pointed to the meat hanging in the tree and said, "Right up there. Are you hungry?" We both dissolved into laughter.

They looked up at the tree and back at us, unbelieving. "Sure it is," one said. Tonette went and took care of the horses and I went back in to finish cooking dinner.

As they came into the cabin and smelled the rich aroma coming from the skillet on the woodstove, they knew! They *knew*!!

They had been shown up by a couple of teenage girls. They even asked us not to tell anyone about it. Yeah, right! We told everyone!

I never saw those hunters again. They wouldn't have dared to come back. Tonette and I never went on another pack trip together. But what a great time we had on that one. I'll never forget my time with that big redhead who could out-shoot and out-hunt any man I ever met!

Chapter Eight

My First Horse

A lot of my time at the pack station was spent in reflection. How had I gotten to this place? Where was I going? What did I really want out of life?

I had never really thought about my future. The years before I met John had been a blur with "Sex, Drugs, and Rock and Roll." I felt worthless and unworthy of anyone's love, including my own. But John changed all that when he put his faith in me. I started to block out all those bad past experiences and focus just on the things that gave me joy.

"Horses," I told my grandchildren coming out of my memories of the down times. "My life had changed because of horses. Most of my childhood memories revolve around looking at, wanting to be, and acting like horses."

"Just like Lindsey," giggled Kacee. Lindsey gave her a good shove, and then whinnied in true horse fashion. I waited for them to stop "horsing around" before continuing.

"Grandma?" voiced Terry, "Tell us about your very first horse."

"Okay, Terry. I guess you should know about Sparol and how that came about," I answered.

ᔓᔕ

My girlfriend Shellie and I spent countless hours galloping around the playground, snorting and whinnying, oblivious to the taunts of fellow classmates. We lived and breathed horses and no amount of teasing was about to distract us from our obsession.

When I was ten years old and my mom married "that stepdad" we moved a few miles away from Shellie's. Once we were out of grade school our make-believe games ended, but the love and desire for those magnificent animals didn't.

As luck would have it, I discovered that a block away from my house lived an old Australian "Equestrienne." She gave riding lessons and had several horses. Her name was Kanga and she was about sixty-five years old. She seemed much older with her weather-wrinkled, tanned face. She had the appearance of having spent her whole life outdoors. She was very rough and grizzled and to this ten-year-old girl seemed very unfriendly. But I knew the moment I met her that I would learn much from her.

After learning how to scoop poop and cleaning corrals for her for a few weeks, my mom let me sign up for lessons. Up to this point, my riding experience had been limited to pony rides at the zoo, and rented stable ponies that never went faster than the slowest snail no matter how hard you kicked them. That is until you turned them toward home and found yourself hanging on for dear life.

Kanga was such a classic horsewoman. Wearing tan jodhpurs and knee-high riding boots, she was all business when it came to her horses. Being Australian, there was no western saddle in sight. Come to think of it, there was no saddle of any kind in sight. She believed that one learned how to ride much more effectively if one learned with no saddle *or* bridle.

We simply sat astride the horses and became one with them. Feeling the twitching of their muscles and sinking into their backs and thus becoming part of every single movement that they made, we learned to move our bodies in sync with theirs. We learned to anticipate their movement and we learned balance and relaxation all while learning how to ride with our legs and not our hands and feet.

She would have us stand next to our mounts and spread our feet apart then tell us to bend our knees into each other. Holding our knees together we would then have to walk our horses around a few paces. This lesson was to show us what part of our body was used to grip the horse. The thighs, and only the thighs, from the knees up. Not the lower leg and definitely not the feet as one tends to do when riding bareback.

Then we got on the horses and had to sit ramrod straight, arms held out to the side, squeezing our thighs as she gave the lope command to her horses. She had a stout riding crop that she used to rap us on the fanny with if she saw daylight between us and the horse's back.

When she yelled "halt," she would come around to each of us and use her crop to show if we were out of line. There was always to be an imaginary line from the heel on up through the knee, shoulder, and head. Slouching and leaning forward was not allowed. She was a very strict riding master. We learned to excel on small jumps and became proficient at all the gaits; walk, trot, lope, and canter moving around her small arena.

She scoffed at western ways and especially western riding. "Anyone can sit on a western saddle and ride a horse!" she would say. "But, learn to ride my way, and you will be able to ride anything."

And I did. I will be forever grateful to that gruff old Aussie woman for teaching me the art of horseback riding.

After working and riding with her it wasn't long before I was on the lookout for a horse of my own. I stashed any and all babysitting money away, saving for that magical day when I would find my own horse.

I was in seventh grade and had made friends with a girl named Peaches. She had horses and took me riding a few times, and soon her family had a horse for me. Sparol was a little horse, a Quarter/Arab cross, about 14.1 hands tall. I forked over all of my babysitting money, my $125.00 fortune. He was dark bay and full of piss and vinegar.

He had a habit of trying to run away with people when they least expected it. I didn't have a saddle, so I rode bareback most of the time and could usually sense when he was getting into that runaway mood. I could take evasive action and derail his plans. It was great fun to take him down to the Rose Bowl Riders arena with all my friends and watch them ride him around in the arena. He usually pulled his stunt on at least one unwary rider. Pretty soon I would hear "Help! He won't stop!" and we would jump down off the rail and try to block his way and grab his reins. We would all have a good laugh about it.

When I first got Sparol, I boarded him at Peaches' house about a quarter mile up the road from my house that was on Loma Alta Drive in Altadena. I would walk up after school and clean corrals, then ride him down to my house to play with him or ride on down into the canyon.

One summer afternoon, I was riding him bareback to my house just minding my own business, when a car full of teenage boys pulled up to the stop sign I was approaching. They were hollering and shouting at me and made me pretty nervous. Then they took off peeling rubber and honking their "AAOOHHGA" horn.

I don't believe Sparol had ever heard a horn like that before. He took off like a racehorse out of a starting gate. I was lucky to not be unseated as I tried to pull his reins back, but it was all I could do to hang on tight to his mane. He was racing down the street as if a monster were on his tail, which he probably thought to be so.

My house was a block from that stop sign and as we raced past it, my mom was out in the front yard watering the lawn. I saw out of the corner of my eye her mouth drop open and she yelled, "Roni?"

I couldn't get anything to come out of my mouth. I was too busy thinking of what to do to get this runaway steed to stop. Another two blocks and I decided I was going to have to bail out. I pictured us being hit by a car if we continued on down this street. I was scared to jump off, but more scared to keep going.

So I mustered all of my courage and lifted my right leg over his back and sort of threw myself off of him. I didn't know what he was going to do. I tumbled to the curb and let go of the reins. I was sure he would keep on running. But I was wrong. As soon as he felt me jump off, he stopped. He let out a huge snort and looked back around at me as if to say "Why didn't you do that sooner?"

My knees were pretty scraped up and I just sat there for a few minutes. As I was thinking about getting up, a Fire/Rescue truck came driving by. They had seen what had happened from several blocks away. While they were tending to my wounds, my mother came screeching down the road and jumped out of the car with a panicked look on her face.

"I'm okay, Mom. Just lost control there for a little bit. You looked pretty funny when we ran by though!" I said to her.

It just seemed too unreal to me. I tried to figure out what I could have done differently. Then I laughed.

This horse loved to run away with people. He thrived on it. Chances are, there was nothing I could have done to stop him. Once he got that bit in his teeth, it was all over. But now that I knew I could just jump off and he would stop, I felt much better. It was a real learning experience for both of us. He never ran away with me again.

Not long after, we moved to that house on Mariposa Street, just two blocks from the canyon, and street traffic was no longer an issue. Cars and horses just did not mix very well. But, best of all, my horse finally got to live with me!

Chapter Nine

Dogs, Cats, and the Farmer's Almanac

There were always dogs that came along on pack trips with us, except during hunting season. The hunters' eyesight could never be trusted, so for the dogs' safety we left them home. But during the spring and summer, there were kids and dogs everywhere.

John had a big, gray Weimaraner named Luke. He was a powerful dog and very majestic. He became one of my favorite dogs. He had the most authoritative face. He always had his nose to the ground, on the trail of anything that had been there in the recent past. And when he sat there with his head held high, sniffing the breeze, you just knew that he knew what was going on and who was in charge.

"Did you have any dogs of your own, Gramma?" asked Alli.

"I sure did," I told her. "My dogs during those years were Hobi, Sheridi, Frosty, and Laddie." My mind drifted back as I thought of those long ago dogs of my teen years.

ɞ

Hobi was a silky, wirehaired stray mutt who resembled an Airedale. He had been a family member for many years and was the calmest, mellowest dog I ever had. He had the gentlest soul I have ever known a dog to have. He never bit or growled. He just loved everyone! When he went to the pack station, it took weeks to get all the burrs out of his long, fine-haired, scraggly coat. He liked to wander off and follow the scents of all the critters that lived there.

Sheridi was a beagle mix that I got as a puppy. We had so many animals at the time that I promised my mom I would even quit smoking if she would only let me have that puppy. I was fifteen and whined a lot. She caved in and I got the pup. Much as I should have, I didn't keep my part of that promise. Sheridi was a great dog. She loved to be at the pack station and spent untold hours lounging on her back in the sun. We had a couple of litters of puppies from her and, one summer, there were several of them at the pack station, too. Sheridi and Hobi both died of old age in my care.

Frosty was five weeks old when I got him from a girl at the stable. He was a little white round ball of cuteness. By the time he was full grown he was the size of a small beagle, but shaped like a miniature Lab. He was pure white with big brown eyes that would look to your very soul when you stared into them. He was as much a part of the pack station as the horses were. He was always so busy protecting us from all sorts of vermin. He chased mice, rats, and lizards from sun up to sun down. His favorite thing was to be the first one into the cabin when we arrived, so he could seek and destroy any and all living things that had invaded his space while we were away during the off season. His nose would start twitching the moment we turned off the highway onto that three-mile long, rutted dirt road. We would have to listen to him whine and whimper every second of that long slow drive up to the cabin at the foot of the mountains.

With a truck full of horses, that drive could take ten or fifteen minutes. By the time we got there he was a frantic, frenzied, jumble of rat-killing nerves. He would be out the window before the truck stopped and off he'd go sniffing out any squatters who had moved into his territory over the winter. He would race from rock to building to bush to woodpile with his nose never leaving the ground. Then he would do it all again in case he missed something. When he found a good smell, he would dig and dig until he was certain he had demolished any home that creature had created. After he was certain he had rid the outside of any interlopers, he would sit at the front door and wait for us to finish getting the horses situated. Once I let him inside, it was best to follow him around to make sure he didn't destroy anything we needed.

One particular year, he made his rounds around the cabin and, oddly, there was not a rat's nest to be found. Frosty was lying by the couch with disappointment written all over his face when I went to light the pilot light on the stove. I opened the oven door and there was the biggest rat's nest I had ever seen. Leaving the oven door open I yelled, "Frosty, get 'em!" He jumped up with such velocity that all I saw was a streak of white propelling itself to the stove, and right into that oven. The tumultuous noise coming from within that old metal stove was deafening. As I waited for the din to die down, I was looking around for a bucket and broom to clean up the mess that was sure to follow this miniature assault. He ripped that nest to pieces with it flying everywhere as he dug farther into it. Soon, he backed out of the oven with rat nest all over his face, but no animal parts in his mouth. It was, thankfully, an empty nest. It could have been very messy to clean up. Yep, rat killer!

One of my most enduring memories of Frosty is of him sitting out front of the cabin in the middle of the road. He often did that, just staring down towards the highway as if waiting for someone special to arrive. He would sit there for hours. I wish I could have crawled inside his brain and found out who he was waiting for. Did he sense some of those shadows that were in my head? I often thought he did.

Long after pack trips were over for us, he remained a part of my family. He tolerated the births and toddlerhood of my four children and lived to tell about it. He lived a long seventeen years and had happy life.

Laddie came into my life quite by accident. John and I were making a trip up north of Mojave to get a load of hay. The nicest man owned the ranch where we went and I always loved to go visit him. He had this black and white collie that I really liked.

This trip would turn out to be very different from the rest. It was Feb. 9, 1971, and when we arrived in Mojave to gas up, we found out there had been an earthquake in the San Fernando area. A big one, 6.6! A freeway overpass had collapsed and there was widespread damage. We had driven through the area hardest hit about an hour before. We tried to call home, but the phones were out. We decided to go on to the ranch and get the hay and then keep trying to get through.

When we had loaded all the hay, Lowell asked me if I still wanted that "blankety blank collie dog." I said yes, and he said "take him!" We had my yellow Dodge truck and had the back stacked high with hay. "Well, I guess he could ride in front with us!"

This was before the days of crew cabs! So we loaded up the dog and ourselves and headed back to Mojave. It was just for a couple of hours, so we could manage to be comfy-though-crowded on that front seat with that big collie.

As we approached Mojave, we heard on the radio that all roads into San Fernando were shut down. Oh no! What did that mean? Well, it meant that we had to take the long way around. Down Highway 395 on the east side of the San Gabriel Mountains towards San Bernardino, then back up north to L.A. County and Altadena. This was going to be a very long trip, especially with this large collie taking up more than his share of the front seat.

We finally did get through to my mom and John's wife, Normalee, to let them know that we were *not* in the truck crushed by the freeway overpass that we had heard about on the radio's news. I guess my mother had been frantic not knowing our whereabouts. Thirteen hours later we arrived home safe and sound with my new dog.

Laddie was about one-and-a-half years old, and it quickly became obvious why Lowell had wanted to ditch him. He barked. And barked and barked. He barked at people. He barked at birds. He barked at bugs. He barked at imaginary monsters. But the absolute worst thing he did was he barked at horses. He would bark, they would kick, and he would bite their heels, bark some more, and usually end up getting pitched over a fence. I watched him get kicked right square in the face once, turn around and go right back for more. I ended up having to tie him up most of the time. We did everything we could think of to break him of that habit, but to no avail.

Oh, another bad habit of his was biting. That dog seemed to have it in for anyone who was not from his "family," regardless of how many times he had met them. Yep, he lived most of his life on the end of a rope. He was not at all the dog I thought he was going to be. I let my good friend Arlene have him. He was a good dog for her and she had him the rest of his life.

During the winter, spring, and summer of my seventeenth year that I lived at the pack station by myself, a small menagerie of critters also came along for the adventure. So I was never really alone.

Besides the dogs, there was Tex, the goat, and my cat, Tabby. The goat was always good for a laugh. He was a little angora goat with horns and a typical male goat stench. He was always doing disgusting things, as male goats are prone to do, and would gross out most of the kids around the stable. He really belonged to the stable, but always seemed to live where I did, so up to the pack station he went. He really loved those horses, and they tolerated him.

My cat, Tabby, had never been anywhere but the house. He was my favorite and I didn't want to leave him for all those months I would be at the pack station, so I took him along. He was about one-and-a-half years old and was still a tomcat. He stayed in the cabin for the first week or so, and then he gradually ventured out to his new world. He adapted well as I knew he would. Soon he was out chasing bugs and mice right along with Frosty.

ღ

The small town of Olancha was just shy of ten miles north of the pack station, and through the years I got to know many of the local town folk. I became good friends with several of them.

One of my favorite local people was Don Lutz. He ran the local garage and tow service in Olancha. He would do work on John's vehicles and we would hang out there at his place and wait. He was a large man with a great sense of humor. He had a mare that rejected her foal and he and I wrestled with that foal and mare for a day and a half before finally separating them and bottle feeding the foal. It gave me something to do when I got bored. I could always go to town and play with the baby!

He would come up and check on me every few days as well. If it had been more than three days without seeing me in town, he was up there looking for me. And I had better be there or I was in big trouble! He and his wife would have me to dinner once a week or so. Most of the junk I ate when alone was canned stuff or mac and cheese, so her home cooking was the very best!

One day while at Don's I mentioned that I had a cat to neuter and did he know a vet?

He said, "The closest vet is in Lone Pine and the ranchers around here pretty much do all those things themselves."

"They do?" I asked, surprised, because I thought only vets did those things.

"I can cut your cat for ya!" he volunteered.

"Really? When?"

"Well, let me get my book," he said as he rose and walked over to the bookshelf. He pulled out an old worn softbound book and thumbed through it a few minutes before finding the page he was looking for.

"Here it is. This chart says we can do it a week from tomorrow."

"What do you mean the chart says?" I asked. I was suddenly having second thoughts about the advisability of putting the life of my beloved pet into the hands of this man who apparently did these sorts of things only after consulting an old book.

"That's the Farmer's Almanac," he told me. "All the farmers and ranchers refer to it before doing anything."

To me, it sounded like some kind of a witch's spell book or something from fairytales.

"Yep, that will be just right," he beamed.

"Why is that?" I asked suspiciously.

"Because, when you do it according to what phase the moon is in, they don't bleed as much!" he answered.

All I could think of to say was, "Oh."

"So bring him along with a burlap sack and I'll take care of him for ya! We'll have dinner first."

"Okay, if you're sure." And I headed for the door.

On the appointed day, I arrived at Don's house for dinner. Tabby stayed in the truck. He seemed a little nervous for some reason. Finishing our meal, Don said, "Well, girl, get your cat."

I dug him out from under the truck seat with him frantically trying to grab hold of anything to keep from being pulled from his secure hiding place. We traipsed into the front room and Don took the burlap sack from me and cut a hole in one corner of it.

He then took my frightened cat and stuffed him into the bag, pulling his tail and the "stars of the show" through the hole. He tied a knot in the open end and then wrapped the whole bundle up tight with a towel and handed the tight little bundle to me. The muffled yowls coming from that cat were heart wrenching. I was about to cave in to them when I heard Don say, "Hold onto him real tight now!"

I squeezed tighter and then the yowls got very loud as he jerked and struggled to move out of my death grip.

"All done. See? That wasn't so bad, eh?" Don said as he put his pocketknife away. I peered down to where my cats little gonads had been, and there was nothing there. Only a fresh little cut with not one single drop of blood.

The enraged cat was now quiet as we started peeling the towel and burlap off of him. I think he was more upset at the indignity of the confinement than what had happened to him.

We went home and he curled up on the bed next to me and didn't move all night. My heart felt like he had forgiven me. But he never stayed in sight after that when Don would visit.

A year or so later we had a couple of kittens that were to be "pack station" cats. Don checked his almanac and we neutered them. They were small enough that he did it the easy way. He shoved them head first into a cowboy boot with their little hind ends sticking up out of the top. Then snip, snip and out they came. It happened so fast they never knew what hit them. So much easier than the trauma Tabby went through.

But it always had to coincide with the phase of the moon as stated in the Farmer's Almanac.

Chapter Ten

Big Daddy

"What other horses did you have, Gramma?" Lindsey asked. "Tell us about your pretty horses. I've seen pictures!" Her cousins nodded in agreement.

"Yeah, we seen pictures!" squealed Alli.

"Yes, I had some pretty horses all right. And there were some who were all pretty and no smarts!" I told her. "Here's the story of one of them."

ᔕ

It was a bright October day, midway through the hunting season. We weren't packing any hunters in that day so the morning was very calm and devoid of human sounds. My tired body rebelled at the thought of getting up until the realization hit that there was no need to get up right away. Instead, I languished in my bunk for an extra hour or so, listening to the sounds of the morning. The raucous chirps of insects were deafening, yet comforting at the same time. The birds were crooning and warbling as the sun peaked up over the crest of the Coso Mountains, swallowing up the shadows of the valley floor.

On this day there was none of the frenzied excitement of people packing in for the first time, nor the hunters anxious to get up to the high country and try out their new rifles. No, there was none of that. Just the vibrant sounds of the high desert in the fall when there is crispness to the air and you can almost *feel* every living thing that dwells there frantically preparing for the winter and its bitter cold.

Reluctantly, my senses full, I finally crawled out, dressed, and went to feed my four-legged friends who were a might impatient with me for being late!

As I was throwing hay out to the horses, my serenity was interrupted by the clamor of a vehicle bumping and bouncing up the rutted dirt road. People often came up with their own horses to pack into high country. It just surprised me that someone was coming so late in the season. Most hunters arrived by the end of September or first week of October.

It was an old, rickety stock truck, the type that is open on the top and has wooden slats for the sides. Two curious heads peered up over the side of the truck as if wondering what excitement was in store for them.

The rig pulled up to the area next to the old loading chute and backed up to the hillside so it was flush with the back of the truck to enable the horses to walk right out and not have jump down. A couple of old cowpunchers got out and went around to unload their horses.

It was love at first sight.

My heart melted over Appaloosa horses. John was always teasing me about loving "those big-headed Appies." My enthusiasm for the breed probably stemmed from the fact that Hellzapoppin' was without a doubt the best horse on the planet. So, if he was the best, other Appies had to be up high on the list, right?

I had been on the lookout for a black Appaloosa with white spots to complement Poppin's white body and black spots, so when my eyes fell on that huge black Appy getting out of that truck, my heart did a little flip-flop. Absentmindedly tossing the rest of the morning's rations, I scooted over to the truck to check him out.

He was enormous. He stood close to seventeen hands and must have weighed well over thirteen hundred pounds. He didn't have very many defined white spots on him, except for a few on his rump. Mostly, he looked like someone had flicked a paintbrush at him over and over again to give him a look of splattered white flecks all through his shiny black coat. The speckles got more pronounced as you got to his rump. He didn't have a true Appy "blanket," but rather a smattering of larger speckles. He had a large head (John always complained about my love for those "big headed Appies"), but it really fit his large frame. He was stout and burly looking. I could just imagine how effortlessly he would probably climb up that mountain.

Once the men had unloaded their horses and tied them to the outside of their truck, I approached. "May I pat the Appy?" I asked.

Given a nod, the horse and I quickly became immersed in hand and lip play. I talked to him, patted him, and stroked his nose, with him mouthing my hand as horses do.

"How old is he?" I inquired of the men who were getting their packs ready.

"'Bout four now would be my guess," said the seasoned old cowboy.

"Have you had him up this trail before?" I asked.

"Naw, just got him. We'll see how he does," came the reply, as he hoisted the saddle up and over onto that wide back.

"Well, I'd sure be interested to hear," I said watching them tighten their saddles and sliding their rifles into their scabbards. They then mounted and tipped their hats to me as they started up the trail.

"What's his name?" I yelled after them.

The cowpoke on the big black horse then turned around in his saddle and grinned, "Big Daddy is his name, little miss, and he's for sale!"

Oh, my. What did he just say? For sale? My feet wouldn't move fast enough down to the cabin to tell John about what had just transpired.

"John! John," I yelled, bursting through the door. "Did you see that horse? He's for sale John! For *sale*! I don't have any idea how I am going to buy that horse. Heck, I didn't even ask how much. I just know I have to have him." I turned and went back out to the corrals leaving John sitting there with his mouth open.

That horse occupied all my thoughts in the next days and weeks.

We weren't there when those cowboys came back out. John and I had gone back into the high country with a group and had missed seeing them return. I had been hoping to run into them on the trail. But no such luck.

Several days later when we returned to the desert, my heart sank with disappointment to see their rig gone.

After a few weeks, the image of me astride that big black Appy started to fade, and we were too busy with deer hunters and horses, cooking and wrangling to think much about him anymore. We had never seen them there before and chances were we wouldn't see them again.

The last weekend of hunting season we brought one last group up from the city to try their luck.

As we pulled up to the corral, we spotted that truck that belonged to that "big headed Appaloosa." I started to get excited until realized that no one was around.

I tried to hide my disappointment, but while packing up horses and hunters, John asked, "What are you so down in the mouth about?"

"You know," I snapped.

"Well, I'm not a mind reader and I'm afraid I don't," he said in his usual calm voice.

"Well, you can see that truck over there. It's the same rig that had that black Appy I told you about a few weeks ago that I liked. And now I'm probably going to miss seeing him again because of *these* guys. Why do I always have to babysit the city guys?" I pouted.

"Because it's your job!" he countered. "Someone has to be up there with them to make sure they don't shoot themselves or get our horses killed."

"Fine!" I protested, and went back to tightening my cinch. I checked all the other cinches, got the riders on, and adjusted their stirrups, and soon we were headed up the trail.

There were four or five police officers on this trip. They were there to hunt and party, but not necessarily in that order. As it turned out there was very little actual hunting and a whole lot of partying going on. Oh, if their wives could have only seen them. It always amazed me how grown men could act when out of sight of their wives and with enough alcohol in them to take away their common sense. These were the kinds of hunters John had been talking about when he said to protect them from themselves and take care of our horses.

Somehow, I survived the weekend with them and managed to keep every living thing alive, including the deer. As we neared the corrals on our return to the desert, my eyes took in the empty spot where that rig had been parked. John was coming out of the cabin to give a hand with the horses.

I dismounted without looking up, tied up Brownie, and went to help with the other horses.

It was always easier to unpack and unsaddle all the horses ourselves rather than let the greenhorns undo every single little buckle and strap that the saddle and bridle had. It could take days to put stuff back together once they got done with things.

We got everyone unsaddled and rubbed down and I was starting to lead the horses toward the gate into the corral. John had thrown hay out and the tired horses were anxious to get in to eat and drink.

As I was almost inside the corral, John yelled, "Hey, take care with that new horse in there."

"What new horse?" I hollered as I looked up and saw a big black Appaloosa not fifteen feet away from me. He had his head in the feeder and was not the least bit interested in anything except that hay in the feeder. He raised his head, made note of the new arrivals to his corral, and went back to his dinner.

Rushing to finish getting the horses in, I excitedly went over to acquaint myself with our new friend. He seemed like such an easy-going guy for such a big horse. In my mind's eye we were riding effortlessly over hill and dale. Yes, I had big plans for this gentle giant.

The phrase "looks can be deceiving" rings so true sometimes. In this case he *looked* great, but oh the problems we had with him.

I didn't have a chance to ride him before we left. We headed back to Altadena that night. Deer season was over and there were no more trips scheduled until spring, so we had plenty of time to get used to each other, him and me. I rode him around the stables and out on the trail up and down the canyon a few times.

About two months after his arrival, I was working him at the stable. He had a slow lumbering gate and I was trying to get him to go faster.

"Come on, boy, let's go," I told him, but he was indifferent to anything I would do to try and convince him to turn up the speed. He was just starting to shift gears when we were approaching the fence. I pulled up sharply on the reins trying to get a sliding stop out of him when his hind foot hit a fresh manure pile. Both hind feet went right out from under him and down he went.

I found myself on the ground with this big monster of a horse on his side with my right foot pinned underneath him. My left foot was still in the stirrup at such an angle that if he had gotten back up it would have been caught.

By some miracle, he stayed perfectly still until a couple of the kids watching ran over to calm him and disentangle me from those stirrups. If he had gotten to his feet with both of my feet still caught in the stirrups, I could have been pretty seriously injured.

As it was, I had a very badly sprained right ankle and my right knee was severely tweaked. I spent the next six weeks on crutches. It put an added burden on John with me unable to ride and feed. All because I was showing off.

Big Daddy went to stay at John's place on Ventura Street so no one else would be tempted to get on him until we were sure he was safe. So far, I had been the only one to ride him, and I was anxious to get back on that big monster of a horse.

That day came about five months later at the first pack trip of the year.

I was a bit apprehensive climbing back up on that tall horse after so many months. He hadn't been ridden at all in that time. And, I had never been hurt that bad on a horse before. But, like they say, you've gotta get back on. So, John got him all saddled up for me. I walked him around for a bit, talking to him and reminding him of our "love at first sight" meeting.

Then I decided it was time. I couldn't put it off any longer. I held the reins in my left hand and reached for the saddle horn. He tensed a bit. I kept talking as he twitched his ears back and forth. I felt him relax and I heaved myself up and over into the saddle.

As my right leg came down on the other side of him and my foot searched for that illusive stirrup, several things happened that would cause the time bomb inside this antsy horse to go off.

John, who had been cutting firewood behind the corral, started up the chainsaw. Laddie, that darn collie that I just had to have a year earlier, and who could never control his herding instincts around horses, ran up behind Big Daddy yapping his head off.

That triggered the big horse to lurch sideways, which caused my unstirruped foot to lodge deep into his side.

All of these things combined were just too much for him to bear.

He exploded.

He started bucking so hard and so high, that when he ducked his head down, I couldn't even see it. He was bucking and leaping and I had absolutely no control. Laddie kept barking and John looked up and killed the chainsaw, then watched helplessly as I tried to stay on that wild-eyed rodeo bronc.

Soon, he was headed for the fence probably figuring he would be safer inside the corral. I was sure he was going to go right through the fence. I think I closed my eyes at that point. Then he launched me, and a second later, I was draped over the top rail of the fence as if I was a saddle blanket. I opened my eyes in time to see this massive black belly sailing over me with only inches to spare, blotting out all light.

It was all in slow motion at that point. I was sure I would never see daylight again because he was certainly going to clip my head with his hind feet. I squeezed my eyes shut and waited for the pain that was sure to come. It didn't.

The next thing I knew John was right there peeling me off the fence, being careful in case something was broken. Luckily, the only thing hurt was my pride.

After giving me a pretty good once over, John turned his attention to the big horse. He got on him and rode him and rode him hard. He had him running full out up and down the road, spinning and stopping.

After about thirty minutes of "schooling" he stopped and dismounted. Big Daddy was dripping sweat, and his powerful lungs were heaving trying to gulp in air that couldn't come fast enough. His muscles were quivering and his head was hanging low. I don't think I had ever seen John ride a horse that way.

"Okay, you ready to get back on?" he asked.

John knew he had to get me right back up in that saddle, because if I'd had much more time to think about it, I probably wouldn't have gotten back on that horse. Ever. All the kids were a little scared of him anyway, because of his size and that fall. And now, with this bucking incident, no one wanted to mess with him.

"Sure," I said, as my mind was saying, "Are you crazy?" I walked over to the horse and said, "I'm ready."

Big Daddy was recovering from his little lesson, but was still pretty tuckered out. He stood perfectly still while John held him as I got on. This time I felt none of the tight muscles and tense nerves I had felt the last time. He raised his head and looked around at me as I gently nudged him with my heel.

"Come on, big fella, it's just me." I whispered, "Let's go for a walk." And we did.

I rode him down to the power line road. It was a wide dirt road where the big transmission lines ran perpendicular to the mountains about halfway up from the highway. We just walked and talked. His ears were perked up, twitching back and forth so I knew he was listening to every word I was saying.

"There are spirits around here in the desert," I told him. "I can hear them and feel them. They're getting stronger and I'm trying to learn about them. I still need to learn to be in tune with Mother Earth as well as myself and with you." I just talked about everything I had felt about this place from the very first time I laid eyes on it. How the only person who seemed to know of these things was Jim, and he was hardly ever here.

We rode for a couple of hours and during that time we rebuilt the trust in each other that had been lost so many months ago when he fell on me.

We packed into the high country the next day and he was a perfect gentleman. We were both very relaxed and I was so amazed at his power on that steep trail. With his big barrel of a chest, he didn't seem affected by the altitude. I felt like he could just go on forever.

We did eventually find a few flaws in Big Daddy though.

When we tried to use him as a packhorse, he had other ideas. We packed him up on the desert for his first trip. He certainly seemed to be *made* to be a packhorse with his build. Plus, his easy way of going lent itself to the slow going of a pack animal. So we hoisted up two bales of hay on him with other assorted items and got him all tied down and ready to go.

John untied him and started to lead him over to me, when all of a sudden Big Daddy exploded. "Hey, whoa, easy boy," yelled John, but to no avail. Big Daddy started bucking and kicking and took off across the desert trying to dislodge those big scary bales of hay from his back. Pretty soon we saw hay flying everywhere.

After a few moments, he calmed down and we caught him and switched horses. "Well, okay maybe this is a little new. We can try again later." John said.

A few weeks later, we decided to try again and packed him up at Dutch John Flat to go up to the higher cabin at Deer Mountain. "We've got him settled in with his surroundings some. It's time to see what he's made of," John told me. "A horse built like him *has* to be a packhorse!"

As soon as we started up the trail, something unknown to us set him off. He started bucking as if he was the rankest bronc in the Cheyenne Rodeo. The chainsaw that had been on top of the pack was soon down under his belly swinging back and forth. And to further infuriate him it was banging into his legs as he spun around trying to dislodge this monster from his back.

There was nothing any of us could do except wait him out and hope it wasn't the last of our chainsaw. Priorities you know. I'm not sure how long it was. Maybe five minutes, maybe twenty.

We were lucky he didn't take off running and bucking, headed for the distant hills. He just sort of eased up the trail as he bucked, so we were able to follow him.

He finally stopped back behind the pasture, exhausted, and I was able to grab him. We disentangled the chainsaw and various other pieces of camping equipment and calmly walked back to camp, picking up all jettisoned items from his pack on the way. The chainsaw by some miracle was undamaged.

We tied him up at the hitching rail and removed the remains of the pack, as well as all of his tack, and let him stand for a while. He had a few nicks and cuts on his legs from the chainsaw banging around underneath him, but was otherwise unhurt.

About an hour later I saddled him up for me to ride and we packed up Poppin' and headed for Deer Mountain without any further setbacks.

It was such a shame that a big stout horse like him, the epitome of what a pack horse should be, couldn't be used for packing. He had seemed to make that perfectly clear.

The other minor flaw in Big Daddy was that he was blind at night. Yep! Blind as a bat! This came to light one night when a bunch of us kids were going to ride in. We were all having a great time getting the horses ready. Everyone was excited, since some of them had never ridden in at night before.

Once on our way with me in the lead, I started to notice that he was increasingly all over the place. He couldn't seem to stay on the trail. I had to constantly turn him and guide him and tug on the reins, steering him back onto the trail. It was a moonlit night and he should have had no problem seeing, but it was getting clearer by each step he took that there was definitely something wrong. I kept at him, watching each step as we got farther up the canyon. "You can't see where you're going, can you fella?" I asked finally.

He would walk right into trees and bushes and if I didn't turn him away he would probably walk right off the trail and keep going.

He never acted like this during the day. "I don't think I want to attempt taking him any further up. I sure don't want to tackle the shale switchbacks with him under these conditions," I told the rest of the group. "He doesn't seem able to see a thing."

We left the group and turned around and headed back down the trail very slowly.

Riding down the canyon alone on a blind horse at night is an experience that I don't ever want to repeat. All of my senses were on guard, constantly watching where he put each foot. He was like a drunk, wobbling and weaving back and forth, totally disoriented. At one point he started getting all snorty and huffy like he was really unhappy about something. I scolded him for being such a sissy.

"It's only a bobcat, you big paranoid galoot. They don't go after big strong horses like you."

We finally got back to the corrals. I unsaddled him, put him away, and headed for the cabin.

John was there and looked surprised as I walked in. "What in the tarn hill are you doing back?"

"When those guys sold you Big Daddy, did they happen to mention that he couldn't see a hand in front of his face at night?" I asked.

"Why, no I don't believe they did," he said shaking his head. "I guess now we know why he was so easy to come by!"

So, we couldn't pack him and we couldn't ride him at night. That sort of limited our uses for him. But I loved him anyway. And he sure was nice to look at, and fun to ride.

Chapter Eleven

Jinx

"You must've had a great time at the packing station, Gramma," said Lindsey. "I hope someday I can have a job like that and ride horses all day."

"Yes, it was great," I told her. "But life at the pack station wasn't all play. We actually had to earn our keep once in a while. During the summer and fall it was very busy with grooming, packing, cooking, cleaning, trail repair, replacing doors and windows on cabins, acting as guides, and babysitting."

"Babysitting?" she asked, looking puzzled.

"Well, that's what it seemed like when the city folks that didn't have any idea what they were doing would come for a pack trip."

ᔕ

One day while I was being driven insane by a bunch of city folks, I needed to get off by myself for a short time. After unpacking and unsaddling their horses, I bid them farewell and left them to John.

I hopped on Brownie bareback for a short ride just to get away. I loved Brownie when he was by himself. He would really stretch his stride out and walk fast. The only time he would do it was when he was in front of the group or alone. It was a real long, even gait and I tended to daydream when he got into that stride.

We found ourselves down to the power line road in no time, so we turned north. He continued his fast-paced tempo. I continued to daydream.

All of a sudden there was this screeching noise that I had never heard before off to the left of us. Brownie, being the Nervous Nelly that he was, jumped out of his skin. Luckily I had anticipated it a fraction of a second before he reacted to it. I tightened my grip around his ribcage and hung onto his meager mane, determined not to fall off.

The noise came again and this time Brownie swung around to face it. The sagebrush and Joshua trees grew high on that side of the road and I couldn't quite see what was making those awful sounds. It sounded like brush was being trampled and it was getting closer. The braying I was hearing then registered in my head. I gripped even harder not knowing how my skittish horse would react. Surprisingly, Brownie was actually somewhat under control. He was snorting, but not quivering. His ears were twitching back and forth, as he stood frozen in that spot.

"It's okay, fella," I told him. I kept patting him and telling him, "It's gonna be okay. You're about to meet some new friends."

Suddenly, we saw four very large ears emerge out of the sagebrush connected to two very cute burros. They were braying away as they came crashing out of the brush and greeted us as if they had found their long lost mother.

Brownie thought he would twirl and whirl and run, but I outmaneuvered him and gathered him up just in time.

"Easy, easy boy," I told him. I kept talking to him as the donkeys trotted right up to him.

There were several minutes of snorts and sniffs and squeals, and then by some miracle, Brownie finally decided they were okay.

I had no idea where these donkeys came from. There weren't any ranches between the pack station and town. I had heard there were some wild horses and burros roaming the desert, but these two certainly didn't look wild. They looked like they were in love.

The sun was starting to slide behind the mountains and dusk was fast upon us.

"Come on, Brownie boy. It's time to head back," I told him as we turned and headed south along the power line road. I wasn't sure what the donkeys would do. Brownie kept looking back and, sure enough, they were following us.

When we got to the pack station, all the horses were lining the rail checking out the new arrivals. My little tag-alongs trotted right up to all those big horses and greeted them. More squeals and snorts and sniffs, and by the time I had brushed Brownie down all was calm on the desert once more. When I led him around to the corral gate, they tried to follow. I closed it before they could squeeze past me. The horses were a little leery of newcomers. Most of them had never seen a donkey before, much less *two* of them.

John sat and watched this whole scene unfold with amusement. As he threw out the evening feed, he said, "I don't think they should stay in with the horses tonight. I don't want them to get hurt." So he threw a few flakes of hay outside the gate where they were standing. They dug in like they hadn't eaten in days. I grabbed a couple of water buckets and ducked into the corral to fill them from the tub.

"Where do you think they came from?" I asked as I carried the buckets over to them.

They both drank the buckets dry and went back to their hay. I repeated the task once more as John said, "Beats me. I'll ask around in town tomorrow. They sure don't seem wild. Wild ones wouldn't let us within a hundred yards. These guys are pretty tame."

As he said that, I put the water buckets down once more and stood by as one of the donkeys put his nose down to drink. When he was done, he reached over and rubbed his face on me.

"Like I said, tame!" John said with a wink. "Come on, let's get some dinner."

Those donkeys hung out with us all summer. Some of the younger, more adventurous boys would try to ride them. They would buck and run and no one ever stayed on. They were very sweet and loved to be groomed and played with, and were in heaven when their long furry ears were stroked. They even went up into the mountains with us. Our own little mascots!

At the end of deer season we were left with a dilemma.

"It seems no one has missed the donkeys or come around looking for them, and I haven't discovered where they came from. So what are we going to do with them?" I asked.

John didn't even think twice. "Guess we'll take them home with us," he answered as if he read my mind. "We can't just leave them alone to starve in the desert with a cold winter coming."

The morning we were leaving, John came up to me and said, "You know we have a slight little problem, don't ya?"

"What are you talking about?" I replied.

"Well, little lady, we have *nine* horses here," he answered.

"Yeah? So?" Then I did the math and thought it through. "Oh! Oh, crap! The donkeys make it eleven. How are we going to do that?" I asked.

"Well, I could split the load and come back. But we don't have any food or supplies left here to hold you over for a couple of days. Or, we can load them all. They are smaller than the horses. It'll be cramped, but I think it will work."

"Whatever you want to do, John, I'm for it." I started putting halters on horses.

John backed the big rig up to the loading spot and one by one we started loading horses into the back of the truck designed to hold ten. We put all the heavier horses in front. Then the donkeys went in the middle (who loaded just fine by the way!).

"The toughest part will be getting that last horse up in a spot that has no more room," John told me.

We left Jinx for last because he was the smallest, thinnest horse of the herd. As I shoved the tenth animal over, John led Jinx up the ramp and he had to step up sideways into his spot. Then we both pushed on him, fastened the cable, and quickly jumped down and raised the tailgate as fast as we could.

"Whew! We did it!" I said as I grabbed Frosty and threw him up into the cab, then climbed in after him.

John jumped in and off we went down that bumpy dirt road with eleven equines in the back of that truck.

We heard occasional hooves scrambling. We knew they probably weren't very comfortable. John had said, "No stops. Let's get them home as fast as we can. I don't like this."

We reached the highway and turned south without any hesitation.

It was about an hour's drive to Mohave. We usually stopped there for either gas or food. This time we were going to drive straight through. Or so we thought.

About half way through town, there was a great amount of scrambling in the back of the truck. So John pulled over at a big wide dirt area between the highway and the train tracks.

As we both got out to go back to see what was going on, a feeling of dread came over me. I heard John whistle as he neared the rear of the truck. That produced immediate quiet from the horses.

John and I rounded the rear corner of the truck at the same time. Both of us, instead of looking up into the back of the truck were stopped in our tracks by the sight of Jinx's hind foot and leg sticking out between the tailgate and the bumper.

I thought I was going to throw up. There was this poor horse's bloody foot, his fetlock joint with half the hide gone and his cannon bone pretty well stripped to the bone.

John saw my white face and said "Don't you go sissy on me now, young lady. We gotta figure this out."

"But John, how?" I asked.

We couldn't lower the tailgate, because his leg was in there. The tailgate was too heavy for John and me to remove. I wasn't sure if those hinges would have come off anyway. I climbed up on the bumper at Jinx's head to talk with him and try to keep him quiet.

Horses when trapped or stuck will keep trying to free themselves, sometimes doing even greater damage. Jinx was no different and kept trying to pull up his leg and each time it caused more tissue to be stripped off. I just didn't see any way we were going to free him.

After about ten minutes or so, John finally said, "Well I think the only way that leg is going to come out of there is by the same way it got in there!"

I wondered what he meant and looked down at him, but he had gone back to the cab of the truck.

"Oh Jinx, what happened, fella? How are we going to get you out of this?" I cooed to him.

Then John reappeared with a hammer in his hand. "What?" was all I got out before John started pounding on the bottom of Jinx's foot.

I had a sick feeling in my stomach when I thought about what would happen to that leg when it got pulled back through that rigid, unmoving space.

Each time he hit the foot, the horse let out a grunt. The look in his eye was dull, and I knew he must be in shock.

Another bang on the hoof. I started to cry. My stomach lurched. Pounding, metal hammer against the metal of his shoe. Pounding.

It was reverberating through my whole body, through the whole truck.

I yelled “Please God! Help this poor horse.”

I looked down at John who was determined to get that foot out. And in the next instant, John’s hammer hit the truck. Jinx had jerked his foot back up. He was shaking. John had sweat pouring off his brow. I had tears streaming down my face.

We were quiet for just a few moments, trying to catch our collective breaths.

Then John lowered the tailgate. I held Jinx’s head until he had the ramp out. Then I untied him and brought him down the ramp. He didn’t put any weight on the leg. I took him to the front of the truck and tied him for a bit while we unloaded the rest of the horses. We couldn’t leave them all in there. They would get too restless and want out. So we tied them all to the outside of the truck.

I was leading Jade down the ramp when one of the many freight trains that passed by hourly came whizzing by and the engineer thought it would be a great idea to sound the whistle. Jade almost ran right over the top of me and to this day I don’t know how I hung onto him. That would have been just perfect, loose horse running down the highway along with one injured three-legged horse to care for. Disaster averted. Well, one of them anyway.

John and I then examined Jinx and his bloody mangled leg. I grabbed one of the buckets from the truck and went to a service station across the street for water. While I was there, I called Jim to come with a trailer. We weren’t going to load eleven back into that truck.

Once back with Jinx, I found a t-shirt in my bag and soaked it and tried to put it around the wounded leg. He kept shaking the leg, as if trying to shake off the skin and tissue dangling from it. He did not want to put weight on it, but John manipulated it and checked it out as best he could.

"Well, can't feel anything broken," he told me, after a careful evaluation. "It sure would have been if we had lowered that tailgate!"

John finally lifted Jinx's other hind leg, causing him to stand on the injured one while I washed some of the blood off and tried to assess the damage. He quivered, but did bear the weight for a few seconds.

I finally got the bleeding stopped and we could see that he had stripped virtually all meat and hide from the cannon bone. His fetlock joint was missing most of the tissue and what was left looked like hamburger meat. The bone of his pastern joint was exposed as well.

"Boy-oh-boy, you really did a number, Jinx!" I said. I grabbed another t-shirt from my pack and wrapped it around his leg. That would have to do until we got him home.

Jim arrived with the trailer and we loaded all the horses back up with no problems. We put Poppin' in the trailer with Jinx and took them to my house. John went to the stable with the rest of the horses and the donkeys.

As Jim and I unloaded Jinx, my mom came out to greet us. "Got a patient here for ya, Mom," I told her. "Ol' Jinx here tried to take his leg off. He's going to need a lot of your nursing TLC."

Mom watched as I took off the shirt. She went almost as white as I had at first. "Well," she said, "This is going to take some time."

She disappeared into the house and returned with an armful of medicines and bandages. I got her a bucket of warm water as directed, and she got to work.

"I bet you never thought you'd be doctoring horses when you were in nursing school huh?" I asked as she scrubbed the wounds clean.

"Nope, sure not anything like this anyway!" she said as she started bandaging the leg.

We gave Jinx some Bute for the pain and then took him into the back and padded a nice thick layer of straw in his stall.

Jinx remained at my house for the next eight months. My mother religiously doctored that leg every single day until it granulated back in and healed. Jinx became spoiled rotten, knowing that every time she came out to the backyard, he would get a treat. She gave him treats before and after taking care of his leg. He even started nickering when she appeared in the doorway.

Jinx rejoined the herd at the pack station the following year. He had a scar on that leg, but was not lame on it once it was completely healed.

John and I both know that his recovery and return to normal was only because of the diligent nursing care he got from my mother the nurse!

Chapter Twelve

Brownie and the Scary Night

August of 1969 was one of those long, hot summer months, very typical of the Owens Valley. It was never boring or quiet around the pack station. The heavy afternoon air on the high desert would sometimes take your breath away. The incessant noise of the insects mingled with the shouts and giggles of children and teenagers feeling freedom from the shackles of the city, some for the very first time. We had kids coming and going all summer, as well as "paying customers" to pack in.

I had spent a very busy week tending to the needs of horses and campers up in the high country. After lunch, I got ready to take a group of departing people down to the desert. I got the horses rounded up and we saddled up, packed their gear, and headed out.

The trip was pretty routine, but it was hot and I couldn't wait to get down to the bottom of the canyon and take a shower. It had probably been a week since I had last been out. We had an outdoor shower rigged to the hot water heater on the outside of the cabin on the desert. It wasn't good for a long shower, but *any* shower was appreciated. That was one amenity we didn't have in the high country.

We reached the desert, got all the riders squared away and watched them drive down that dusty dirt road. You could follow a car all the way to the highway just watching its dust.

I unsaddled all the horses and rubbed them down, then turned them in with a few of their friends who had stayed in the desert with John, awaiting a group coming to be packed in the next day. I wolfed down some dinner and took a luxurious three-minute shower. My tired, trail-weary body just needed to kick back and relax. But it was getting dark, and I had to get back to the high country to all those teenagers who had been left unattended up there.

One could only imagine what trouble they could get into. Maybe they were horseback riding and communing with nature. Or maybe they were sitting around the table playing cards and seeing how life was when not complicated by TV and all the modern inventions that took one's mind away from the simple things in life. Yes, I had better get back up there.

After Brownie had eaten a big dinner, I saddled him up for the trip back into the high country. He didn't seem too happy about this, but I kept telling him how lucky he was to be going out during the cool evening hours instead of during the day. He didn't seem impressed. After filling the packs with needed supplies for the cabin, we headed up the trail as it approached 10 PM.

The landscape around me shimmered from the light of the biggest full moon I had ever seen. There was no need for a flashlight. It was very bright yet colorless, like a black and white movie. The sounds of the night were so different than those during the hot day. The croaking frogs and toads along the canyon bottom were like a musical being performed just for Brownie and me. The crickets would chime in and soon we had a symphony singing us along the trail. I had ridden this trail before at night, but never alone. The sights and sounds told me I wasn't really alone, but I was completely at ease.

ᔕ

When we started to climb out of the canyon, the songs faded and the trail grew brighter. There was a small stand of trees that opened to what we called Deer Point and a resting spot. A place to dismount, tighten cinches, and let the horses rest for a few minutes before starting the hardest part of the ride. From Deer Point, the trail went up through steep and rocky switchbacks. This side of the canyon was devoid of trees, and the meager bits of sagebrush were surrounded by loose rocks and shale. One stray foot off the trail could cause an avalanche of rocks and dirt crashing down the side of the mountain. Riding up those steep switchbacks, the trail was still bright, and it seemed as if we were climbing the stairs to heaven. The lighter it became ahead, the darker it was below. The canyon became nonexistent as it fell into the shadows of the moonlit night.

Brownie and I finally made it to Halfway Point. It was unknown if this actually was the halfway point, but it had a nice wide area to dismount to let the horses rest. It also had a small creek going through it that allowed for washing the dust off your face and filling up canteens. The horses in the pack string would sometimes drink, but they mostly just rested. Brownie took a few sips and grabbed a short nap while I listened to the sounds of the night.

From that point, the trail grew heavily forested. The ride from Halfway Point to the summit was also filled with switchbacks, but not as steep and treacherous as the ones we had just conquered.

Once we reached the summit, we stopped for a rest. While Brownie caught his breath, I sat quietly on his back taking in the quiet stillness that surrounded me. The panorama before me had an almost holy feeling. It was as if this scene had been placed there at just that moment just for me. I could even see the reservoir on the desert floor twinkling as if it wanted to dance with the moon beams. I was unable to move forward. The power of my surroundings engulfed me. I had never had that overwhelming sense of the universe before. It was mesmerizing. I felt as if this was my first trip and I was seeing everything for the very first time.

I have no idea how long I sat there. With no watch to tell me, it seemed about midnight. The moon at seven-thousand-plus feet was close enough to put my arms around. All the craters and shadows were jumping out at me as if it were a 3-D picture from a book.

I finally came back to the present and decided it was time to be on our way. The trail from the summit takes a rather flat route as it wanders through sage and manzanita atop the mountains, before it gets to the ridge above the river. My thoughts were still on the scene at the summit and my body wanted to stretch a bit, so I got off to walk and let Brownie have a rest. With the loop of the lead rope hooked over my shoulder, we started walking the moonlit trail at a pretty good pace. We walked briskly, my eyes down watching the trail. I was wrapped up in the rhythm of Brownie's footsteps and the creaking of the saddle as we kept up our pace. It had the most hypnotizing effect.

I'm not completely sure how it happened. One minute we were walking in rhythm and the next I was flat on my backside in the middle of the trail. The lead rope that had been looped over my shoulder had pulled me down as my brave steed had come to an abrupt stop. Stunned, I looked over my shoulder to see what the problem was. All I saw were two huge eyes, shining like silver dollars with a look of terror in them.

Now, my history with Brownie and his scaredy-cat tantrums told me that it was probably a mouse or, worse yet, a deer that had spooked him. I'd had such misadventures with him many, many times. There was no end to what he might do to avoid such encounters. Especially fun were the stationary garbage-can boogiemen, encountered on trash day when I would have to ride to the stables to feed the horses. He would stare at them all, standing guard at each driveway, his ears forward, snorting menacingly while at same time side stepping halfway across the street so that "they" wouldn't get him.

So I didn't feel particularly worried when I looked back around to see what had upset him, and found myself face to face with a mountain lion whose eyes had that same silver dollar look of terror in them. He was about ten feet in front of me on the trail. His pungent odor filled my senses. I could hear him breathing and I am sure he could hear my heart pounding. Brownie's breathing seemed to have stopped, and I was sure he would drop dead from fright. Still on my backside, the cat and I warily eyed one another for what was mere seconds but seemed like eternity.

What happened next was inexplicable. As I stared at the cat and the cat stared back, there was a movement of air, almost a swirling motion that passed between us. Watching the small vortex continue off the trail for a few yards it seemed to turn into the shadow of a man on an Indian pony. When I glanced back towards the lion, it was gone. I heard it crashing through the brush on the opposite side of the trail running from whatever it was that had come between us.

I was still sitting there when I remembered my horse. I found him frozen in his tracks. What had just happened? Was it a dream? As I slowly rose and brushed off my jeans, Brownie came to life, snorting and acting the fool as usual. Things were back to normal. We stood in the middle of that dusty trail, looking off in both directions. There was nothing on top of that mountain but me and my chicken horse. But there was something that filled my senses. Something ancient. Something that made me feel I belonged on that trail. That we were accepted and welcomed into a sacred world that few people had encountered in that rugged high country.

There had always been stories floating around about ghosts and spirits in the Sierras. On this night, I believe I met one. And he protected me from that mountain lion.

There is no way to know how long we stood there. Brownie's gentle nudging stirred me back to the here-and-now.

"C'mon, let's get going," he seemed to say. "Too many spooky things up here and I just want to get to the safety of the pasture and my friends."

"Okay, boy. Let's go. You'd better stand still and not act like an idiot while I get on!" I told him as I stretched my leg up to the stirrup. To my surprise, he stood perfectly still.

The pace was then very fast as we transversed the last of the trail down to the river crossing. It was another mile to the cabins. Then I slowed down to make the trail last longer. I wasn't sure I wanted this night or this ride to end.

It was probably one or two in the morning when we got there. The camp was dark and quiet. There wasn't even a horse in the corral to welcome us.

I got Brownie unpacked, unsaddled, and then led him out to the pasture where the other horses were grazing under the full moon light with several deer for company. All of their heads popped up as we approached. They nickered a greeting and went back to their grazing. Brownie trotted off to join them and no doubt share his story of how he saved his mistress from a mountain lion. Tales of bravery, the likes of which they had never heard before.

I gathered my stuff and walked over to the quiet cabin. Not wanting to go inside and wake anyone, I left my things by the door and walked near the hitching post and sat down. The tranquility of this place enveloped me as I stayed there until almost dawn contemplating what had happened to me on this night. It would forever be my most memorable ride in the high country. Yet, I didn't feel I could share it with anyone. I eventually told about seeing the lion, but remained a bit reluctant to talk about the ghost. In later years as I heard similar stories from others, I let mine be known as well. Jim told me my apparition was a native called Running Bear. He had seen him too.

As badly as I wanted one, I never had another encounter in that high country. Many, many times on the desert I had "felt" spirits and would commune with them. But it was never as profound as that bright moonlit night on the top of the mountain.

Just me and my horse, Brownie.

Chapter Thirteen

Dust, Grime, and Supplies

It's funny, looking back, how carefree and, sometimes, careless we were. We thought nothing of riding into the high country for two weeks with only one change of clothes. Hygiene was not a priority when camping in the mountains. There was no shower, no tub, and certainly no silk sheets at the end of the day. We spent our days getting horses ready for various activities.

Anyone who has been around horses knows that grooming them is a dusty, dirty job. These were real horses after all, not namby-pamby show horses who are allergic to dirt. So, after breakfast, we went to catch them and give them a quick once over for any possible problems. Then we'd brush and saddle them up for the day. Often, we worked up a good sweat just trying to catch the blasted animals! Then, as we brushed them, depending on how much they had rolled in the dirt during the night, we were soon covered with a fine dust. Saddles and blankets were dusted off and hoisted upon their backs as even more dust flew off when the saddles landed with a dull poof. We had probably been up only an hour or so and already we were covered head to toe with dirt and dust. After the riders headed out our time was our own.

"Come on," one of the kids hollered. "Let's head down to Strawberry and go skinny dippin'. See if we can't get some of this dirt off."

Strawberry was our favorite swimming hole. For the life of me I can't remember why it was named that. Even though it was cold, it felt good to get the dust and grime off. A full dip in the river, no matter what time of year it was, awoke the senses. It was never warm, but sometimes a bit less chilly than other times.

We were never really shy with each other. After all, this was nature and we loved being "natural." Boys and girls "skinny dipping" together was never a big deal. We would "wash" our hair with a bar of soap and call it good. Then, when we were dry, we would put our same old dirty clothes back on and ride back to the cabin.

When the riders returned, we unsaddled the horses, put the gear away, and rubbed them down just a bit. We didn't groom them as nicely, knowing they were just going to go out and roll.

Several of us would bring in wood for the stove; others would get dinner going and get things settled down for the night. Everyone had their chores to do.

After dinner and dishes it was time to relax and play cards and gross each other out about how dirty we were. And then we would crawl into our sleeping bags, unsure at times if there weren't other creatures in there with us. If we weren't completely exhausted from the day's activities, we would tell ghost stories in the dark until we drifted off to sleep. I can remember being so wiped out that I would simply fall onto my bed, too tired to even take off my boots. I would often be in the same spot next morning at first light.

Sometimes there were only a couple of girls up there. And often, I was the *only* girl there.

There were many trips where we had groups of unruly hunters. Especially after a long day of not seeing any deer, which could lead to a long night of drinking. They would often do their best to try to get their hands on me when John wasn't around. They would make rude remarks and brush against me acting like it was an accident. I was very careful not to lead them on, though there always seemed to be a certain amount of flirting between us wranglers and our charges. But I never acted that way when I was the only girl. I was already aware of what men could do to me against my will. I didn't want to ever go there again.

On one particular "only girl" trip, the group of hunters had one surly member who made it known to everyone that he was after me. John had overheard him talking and warned me to be careful.

"It's better to be safe than sorry," he told me. "You just make sure you watch out for yourself."

I wasn't too afraid because I had the cutest little knife that was about three inches long and sharp as a razor, and I always slept with it.

One night after he had too much to drink, this guy thought he would quietly slip into my bed. Everyone else was snoring away when all of a sudden he let out some very loud, choice swear words.

John sat up with a start and shined his light in the direction of the disturbance and laughed when he saw that man's extremely pale face as well as the tip of my knife threatening to pierce his throat.

That was the last trouble I ever had with the men I packed in. I guess word got around about my little sidekick and that I wasn't afraid to use it. It was always with me, just in case.

∽

I don't remember ever running out of the necessities up there. Oh, sometimes we would have to ride to the Kennedy Meadows store for beer and such, but mostly we were well stocked and prepared.

Well, most of us were anyway. There was one occasion where poor planning led to a most embarrassing ride to Kennedy Meadows, twenty-five miles away.

Jim, Julie, and Cheryl were in the high country for an extended stay, but it seemed that Julie didn't look at her calendar before she went and her "time of the month" snuck up on her. They had been there for a week or two and Jim was looking pretty scruffy by that time. So, desperately needing her feminine supplies, she begged Jim to ride to Kennedy Meadows to get them.

Jim was a very quiet, intellectual type, who was very happy being off by himself, deep in meditation and not having to worry about anybody else. His first reaction at her request was, "You're kidding, right?" But after being assured she was serious, he grudgingly saddled up, strapped his rifle to the saddle, and rode off. This was a trip that took most of the day mind you, so he would have plenty of time to himself!

I wish I could have been there. Jim rode up to the hitching post, all scruffy looking like a mountain man out of the old west. He climbed down, and tethered the horse, grabbed his rifle so no one would take it, strode menacingly into the store, and looked around before asking, "Can you tell me where the tampons are?"

I can only imagine the look on the shopkeeper's face. We were rolling on the floor as he related his embarrassing story to us that evening.

Yes, he was a true knight in shining armor that day.

Chapter Fourteen

Birthdays, Snickerdoodles, and Blackberry Brandy

"What did you do if it was your birthday and you were at the pack station, Gramma?" asked one of my grandchildren. "Did you get your presents then or did you have to wait until you got home?"

I smiled. I knew that having to put off a birthday celebration until later was paramount to a national catastrophe at their young ages.

"Actually, I spent *several* birthdays at the pack station, since it fell right in the middle of hunting season," I told them. "And usually it was a great thing when that happened. It was like having two birthdays in one year. One up in the mountains, and another when I got home with my mother. Let me tell you about a couple of the memorable ones that I had here."

ᔕ

I was looking forward to my 18th birthday. It represented my "official" freedom from my mother's apron strings even though I had basically been free of them for over two years.

No longer searching for my niche, I knew where I belonged and where I wanted to be. Around John and his horses.

My mother knew it, too. I think she was just happy that I was no longer hanging around with the gang who I had gotten into trouble with. It was 1969. She was very worried about the drug scene and hoped I would steer clear of all of that, though I have to admit there was plenty of recreational drug experimentation at the pack station, but none that turned into a problem.

As my birthday approached, I was excited that we would be in the mountains for it. It was a hunting trip, as most of the October trips were. But on this trip, several of the girls were also going. Katie and I were very close at that time and I was glad she'd be there.

We wranglers were busy packing up and getting hunters onto their horses. John was loading Sandpiper, who was the usual pack-horse. I was finally mounted and ready to go, bringing up the rear of the line, while John was out front leading Sandpiper.

As we settled into the steady clip-clop of the dusty trail, my eyes were focused on a long skinny roll about four feet long that was on the top of the pack on Sandpiper. For the next forty-five minutes or so until we got to Deer Point, I was trying to figure out what the heck it was.

Curiosity finally won, as we all got off to adjust cinches, I hollered at John, "What is that thing on top there?

"A fishin' pole," was his short reply.

Oh, well, okay. That makes sense, I thought to myself. We had taken rods in before, just not like that. But I didn't think any more of it.

The rest of the ride just blends in memory with so many others.

They were all so special, yet so ordinary in that nothing very exciting ever really happened. We simply rode in silence and enjoyed the ambience of our surroundings. The oneness with nature we felt on that trail I have never in my life experienced anywhere else. The canyon and trail were devoid of any motorized sound. That is hard to find in this day and age. Even forty years ago, no motor vehicles of any kind were allowed on the trail. Up top they could come in from other places, but not on that trail that rose from the desert floor up over the summit. Our peace and quiet was always intact.

We uneventfully got to camp and unpacked the horses. I started to help with the packhorse, but John stopped me.

"I've got it handled," he told me. "You go in and get dinner started."

I did as I was told.

All of us had a filling meal and lots of chatter around the table before the weariness of the trail caught up with us and we headed off to bed.

The next day was my birthday. I was excited because I loved to celebrate up in the beautiful high country where I felt the closest to God that I have ever felt in my life. It wasn't that we were going to *do* anything to celebrate. We spent the day riding and loafing while the hunters went out to try their luck. That was celebration enough for me. It was really just like any other day, since we always rode and loafed. Our work centered on taking care of the hunters' horses and meals. Our time was our own once that was done. Life was easy in the high country.

That night, after we had cleaned up the dinner dishes and were gathered around the table playing cards, John and Katie went outside, but soon returned with several packages.

Everyone started singing "Happy Birthday," and a long skinny, rolled up package was placed on the table in front of me. That same "fishin' pole" package was sitting right there in front of me, and all eyes were on me with big smiles.

Katie set a box with birthday wrapping paper on it next to the "pole." Everyone yelled, "Open 'em! Open 'em!"

I opened the small box first.

As I ripped off the paper, the scent of a Christmas kitchen drifted up. Cookies? Yes, Katie's famous Snickerdoodles. Oh, what a great gift. I started munching away, oblivious to the drooling faces around me.

The long parcel then beckoned me.

I tore off the paper and found what looked like a rolled up rug. Unfurling it, I saw that it was a specific tapestry that I had wanted. It had been displayed in the little diner down the highway. It was of a Bengal tiger crouched over his kill as an elephant with hunters approach. For some unknown reason I fell in love with that silly tapestry.

Unbeknownst to me, John bought it when we stopped for burgers before reaching the pack station. I was shocked and surprised. I couldn't believe he had managed to pack it in without me knowing.

Now, forty years later, it still hangs in my house. A reminder of those carefree days in the high country.

ᔕ

My 21st birthday came when I was in the high country with a couple of our regular hunters. I was married by then, but still working pack trips for John.

Vic had been coming up with us for years. He seemed to always remember my special day and somehow he knew it would be my "big birthday" while I was stuck in the mountains, and he was determined that I had a good time.

The night of my birthday, he came in with a big box. He opened it and lifted out a perfect, undamaged, beautifully decorated birthday cake with my name on it.

"How on earth did you ever bring that cake up here without me knowing about it?" I gasped. Vic just grinned. It sure seemed like people could keep secrets from me with ease.

Along with the cake he brought a seemingly endless supply of blackberry brandy. We always had a bottle stowed away in case someone got a deer, since it was a ritual to cook the fresh deer liver in blackberry brandy with onions. But I had never drunk it straight from the bottle. On this night I was intent on celebrating this milestone in my life, and Vic had the means for me to do it.

I started downing it by the cupfuls. I don't remember anything after those first few swallows. The pictures I have of that night show me with quite a bright red face though. I wish I could remember if I had fun. I do recall that Vic got his deer, at last, on that trip. But I don't remember if we had any blackberry brandy left to fry his deer liver in!

We found one more bottle in his truck. Standing in the desert drinking straight out of the bottle, I didn't have a care in the world. I was in this magnificent country with an unending panoramic view of the Owens Valley. The world was mine! I was now twenty-one years old. I was an adult! Of course, I had been married for ten months, but so what. It's that big birthday that somehow means you have crossed the threshold to adulthood.

That was the last birthday I spent in the high country, and the most memorable (in spite of not remembering all of it). I owe my thanks to Vic for taking the time to make my day unforgettable. And to this day he still remembers my birthday with a card that arrives every year for the last thirty-nine years. He's so awesome! Thank you Vic!

Chapter Fifteen

Missing Horses

I began the evening's story as the children settled around me

"One fall there were so many hunters in the high country that we had them scattered all over. We had about two-dozen horses up there and I had to keep track of all of them."

"Wow, that's a lot of horses, Gramma," said one of the younger children. "That would be at least eight, wouldn't it?"

"Two dozen would be twenty-four," I told them.

"Wow," said the kids.

"Did you ever lose any, Gramma?" asked Lindsey. She is my horse lover and I can see a lot of myself in her in that respect, just as I can see bits and pieces of myself in all of my grandchildren.

"Well, we did have some that turned up missing once in a while," I admitted.

ഗ

The cabins at Dutch John had a nice big pasture behind a hill that was all fenced in. So when the horses were in that one, we didn't worry too much about them. But at the cabin on Deer Mountain, well that was another story.

Deer Mountain had the most beautiful meadow I had ever seen. The horses were usually so hungry that we didn't have to worry about them going anywhere. There were no fences, just lush green grass. When we neared the cabin and meadow, the horses always sensed that they were in for a yummy treat. They would get excited as we came out of the trees into the open meadow with wildflowers everywhere. After we unpacked them, we would barely get the last of the tack off before they tried to bolt for the grass buffet awaiting them.

On one such trip I was leaving the hunters and horses at that cabin for a few days. There were four horses and I made sure to teach the hunters how to hobble them at night, just in case anything frightened them.

Hobbles are made up of two cuffs that are connected by a chain or leather that are wrapped around the horses front pasterns (ankles). When they were hobbled they couldn't take off running and were limited to hopping instead of moving normally. They could move around freely to graze, they just couldn't go anywhere very fast. It's an old cowboy method of keeping the horses close but allowing them some freedom at the same time.

They had enough supplies for three days and knew the way back to the main cabins at Dutch John if they had any problems. I wished them happy hunting and left them reluctantly with Tammy, Little Oats, Cindy, and Sandpiper. I told the horses to take good care of them and stay out of the way of any stray bullets.

Poppin' and I loped most of the way back to Dutch John. We passed a few of the hunters from that camp heading out to try their luck, but I would say ninety percent of the time, the deer were more lucky than the hunters.

The next day, one of the hunters from Deer Mountain showed up on foot at our cabin. He was out of breath and red-faced as he tried to tell us what happened.

"The horses are gone!" he was finally able to spit out.

"What do you mean 'gone'?" I asked.

"We got up this morning and they were gone. We looked all over for them. We couldn't find any tracks, nothing. All four of them…gone," he replied.

"Did you hobble them like I showed you?" I asked.

"Well, we ate dinner, then got to playing cards and having a couple beers. The next thing we knew it was morning and they were gone. We meant to, but I guess we fell asleep." He lowered his head, embarrassed.

I walked out and whistled for Poppin'. He hadn't been too far out in the pasture and came running as soon as he heard me. I saddled him up, grabbed a couple of scoops of grain, and put it in my saddlebags.

As I started out on the trail, I hollered for my teen wranglers, Cary and Clark, to saddle up another horse for the hunter and bring him back up to Deer Mountain. Then they could help me look for the horses.

"Leave it to those idiot hunters to make my life harder," I thought to myself. "Why can't people just follow directions?" It seemed like every time something happened it was because someone wasn't doing what they were told. My mind raced back to Blaze falling down the mountain. Yep, not following directions.

I eased Poppin' into an easy lope and headed up the trail to the high cabin. I knew Cary and Clark would not be far behind. "Hopefully those horses will be back at the meadow by the time I get there," I thought. "There aren't a lot of other places for them to eat on that mountain."

When I approached the meadow, I could see there were no horses. The hunters were outside the cabin cleaning their rifles.

"Any sign of them since your buddy left?" I asked.

"Nope, not a thing," came the reply.

"Well, I'm going to ride around a bit and see if I can pick up any trail or direction they went. I'm surprised they didn't head back down to Dutch John where they know there's food, as well as their buddies," I said as I headed out on the trail from the cabin.

I rode around the perimeter of the meadow looking for tracks or any sign at all of the horses. At the north end of the meadow there were a few deer trails leading off into the brush, and at the western edge was a small trail eventually leading to the Pacific Crest Trail. It was all overgrown and had no fresh tracks on it. The southern edge of the meadow had no trails leading out from it but went from meadow to trees and forest. The horses could've possibly gone that way but, again, I saw no tracks.

"How could they have just vanished into thin air without a trace?" I rode around again. Maybe I missed something.

About that time, Cary and Clark arrived with the hunter. They got him settled with his friends and tied the extra horse to the hitching post.

"Anything?" Clark asked as they rode towards me.

"Not a sign of horses anywhere," I replied. "It's like they said 'Beam me up Scottie!' and poof, gone! Why don't you two go back down the trail and look real close for any signs between here and the cabins? Maybe they're making their way back to the other horses, took a short cut, and we missed seeing anything because we were so intent on getting here. I'll ride around a bit more up here. Let's meet back at Dutch John in two hours."

We went our separate ways. I spent the next hour riding in circles and found nothing at all. I finally gave up and decided to go back down the mountain. I was almost to the pasture when the boys came trotting down the hillside out of the timber.

"We followed a couple of small deer trails on our way and didn't find anything." Cary said, as they caught up with me.

"Well, we'd better get back and tend to the horses we still have. We'll look again tomorrow. Maybe they'll come back to the meadow by then," I said as we turned for the trail back to Dutch John.

As we approached the hitching rail, I said, "Let's turn these guys out to graze and get some chow. I'm starving."

After lunch I got out my map of the high country and laid it out on the table. There was just so much open country with no trails at all and horses could easily get lost forever. We had to have a plan.

I gathered the two boys, and the other girls on the trip, Pam and Terri, around the map.

"Okay, here's what we're going to do. There are a lot of packers to the north of Deer Mountain, as well as here at Kennedy Meadows to the south. Let's post some 'lost horses' signs on some of the main trails. Terri and Pam, I want you to ride to Kennedy Meadows in the morning and put a notice on their bulletin board at the store. Since it's a central meeting place, any hikers who see the horses will know who to contact. And be sure to tell everyone you see along the way. Get the word out to as many people as possible that there are three mares and a gelding missing in the high country around Deer Mountain, and that our main camp is at Dutch John if anyone hears anything. Clark, Cary, and I will scour the area around Deer Mountain."

"Sounds good." they all said in agreement.

The rest of that day was spent taking care of the hunters and horses at Dutch John.

At first light the next morning, we all headed out. The boys and I wasted no time getting up to that mountain. They took off on one of the first deer trails to the northeast and I told them to meet me back in the meadow in two hours. I continued to the northwest corner and followed a deer trail from there.

Poppin' and I plodded along warily on that little-used trail. I saw no signs of horses at all, but I figured "what the heck, I have to look somewhere." We rode and stopped. I listened for any sort of out-of-the-ordinary noise. It was so eerily quiet. No birds singing, no deer spotted. No living creatures seen at all.

At one point the trail went up and around a rocky outcropping. It looked narrow and not very safe. We soon reached a narrow passage with a sheer drop beside it. I decided that we had gone far enough.

Poppin' and I carefully backed up as there wasn't room to turn around. "Thank goodness I'm on you and not that squirrelly Brownie," I told him. "He would have danced and pranced us right off the trail."

Then something tugged at my mind. What if they had run up here, spooked at something, and had slipped and fallen? I had to look.

I got back to a safe place and dismounted. I dropped the reins so Poppin' would stay put, and walked back up that narrow path. I approached the ledge and got down on my knees and crawled to the edge to peer over.

In my mind I saw four horses sprawled at the bottom of that steep canyon. I cleared that image from my head, held my breath and looked down. Nothing. My heart did a little flip-flop of thanks. I backed away from the ledge, got up and ran back down to Poppin'. He was standing right where I left him, and together we walked back down the path. I stayed on foot the rest of the way trying to see if there was anything I had missed.

I reached the meadow about the same time as the boys. They were trotting toward me, waving.

"Come and see what we found," Cary said to me as I jumped back up on Poppin'.

They led me down one of the deer trails they had followed for about a quarter of a mile.

"Check it out," said Clark as he pointed to a brush mound just off the trail.

It was a mountain lion kill. Under the brush was a half-eaten deer that had been "buried" to eat later. It looked to be a day or two old.

"Well, that explains why we haven't seen any deer for a few days up here. And *maybe* it explains why the horses are gone. Scared off?" I said. "Let's go tell the hunters to watch out and get back down to the cabins."

Later that afternoon the girls returned from Kennedy. "No one we ran into has seen the horses," they told us. "We posted notices with their descriptions and talked to several people along the way."

"Well, there's not much more we can do but wait, I guess." I told them. "John is going to tan my hide for sure for losing his best pack horse. Tomorrow those hunters need to be packed out. So Cary and Clark, first thing in the morning take four horses up there and bring them out. When you get down to the desert maybe John will be there, maybe not. If he is, tell him what happened. If not, don't call him. I'm still hoping for a miracle."

The next day was spent much like the one before. The boys took the hunters out to the desert and I rode Poppin' all over Deer Mountain looking for the missing horses. After several hours of fruitless searching, I rode back to camp frustrated that there was no sign of any living thing on that mountain.

I turned Poppin' out to the pasture and went back to the cabin. The girls were finishing up the dishes from breakfast and lunch.

We still had a few men with us who were out hunting for the day. Since we were short of horses, today they were on foot. I liked it best that way. It meant our horses were out of harm's way!

Late in the afternoon the hunter's returned with news that they had gotten a deer. They needed us to bring a horse to pack it up the hill to the cabin.

"You got a what?" I asked incredulously. "You actually shot a deer?"

"Yep, sure did," the proud hunter replied.

"Well I'll be. That's a rare happening up here, you know!" I laughed as I went out and whistled for horses.

Poppin' came running, bringing a few others with him. "Good boy," I told him. "But you don't have to go anywhere." I put a small hand-full of grain in front of each horse that came to the corral. It was a way of rewarding them for coming to me, rather than me having to hike all over the pasture and chase them.

I put a halter on Blaze and led him out, saddled him up and gave the lead rope to the mighty deer-slayer.

"There's extra rope to tie it on with. Just throw it over the saddle, tie it good, and Blaze will do the rest," I said, as I sent them off to gather their prize.

About an hour later they were back with a good-sized buck. They took their kill over to the two trees we used for hanging the carcasses and strung it up to gut it out. I took out a pot for them to put the liver in. The traditional meal of liver and onions sautéed in Blackberry Brandy was on the horizon. It was the only time in my life I *ever* ate liver! It just tasted so different when fresh and cooked like that. Of course we used a whole bottle of Blackberry Brandy so maybe that had something to do with the taste.

They got their deer skinned and quartered and we ate our fill of liver that night. It was good for our morale to not think about the missing horses for a few hours.

After dinner, I lay on my bed and thought about all the possibilities of where those horses could be. They could be all dead somewhere. They could have been caught by one of those unscrupulous packers we had run into occasionally. Or they could just be running free in the high country, never to be seen again!

The next thing I knew, morning sunshine was coming through the small dirty window. The crew had let me sleep and were outside with the men getting them packed up and ready to leave. I went out to help and they said they had it handled.

"We're giving you a day off," Cary told me. I went back inside and fixed a cup of coffee and a bowl of cereal. They hollered a "good-bye" and headed off down the trail.

Well, what was I going to do with myself today? It was a rare thing to not have any chores. The horses had now been gone four days.

I spent most of the day just tinkering around the cabins. It had been so long since I had been alone that I was relishing the solitude. I brought in wood and tidied up the cabin. Not much you can do with a dirt floor but keep dusting everything. I rearranged the cupboard and made sure all the mousetraps were freshly baited and set.

Later in the day I decided to go sit on the rocks behind the cabins overlooking the pasture the horses were in. I took my book with me and laid on a big flat rock for most of the afternoon. There were only two horses left, Poppin' and Jade. They were napping in the late afternoon sunshine just like me. I must have dozed off reading my book, daydreaming about King Arthur and the Crystal Cave…

❦

…You have the answer child. You know how to find your horses. It is obvious. It will come to you. The ancestors are sending you their message. Listen to them. You know what to do…

❦

Suddenly, I was awakened by the loudest whinny I ever heard.

I sat straight up and looked down to see Jade running around with his nose in the air hollering his fool head off. Poppin' seemed unconcerned.

What in the world was going on?

Then I heard an answering whinny coming from down the trail. It was Cary, Clark, and the girls returning from the desert with all of the horses they had taken with them. Jade was ecstatic that part of his herd was home.

As I sat there watching him running around and yelling at his herd mates, an idea began taking shape in my head. "I wonder...." I thought to myself.

I jumped up and ran down to the cabins just in time to greet the returning riders. "Boy, Jade sure is freaking out," Clark said as he dismounted.

"Yes he is," I replied. "It's given me an idea. Tomorrow morning at first light, Jade and I are going for a ride. You all need to stay here and keep all the horses here."

"Why?" asked Clark.

"Not telling. In case it doesn't work," I answered.

We led all the horses out to the pasture where Jade and Poppin' were waiting. There was a happy greeting for each one and then they were all grazing as if they had never been apart.

The next morning, Clark went out and brought Jade in to be saddled. He was fidgety and not happy to be away from all the others. Stallions are like that. They don't like to be alone.

That's the one trait I was counting on.

I hopped on his back and as soon as I was settled, I gently clucked at him and off we went up the trail.

Jade was such a good horse and all business when he was moving and doing something. I nudged him into a slow trot and away we went up the mountain. As we got near the meadow and the high cabin, we slowed to a walk. He was so alert with ears twitching back and forth. His nostrils were flaring a bit from the rapid climb.

When we got to the middle of the meadow I pulled him up and stopped. He stood still. Gradually his breathing slowed and his side stopped heaving. He wasn't really out of shape, just excited to be out. Plus, he put out a bit more exertion knowing he was alone. We stood there for a moment or two and then it got very quiet. I was watching his ears and the way he was sniffing the air. I waited for what I knew was coming.

I didn't have to wait long. With a mighty gulp of air he let loose with a whinny that could probably be heard down on the desert floor. He did it again and again. I was so proud of him. He was snorting and carrying on just like a stallion should; calling his herd mates.

We walked up the trail a bit and he stopped and again hollered. His ears were going every which way. Nostrils flared and sniffing the air, he stood still as a statue, looking for any hint at all of his ladies. When we got to the end of the meadow, we just stood there and I let him holler to his heart's content. Then I quieted him as much as I could so I could listen.

At first I didn't hear anything. But then he whinnied one more time and there was an answering call. It was faint and I had no sense of the direction it was coming from. He spoke up again and this time I heard two horses answer him. Then suddenly his head jerked around looking back to the trail that had the mountain lion kill on it.

I gave him his head and we trotted back through the meadow with him still yelling his head off. The answering calls were coming closer and closer.

Suddenly, the three mares rounded the bend and were running toward us. Jade was just beside himself with stallion happiness! There were nickers and snorts and the girls seemed so happy to see him.

With this happy reunion going on I sadly looked around hoping to see Sandpiper. There was no sign of him.

"Where's your fella, girls?" I asked them. I decided to dismount for a while to let the mares eat their fill of grass. It was obvious to me they had not eaten for days. Jade must have realized his girls didn't need his "attention" right then, since he acted like a perfect gentleman and let me concentrate.

As I tried to piece the mystery together, I believed that the night they were unhobbled the cat probably came through and frightened them and they took off up the trail. Then, with the cat's kill there, they were too spooked to come back to the meadow. They probably just wandered further up the trail looking for food. None of the horses we had been riding in our search had bothered to call out for them. But with their man calling, that was a different story!

"Jade, you did good, ol' buddy!" I told him. "Let's get going down the hill and get these girls settled back in their own pasture for the night."

I was still wondering what had happened to Piper when Jade's head jerked up and he let out another whinny.

I looked around and there, in the clearing, limping over to us, was that big palomino gelding. The mares trotted over to him and then back to Jade. I had tears of joy streaming down my face.

Piper stopped in front of me and put his head against my side. He looked pretty beat up and had scratches on his neck and as I checked him over I saw an injury to his hind leg. There was a gaping wound with torn muscle hanging out. He was still able to walk on the leg, but it didn't look good. Then I realized that the lion had attacked him. There was no other explanation. I bet he was kicking up a storm at that cat! So if he had been hobbled, perhaps he would have been killed. Chills ran down my spine.

"Well, Piper, do you think you can make it down the mountain?" I asked as I stroked his forehead. He nudged me as if in answer. I sensed that he just wanted off this mountain as fast as possible.

I got back up on Jade and started down the hill. We would go as slow as we needed to. All four horses fell in behind me with Piper in the middle and the mares taking care not to trample on him as he limped down the trail. Every few minutes Jade would stop to let the gelding catch up. That was the longest ride I had ever taken down from Deer Mountain.

As we approached the back part of the pasture, the mares started whinnying and Poppin' and everyone else in the pasture ran over to the fence. They followed along as we made our way around and down the last quarter of a mile to the corral. The mares were now out in front trotting to the corral.

Hearing all the commotion, Cary and Clark had opened the gate and were there to greet us. Slowly Piper and Jade reached the hitching rail and I dismounted. The horses were having a party as I unsaddled Jade and took him into the corral and turned him loose.

Off they ran, Jade with his herd once more intact, out to the pasture. At the creek, I saw the mares stop and drink and drink and drink. It had been five days without apparent food and water for them.

"Go and see if you can find some fishing gear," I told the Cary. "We have a horse to try to put back together."

I got some disinfectant out of the first aid kit and started cleaning Piper's wounds. They seemed a bit infected, like cat scratches always seem to get. I chuckled to myself that maybe it made no difference, house cat, mountain lion; a cat scratch is a cat scratch.

I cleaned the wounds as much as I could. We had a bottle of old penicillin in the icebox in the creek. I figured it couldn't hurt. I gave him a shot. By that time the boys had come back with the fishing gear.

I had a needle and thread in my gear, so I took out the needle and the reel of fishing line. I had never sewn anything together before, so I didn't know what made me think I could sew a horse's leg back together. I just knew I had to try and do something for him. If only John were here. He would know exactly what to do.

"You guys need to hold him tight," I told the boys and started trying to put the muscle back together. That horse didn't even flinch. He seemed to know we just wanted to help him.

At last, I managed to piece it back and just tacked it together with the fishing line. I put in big looping stitches to hold it in place.

There was nothing very neat and tidy about it. I felt it would do the trick though, and when I was done, I stood back and was satisfied. Sandpiper didn't seem to feel anything. For that I was happy.

I didn't have anything to wrap it with, so I put a bunch of Furacin first aid ointment on it, and fed him some grain. We brought a bucket of water over to him and then just let him stand for the rest of the afternoon.

"You are a good, brave boy," I told him.

That evening we confined him to the corral. Not that he was going anywhere. He was extremely reluctant to move at all. Several times that evening the other horses came down to check on him. It was obvious they were concerned about him.

The next morning I sent Cary and Clark out to take down the lost horse notices. When Terri and Pam returned from the desert their eyes practically fell out of their sockets when they saw Piper in the corral.

After I filled them in on the whole story we spent the rest of the day just hanging around pampering Sandpiper and watching "the herd."

Life on the mountain seemed to be getting back to normal. All the horses were present and accounted for. The five of us were once again carefree and happy.

Sandpiper ended up healing very well with no real lingering sign of the injury. He had a few months off and then returned to the string.

I never left horses up in that high pasture again after that fiasco. I didn't trust the hunters to properly care for them. And I didn't think I would be so lucky if it happened again. Mountain lions were just too scary to deal with and Sandpiper was a very, very lucky horse.

I thanked the spirits of the mountain for helping me find the horses. I knew they had "spoken" to Jade that day and put that idea in my head. And I thanked them for my continued education in this way of life I had chosen to embrace.

Chapter Sixteen

On My Own

I had never stayed anywhere alone before. Oh sure, I was home alone while my mother worked the graveyard shift, but never any place away from home. I was never away from whatever I knew to be "comfortable" for an extended period of time.

"How would you like to stay at the pack station by yourself all winter?" John asked me.

I looked at him in amazement. I had never thought about doing such a thing. I was a little apprehensive, but more than that, I was filled with a sense of adventure. I was seventeen years old.

The pack station was going strong now. We had people coming and going all summer, along with all of the deer hunters in the fall. Since John was now the official name of record at the pack station, he was free to use the place as he saw fit.

"I think I'd like to winter some of the horses up here," he told me. "That would be cheaper than feeding them in the city. I'll leave six or seven here, but I'll need someone to watch over them. You interested?"

"Oh yeah!" I told him. I jumped at the chance to be away from home and was eager for this new experience.

A few weeks later, after closing down for the season, John drove off with his last load of horses, leaving me alone with my charges and, thankfully, my pickup truck.

Then the stark reality of my situation sank in.

I was totally and completely alone. I couldn't just pick up the phone and call someone. I was used to the isolation here all summer, but honestly hadn't really thought about what it would be like in winter.

Oh, but I wasn't *really* alone. I had my horses, Brownie and Poppin' and seven others, my dogs Frosty and Laddie, and my cat Tabby. Oh yeah, stinky ol' Tex, the goat, was there, too. But for human company, nada!

At first it was kind of cool. I thought I would like having no one to talk to. But after a few days it got old. I often went to town and met some of the locals. Soon people were coming up to see me, and there was often unexpected but welcome company coming up the road.

The Sheriff and I became great friends. He was Paiute Indian and was descended from some of the first people in this valley. I was fascinated by the stories he told.

I started talking more and more to the animals, and soon I was talking to the horses and half expecting them to answer. The dogs thought I was just plain crazy. Maybe I was.

Each day I spent alone brought me closer to the world as it must have been two hundred years ago. The only modern conveniences were my truck, the stove, and a hot water heater. There was an ice-box in the spring. I also had a battery-powered transistor radio that never seemed to work.

I basked in the sound of silence as it echoed noiselessly across the desert valley. I could shout at the top of my lungs and hear my own empty voice faintly answer down the canyon.

At this time of year, late fall, most living things were taking refuge in their burrows and nests, dug in for the long, cold winter. During the spring and summer and even early fall, there was a flurry of insect and wildlife activity, but now only an occasional chirp or click was heard. Sometimes I would see a long-eared jackrabbit by the hay in the early evening but, for the most part, it was just me and the domesticated critters.

Sheriff Wright came up every other day or so to make sure all was well. I never felt afraid or scared that anything bad would happen or that any dangerous people would come around. I just didn't think about things like that. As it turns out it was around the time Charles Manson was causing trouble in Inyo County, so I am fortunate that I had people watching out for me.

The nights were dark and lonely. I'm afraid that most nights I went to bed rather early. As soon as it got dark there wasn't much to do but listen to the dogs snore. I would try to stay awake and read my books or play solitaire, but the presence of the complete and utter quiet would win out and I would turn the lamp off and drift away in my dreams.

My dreams were becoming more and more vivid. When I first came here I sensed voices and colors, now images were coming in loud and clear.

One particular rainy night I kept being jarred out of my sleep by thunder and the heavy downpour on the roof. I was tossing and turning when a calm came over me, telling me to let my spirit rest. The fight went out of my body and before I knew it...

ꟹ

I am walking up the canyon toward the first stream crossing.

It is a bright sunny day. The birds are busy gathering nest materials and food.

I am in awe of my surroundings when I walk around a slight bend and there standing in the middle of the trail is an Indian girl.

She looks a few years younger than me, and seems to be waiting for me. She is dressed lightly in what appear to be rabbit skins. She smiles and motions for me to follow her.

We walk another hundred yards or so and she veers off the trail down a small path and sits by a flat rock that has a few shallow round holes in it.

She motions for me to sit and I obey. She doesn't speak and just keeps smiling as she reaches into a fur pouch she has tied around her waist.

She removes a black flat stone and shows it to me. It has a white line that cuts through the center similar to a lightning bolt. She grins again as she takes a dead squirrel out of her pouch and, within minutes, she proceeds to gut it out and skin it.

Wow! I just stare at her. She scrapes the skin with the tool she holds in her hand, and soon she has the hide ready for drying.

ᔕ

A loud clap of thunder woke me out of my dream. I sat up wide awake, disappointed that I was not on that rock with the young girl. No matter how I longed to go back to be with her, the dream eluded me.

I took great interest in riding and exploring the world around me. Most of the time, I would head off for new territory. I don't think there was any place within a five-mile radius that I didn't explore.

Finding arrowheads was the icing on the cake on these excursions. They were everywhere within a mile or two of the pack station. My horses and I would find gifts everywhere we went. I had never imagined so many relics in one spot.

Sometimes I would just hang around the pack station and look for ghosts from the past.

One day toward winter, I decided to clean out the old storage room and reorganize it. I needed to move the winter's feed inside to keep it dry once the rains came, and it was full of junk that we had never sorted through. Back in a corner there were a couple of ancient, dusty saddles that were falling apart. As I moved one of them, I saw what looked like an even *more* ancient set of saddlebags. When I reached out to open the flap, the once ornate leather pouch seemed to dissolve into a fine dust. As I scooped it up to throw it out, a small bundle fell to the ground. I picked up the object wrapped in a piece of hardened chamois. I carefully unwrapped it and found a chunk of black obsidian with a very noticeable grayish stripe that looked to me like a bolt of lightning. It was sort of round and about palm-sized with one edge knife-blade sharp. Holding it in my hand, I could fit my thumb and fingers in the worn grooves on the stone. I turned it over and over in my hand, marveling at the feelings I had while holding it. It looked very much like the stone tool the girl in my dream had used while working on her squirrel hide. How did it get here? My mind re-ran the dream as I tried to pick out clues as to how it might have ended up in this old shed.

I don't know how long I sat there thinking, but the horses nickering at me brought me out of my trance. It was feeding time. Gently, I rewrapped the treasure, set it down, and went back to work. After I was done feeding and watering all the critters, I grabbed my new prize and headed to the cabin to fix some dinner.

I lit the lantern and settled into my comfy chair to read "Return of the King." I was almost done with "The Lord of the Rings" series. Most of the teenagers at the pack station that year had read it. I must have read for two hours, finally finishing it. It was so good I didn't want it to end. My back was getting stiff from not moving for several hours while I finished the book, so I rose to stretch my legs, walked to the door to let Frosty and Laddie out for one last time before turning in for the night.

With a sense of gratefulness, I looked up into the heavens and said a sincere thank you to no one in particular for the beauty of this place, gathered my dogs, and went back in to go to bed.

As I walked past the table, I grabbed the leather bundle and went into my little room at the back of the cabin, then crawled into my comfy, soft bed. Frosty jumped up and tamped out a circle at my feet. Since he couldn't seem to settle down, I finally kicked him off and he went to join Laddie who was curled up out by the woodstove. Everything was warm and toasty, quiet and perfect. I was content.

I got out the stone tool and turned it over and over in my hands. It was so smooth and the edge was so sharp. It fit my hand so perfectly.

As I drifted off to sleep, my dreams took over and I found myself...

ᔕ

...walking toward the grinding stone. The same young girl appears once more and motions for me to join her.

Hesitantly, I move toward her as she sits on the stone, picks up the stone pestle, and starts grinding some pinion nuts in one of the holes on this massive rock.

Unsure of what I am supposed to do, she looks at me and motions for me to sit next to her. She finishes grinding the nuts into a fine powder, then picks up a rabbit that has been brought to her by a young boy, and starts to dress it out. She has an oblong obsidian tool that comes to a point. She uses it to make a slit from the rabbit's throat down to the bottom of its belly, as well as cutting out to the end of each leg.

My eyes are riveted to what she is doing. She is fast and sure of her task and makes it look as easy to me as pouring macaroni into boiling water.

After gutting the animal, she sets down the pointed tool and picks up a round flat piece of obsidian that is sharpened on one side. It is black with a white stripe. This tool is familiar to me.

This tool is used to scrape the hide away from the meat. She moves effortlessly as she skins the rabbit. She puts the carcass into a basket beside her, then turns the skin over and lays it flat. She scrapes all flesh and tissue away and then rises and goes over to a crude sort of wooden rack, then stretches it up and binds it with sinew at four corners to dry.

She sits back down, picks up another rabbit, and hands it to me. She wants me to skin this one. I take it from her and she offers me the first tool she used. I nervously try to copy what she had done. My fingers won't work. When I try to cut it open, I don't press hard enough.

She is watching intently when I swear under my breath as I fumble with the dead rabbit. I look up at her. She is smiling at me. Her dark eyes are dancing as she stares into mine. She smiles, big as the sky, as she nods. She takes the stone knife from me as clouds start to gather.

Storms can come to the desert in an instant and now clouds are racing overhead. The darkness swallows up the daylight and becomes fierce and menacing.

She hurriedly gathers up the flour she has ground, the skinned rabbit and her tools, then races off to shelter. I start running after her when a loud clap of thunder shakes the sky.

❧

I sat straight up in bed frightened by the piercing sound. My mind was confused and caught somewhere between a dream and a nightmare. My heart was pounding and my breathing felt too rapid.

"Calm down girl," I thought to myself. "It was only a dream." Once fully awake, I told myself to relax and breathe.

A moment later I heard a loud commotion out in the corral. Horses were running around and hollering. The dogs started barking and carrying on. I jumped up and went to the window to see if I could make out what was going on. I expected it to be pouring rain with thunder and lightning, but the dark sky was alive and twinkling with all those ever-present stars.

What in the world was scaring them? They were definitely spooked about something.

John had made sure I had my 30-30 Winchester rifle with me, but even with the gun and not knowing what was going on, I didn't think I should go out there by myself.

There had been bear and mountain lion tracks seen down here at times. And I didn't want to let the dogs out for fear they would get hurt. And what in the world would I do even if I went out and found one of them in with the horses? I mean really, what would I do?

Then I heard a loud kick at the feeders, some squealing and, after that, things started to settle down.

I decided to wait for first light before going out. Of course, time seems to stand still when you want it to rush by the fastest. After what seemed like forever and beyond, the dawn broke. I let the dogs out, grabbed my rifle, and went out to the horses.

The dogs went tearing ahead of me to the corral, quickly picked up a scent, and started to head up the canyon. I hollered at them and they actually, for the first time ever, listened and came back to me.

So, something *had* been here during the night. I felt grateful that I had heeded that little voice inside of me once again. It never seemed to let me down.

I went straight to the fence, ducked under, and was at once greeted by several nervous horses. They came trotting up to me as if they needed to tell me the whole story.

My eyes did a slow scan, checking them all for any kinds of cuts or injuries. I didn't see anything amiss. I leaned my rifle against the fence post as I patted them, talked to them, and then went to the shed to get them their breakfast.

As I walked around throwing hay in the feeders and got to the last one, I noticed Maverick standing in the same spot he was in when I came out.

A feeling of dread came over me as fast as a cloud blots out the sun in a sudden storm. I called to him. He looked at me and perked his ears up but didn't move.

"Come on, boy," I called again. He didn't move.

When I walked over to him my eyes were drawn to the leg he had cocked in a funny position.

"Oh, God no! It can't be. Oh please, oh please, oh please! *no*!"

I just stood there in front of him; he nudged me with his muzzle. I didn't want to believe my eyes, but it was so obvious that his leg was broken.

He nickered at me. My heart dissolved into tears that came pouring out as I crumpled down in front of him sobbing. What in the world was I going to do? How was I supposed to handle something like this? There had been no training in my years with John to prepare me for this kind of emergency.

I looked up into the bright, early morning sky, still sobbing. "I'm alone here!" I screamed to the heavens. "I'm only seventeen! What am I supposed to do?"

Maverick nudged my shoulder. His eyes were full of pain and yet he seemed worried about me. I cried harder.

When my tears at last dried up, I looked around. The dogs were sitting next to me and all the horses were looking at me. They weren't eating. It seemed like they were waiting to see what I was going to do.

I said to myself, "Okay Miss Roni, you were grown up enough to take on this challenge to be here alone. Now grow up, figure it out, and make the right decision!"

Slowly, I stood up and walked around talking to all the horses, my mind a jumble of racing, rambling thoughts. One by one each horse seemed to go over to Maverick to give him support. I know it isn't really like that in the animal world. Is it?

Maverick just stood there as they nuzzled him and then returned to their food.

My mind was clearing a bit, and my chest hurt from crying so hard. I looked around scanning down to the highway hoping to see a trail of dust that would signal someone was coming to help.

There was nothing there.

Then I zeroed in on the rifle leaning against the post. A chill went through me as I realized what I had to do.

There was no healing a broken cannon bone on a horse out here in the middle of nowhere. There was no horse vet in these parts to come put him out of his pain. There was no savior driving up the dirt road to deliver us from this catastrophe. No. There was only me, and a Winchester 30-30.

I walked over, put my arms around him and buried my head in his mane. I could feel the tears welling up again and willed them away. I had to be strong here.

I looked in his eyes and saw the empty, hollow look of a horse in pain. Those eyes were pleading with me to help him. Begging me to release him from his pain.

"Please be strong for a few more minutes, Mav. I need to do a few things," I whispered softly in his ears. He nickered back.

I crawled back under the fence, and called the dogs. They would stay in the cabin for the rest of the morning. Then I went back to the corrals and shifted the horses into the other two corrals so Maverick was alone in the big one.

After I had everyone situated, I sat down on a feeder and said a prayer to whoever was listening. "*Please* let me be strong here. *Please* don't let him suffer. And please, oh *please* don't let me miss. I don't think I can do it twice!"

I felt a calm come over me as I walked over to Mav for the last time.

"It's going to be all right," I whispered to him. "You have to be brave for me. I don't want to do what I am about to do and I hope you understand it's because I love you."

I walked to the fencepost and picked up my rifle. "Oh God, please help me do this," I said.

The gun felt heavy. Oh so heavy. And cold.

I walked back to him and stood about ten feet away. Was I too close? Not close enough?

"How do I know the right way to do this?" I pleaded as I raised the gun up and aimed for the middle of his forehead.

My arms felt weak and shaky. Maverick stood there straight as an arrow looking at me. Waiting for me. Waiting for release.

He didn't move a muscle. I took a deep breath and asked once again for help.

Then I felt them.

The spirits who surround everything here were surrounding me as I raised that gun and held it steady and someone pulled the trigger.

It was me.

I saw it all happen in slow motion as if I were a bystander in this whole affair.

The loud echo of the Winchester; the slow trail of the bullet as it entered dead center into Maverick's forehead; the slow collapse of the stoic animal as his spirit soared to run in the heavens with those who had gone before; the unexpected shake of the earth as the dead horse fell to the ground with a thud, causing a swirl of dust to rise.

I dropped the rifle as all my senses returned to normal, and stood looking at the body of that beautiful horse lying in a heap in a corner of that dusty corral.

Everything was still. There was no sound at all. No birds. No insects. No sound from the other horses.

Nothing.

But the stillest of all was the body of that heroic horse.

"Thank you, thank you, *thank you*! Thank you for letting it kill him instantly!" I said as I looked around and saw nothing but empty desert, and curious horses that were now lining the fences.

Slowly, almost reverently, I turned away from him, ducked under the rail, and sat down right in the middle of the road. I bent my knees, laid my head down on my arms and cried. I felt the whole desert crying with me. And weeping with me were my new friends from eons past. They helped me do what had to be done and now they mourned the loss of the horse with me as they huddled around me sitting there, unable to stop the tears.

They took longer to dry up this time. I don't know how long I sat there.

The drone of an engine brought me out of my stupor. I looked up and saw a trail of dust coming up the road. He was almost to the cabin before I realized it was the Sheriff.

He pulled his truck to a stop, got out, and leaned against it while taking in the scene before him: a red-eyed girl sitting in the middle of the road, two madly barking dogs locked inside the cabin, horses whinnying to be let out of their small area so they could finish their breakfast and, finally, the body of a horse in the corner of the corral.

He looked around as he walked over to me and he said, "I see you've had a rough morning."

I looked up at him with red swollen eyes and nodded.

"Let's get you inside and have some coffee." He helped me up and we slowly walked to the front door.

We were greeted by the dogs. They were wiggling and wagging their tails like crazy as we walked in. They hadn't seen another human for a few days now. Maybe they were tired of me already.

He grabbed the coffee pot, filled it, put the grounds in, and set it on the stove to percolate. Nothing smelled better than cowboy coffee.

We sat at the table where neither one of us said anything for a time.

"Is there anything I can do?" he asked.

I broke down again.

In a caring voice he asked, "Do you know what happened?"

Through my tears I told him of the night before and how scared I was to go outside, so I waited and poor Maverick had to be in pain all that time, and then when I found him I didn't know what to do and, "Oh God why did this have to happen?"

He came around the table and put his arm around my shoulder. I just sat there and cried.

And he let me.

He poured two cups of coffee, set one in front of me, sat down, and waited.

Finally spent, I took a deep breath and went to the kitchen sink to splash cold water on my face. I was exhausted.

I came back to the table and we talked about what had happened. I told him about the calm that had come over me and it seemed to hold up the gun as the shot was fired.

He said, "Ah, the Grandfathers were with you!"

"Who?" I asked.

"My ancestors who have lived in this desert since creation," he answered.

"Well, they sure helped me out here" I replied.

"You believe in them. They know this and sense the spirit in you that seems to come from the past. They trust you. Very few are this blessed," he said in an almost reverent tone.

"What made you come up here, anyway?" I asked.

"Not sure exactly. I had heard there was a teenage girl living out here alone, and I just had a feeling I was needed," he replied.

"Well I am so grateful that you're here. Thanks!" I said. "You can come up any time you feel like it. I've been going a little crazy. Not bad, but it does get lonely."

As we talked I became aware of the horses pacing in the corrals.

"Guess I'd better let those guys back out."

"I'll help," he offered as we rose and went outside.

All seemed to be back to normal out on the desert. It was a fairly warm day, and the insects were back at it. So were the birds. The horses were itching to get back to their breakfast and the dogs were running in circles.

He opened one gate and I the other. The horses all trotted back to the feeders, grabbed a few bites of hay, and then as if someone yelled a silent command, they all stopped and turned towards Maverick with their ears twitching and noses in the air.

Then, as Sheriff Wright and I watched, one by one they all went over and sniffed the body of their friend. They seemed to be paying their respects. Single file, one by one. It was incredible! Laddie and Frosty were sitting there next to Maverick like they were an Honor Guard.

The Sheriff and I looked at each other, smiled, and looked up at the sky.

The Grandfathers. I liked that!

After we watched for a while, we returned to the cabin and a second cup of coffee.

"So, I have a question for ya, Sheriff," I said.

"Which is?" he replied.

"What the heck am I supposed to do with a dead horse?" I asked.

"Oh, you're not going to like this answer," he said. "Out here in this county we have no way to dispose of livestock. So, for some reason, rather than letting them lay there and feed the scavengers, there is an ordinance that they be incinerated."

"As in burned up?" I asked aghast.

"As in burned up," he replied.

"How in the world am I supposed to do that?" I asked while my mind raced a million miles a minute thinking of ways to do it. This sounded way more complicated than starting a campfire!

"Well, I'll help ya. We'll go get a bunch of old tires at the dump," he said. "Then we'll stack them all around him and on top of him and douse them with kerosene and light it. It will burn for days, but it will do the job. We'll do it tomorrow."

He got up and took the coffee cups over to the sink. As he set them down he noticed the small bundle wrapped in leather sitting on the counter. "What's this?" he asked.

"Oh, something I found out in the shed," I replied.

"May I look at it?" he asked as he rubbed the leather in an admiring way.

"Of course."

He unwrapped the stone tool as tenderly as if it were the Holy Grail, and examined it closely, turning it over in his hand.

"Do you have any idea how old this is?" he asked as he stared at it.

"No. Why?" I replied, as mesmerized as he was.

"It's very, very old," he said. "Where did it come from?"

"I found it out in the shed while I was cleaning up. It was in an old saddlebag. Probably one of Sam Lewis's," I answered.

We both sat there looking at it totally transfixed. He broke the silence by telling me a bit of the history of this valley, long before the White man and Sam Lewis came here.

Chapter Seventeen

The Ancestors

Sheriff Wright settled into his chair and started telling me about his ancestors and the first people to live in this valley.

"Estimates are that people have lived in the Owens Valley for more than ten thousand years!" he said. "The local Paiute and Shoshone people are descendants of the American Indians of the Great Basin. Before that, there were the Martis people. That's what the archeologists call them anyway. They were prehistoric hunters and gatherers. They were very intelligent and very adaptable to their environment. They knew more about the use of plants and animal behavior than our society will *ever* know. They spent their summers at higher elevations and winters down at the lower elevations in "base camps" they would use over and over again, much like the later inhabitants, the Paiute, did. I imagine this area at the pack station was one of those base camps. The signs are everywhere.

"The Paiute lived in the northern Sierras from Owens Valley to southern Oregon, and they called themselves 'Numu,' meaning 'the people.' But when the White settlers came to the area they called them 'Paiute,' possibly from an Indian word 'Pah-Yah,' meaning water.

"Did you know that Inyo County is the second largest county in the country? It's so big that several eastern states would fit right inside it. 'Inyo' is believed to be a Paiute word meaning, 'dwelling place of the Great Spirit.' This desert wasn't so dry and arid back then. There was a lake and river. They called Owens Lake 'Pacheta' and the Owens River 'Wakopee.' The valley was lush and alive with all they needed to live a simple life. It abounded in wildlife with plenty of mule deer, bighorn sheep, pronghorn antelope, jack and cottontail rabbits, mountain lions, black and grizzly bears, pocket gophers, and kangaroo rats, as well as ducks, geese, quail, and sage grouse. The lakes and streams were full of bony chubs and cutthroat trout."

I sat on the floor by the wood stove looking up at him, transfixed by the pictures in my mind as he brought my dreams to life. It was like a motion picture racing through the deep recesses of my brain. He got up and refilled our coffee cups.

"Those native people led a semi-nomadic lifestyle, meaning they traveled to where the food was at the time. For instance, in the winter they were most likely here on the desert because the snows in the mountains would drive the game down to the desert for food. They built winter houses from branches and brush on the valley floor. The main diet consisted of stores of food put away in the summer and fall. Early spring was the hardest since winter stores were running low.

"Then, they subsisted on the first tender shoots of wild onions, watercress, and cattails. Melting snows would fill the Owens River and a supply of freshwater mussels and fish were once again abundant. In summer and fall they would migrate into the mountains to gather the pinion nuts as well as other nuts and seeds that they used. The pinion nuts were an important part of their diet. When the nuts were ripe, whole families helped with the harvest. It was a happy time.

"Most families returned to the valley after the harvest. It was an exciting time as there was plentiful food, the days were still warm, and there were gatherings to go to.

"The clans would meet in a specified area (Bishop, Big Pine, etc.), and it was one big party with dancing, storytelling, and games. It was probably their only social event of the year. Then they would go back to their areas to store food and prepare for winter all over again. They learned to use the objects from the land to help them kill and prepare their food. They made dart tips and arrows from the plentiful obsidian around here and they used 'millstones' to grind their nuts and seeds into fine flour to make their breads and mushes."

I perked up and said, "Oh, I found one! It's amazing! I'll show you!"

He smiled at me with a twinkle in his eye. "I know the stone. I have 'talked' with my people there many times."

I was in awe. Why did his words speak to my heart so?

He got up, took my cup, and set both his and mine in the sink. "Let's go sit on 'your' stone and I'll tell you more.

We shut the dogs inside and headed to the millstone. As we got close to it my skin got all "goose pimply." My spirit seemed to soar. I turned to the Sheriff and he saw in my face that his ancestors were around us.

"You may not know it yet, but you are one of us," he said looking from my face to the heavens and back to the stone. He reached down with his outstretched palm and touched the stone. "Feel them?"

"I always feel them here," I answered as I sat on the edge of the huge stone. It was warm to the touch, even though the day was quite chilly. I sat quietly and I could detect a sort of "humming" coming from the stone. It felt like some kind of invisible energy pulling me down into the stone. I had no desire to get up. It felt alive and all I wanted was to learn more about the people who lived here. "Go on. Tell me more, please."

He sat beside me, closed his eyes, and took a big, deep breath before continuing. "Their simple needs were met by Mother Earth and there was balance between all life here. For centuries they existed in this place, adapting to the changing seasons and sometimes harsh land. There were drought years, and years of plenty. The People took each day as a gift from the Great Spirit. The cycle of the seasons never changed. Then, as happened all across our land, White settlers came, and with them, White soldiers. The Paiute people were very peaceful. They lived near each other in loose family groups. Most disagreements among them were over pinion nut territory or hunting areas. The discovery of gold and silver in the lands east of the Sierras brought many White settlers. With them came cattle and livestock. The natives were starting to be squeezed from all sides. The winter of eighteen-sixty-one and two was one of the hardest to ever hit the Owens Valley. The Paiute were in dire straits. Bad weather had driven most game away and killed most of what was left."

He stood to stretch, and turned to look out over the great expanse of desert.

I was mesmerized by his story with those vivid pictures racing through my mind as he spoke. "I can see it all happening. I feel it all happening as you tell it to me," I said.

He looked down at me, paused a moment, grinned, and looked up to the heavens as he continued.

"The White man's cattle were straying and feeding on the Paiute's fields of wild hyacinth and yellow nut grasses. The Paiute figured that cattle feeding on their lands were rightfully theirs to do with as they wished. And they wished to eat!

"A cowboy caught an Indian butchering his steer, so he shot and killed him. That of course ignited outrage with The People, and they retaliated by killing a White man traveling through and, soon, everyone was riding armed with weapons. The White men had rifles and the Paiute had bows and arrows.

"The peaceful Paiute never wanted war. But it was becoming increasingly difficult to live near the settlers who kept invading their lands, and soon war could not be avoided.

"If you want to know more, there is much written on this war in some books I can bring you. The war only lasted about two years. It started because of the settlers' total disregard for the property rights of the Indians. It ended mainly because of the destruction of winter food supplies. It's estimated that about sixty White men died, while about two hundred Indians were killed in the conflict."

I sat listening to him with rapt attention, transported so completely to the time of my dreams. It was like I had lived it *before* he told me the stories.

"Well, no wonder they dislike us so much," I said. "And the fact that those things happened to the natives all over the country is just mind boggling. How could our forefathers treat other humans like that? Oh, yeah, it wasn't just the Indians, was it? The Blacks didn't fare any better. Who gave the White man the right to rule the world?"

"That's right," said the sheriff. "And down through the generations, many of us have harbored such deep resentments that get passed down from father to son."

"So do you feel that way, too?" I asked quietly. I felt the shame of my whole race and what they had done weighing down on my shoulders.

"No, I don't hold anyone responsible. It does no good to harbor hate about things so distant in the past. There is nothing you can do to change them. The best thing to do is try to get people to change the way they feel today; to recognize all races as those of the Human Race," he said as he stood and patted my back. "You're a thinking, caring person. *You* are becoming in tune with the Earth Mother. It's clear to me and the Ancestors that there is no hate in your heart and you have much sorrow in your soul about the evil wrongdoings of men. I can see it in your eyes. You just keep learning and listening!"

We finally went back to the cabin. I let the dogs out and he patted both of them on the head as he headed for his truck.

"I'll see you tomorrow and we'll take care of Maverick. Dream well, my friend!"

I felt so lucky to have a friend like him.

Chapter Eighteen

Winter

"The winter I was alone was long and bitterly cold," I told the grandchildren. I leaned back, thinking in my mind what it had been like.

"It only snowed a few times on the desert, but I could tell there were storms raging in the high country. It seemed like the coldest place on earth. Well, it *was* the coldest place I had ever been," I chuckled at the memory as I continued my story.

ᔕ

It was very hard to stay entertained and escape the extreme boredom of being alone with only the animals to talk to. Every day it was the same conversations with Laddie and Frosty.

"Good morning, boys. Finding anything to chase today? I think every living thing on this desert is hibernating and fast asleep. I doubt you'll be chasing anything but the cats today. And we all know they don't run from you anymore, don't we boys?"

They just looked at me and wagged their tails. Neither dog was the brightest canine on the planet, but I loved them both. I would open the door every morning and they would charge out, falling over each other, yapping and running off looking for adventure.

As I would make my way to the corral to feed the horses, Laddie would beat me there and would waste no time at all in causing a ruckus with the horses. The horses hated him with a passion! He would sneak up on them when they least expected it, nip their heels, start barking, and wouldn't shut up until I was able to get him back inside. It was maddening. Some of the horses would spot him coming into the corral and spin around and keep their heads to him. He would just pace back and forth with his tongue hanging out until he found an opening and then the game was on.

There were a couple of horses who were quick enough to kick him. Once I saw Little Oats kick him clean over the fence, but it never made any difference in his behavior.

The strange thing is that he didn't act like that on the trail. He was perfectly happy to be a good trail dog on rides, and our trips into the high country were pleasant. By the time we got to the cabins he was too exhausted to bark.

Most of the time I went about my chores in the peace and quiet of the still winter air. It was so different with no birds or insects chattering on. The winter desert was a vast, quiet, seemingly empty land.

Occasionally, I saw a rabbit run from its hole, sniff the air, and run right back inside. The deer herds from up in the high country wintered down on the desert, but they stayed well away from the pack station and I rarely saw them. Sometimes, if I let the horses out to graze at the base of the hills, a few deer would mingle with them, but they mostly stayed a few canyons over from us.

The weather was so unpredictable that I didn't ride very much. I didn't want to be caught several miles away from the cabin and have a storm blow in. They could come in fast and furious, allowing no time to run for cover. Great black torrents of clouds spewing rain and hail like an angry volcano. Powerful to watch. Terrifying to experience.

But mostly it was just cold. Winds would blow down from the high country, sometimes with gale force. The ground was too frozen to raise dust clouds like in the summer. But the wind cut like a knife with bone-chilling numbness.

The horses would huddle together for warmth and face east with their rumps against the cold winds coming down from the mountains. Their winter coats were the longest I had ever seen. It was so much colder here than what we were *all* used to in Altadena.

Some mornings the ground was so frozen it would seem to crack under my feet when I went out to feed. Cold, frosty noses and hot, moist breath would greet me. The steam rising from the breath of the huddled horses looked like steam rising from a sauna.

Sometimes the sagebrush shimmered white as if an artist had sketched the bushes there with iridescent paint. A winter wonderland with no snow, but white just the same. The roof of the cabin and sheds would glisten brightly as the morning sun inched its way up from behind the Cosos Mountains across the valley.

By afternoon, most color returned to the desert, but not the warmth. Never the warmth. It stayed cold all day long. The sunlight didn't last long enough to warm things. With the high peaks behind the pack station, the sun was gone by 2:30 PM.

Breaking the ice on the surface of the water trough was a daily chore. I had a hammer out by the tub that I would use, and sometimes I'd have to do it several times a day.

Feeding took longer because my hands would get so cold. Trying to break baling wire was harder when your hands weren't working right. I never used wire cutters because we always had a hay hook to twist the wire and it would break. When your hands are freezing it's hard to get them to do normal things. I had never worn gloves much and found them to be clumsy. But after the first few really-really cold days I discovered that I was going to have to rethink the glove issue. So I settled for knitted gloves and I cut off the fingertips. It was a suitable compromise where I could brush the horses, ride them, and feed them without getting frostbite on my whole hand! Somehow, my hands stayed warmer and my fingertips never froze.

Just being with the horses on those cold days warmed me to the core. The horses and I had a routine, and we hardly ever varied it. After I fed them, we just enjoyed each other. I would brush and talk, and they would nuzzle and talk back. I would sometimes sit on them to keep warm, and we would all walk around in the corral as a group. The unspoken love and respect between those horses and me was never clearer than on those short cold winter days when we would just "be" with each other.

The four walls of the cabin sometimes seemed to close in on me, so I would stay out in the corral as long as I could with the horses until I got too cold. As soon as I went in they returned to their east-facing stance, crimping their tails down tight against their rumps for warmth, then wait patiently for their next meal.

I would grab an armful of wood every time I was outside. That was my main objective day and night…keeping the woodstove going so the cabin wouldn't cool off. There were so many small holes in the thin walls where heat was lost that if it cooled down it would take another day to get it warm again.

If I left for the day, I would stuff the stove full, shut the damper down as much as I could without suffocating it, and hope that I got back before it was out.

I only mistimed it a couple of times. When the cabin got that cold, I even let the dogs under the covers to keep me warm. Not always a pleasant experience if they had been successful at chasing things that day! But I had to make sacrifices; stink versus warmth. I always chose warmth!

I missed seeing Jim. Our relationship was very up and down. One minute we were arguing, and the next making up. He always had other girls in his life and we were never in an exclusive relationship. But when we *were* together it was, like him, very intense. I would dream of the times he took me to the cabin on Deer Mountain, and I finally learned how a man is supposed to treat a woman. I longed for his touch often when going to bed at night on that lonely desert.

John usually showed up once every other week or so. Don Lutz would visit once a week or more. They both always arrived with big bundles of firewood, more food, and more things to read.

But Sheriff Wright usually came up at least three times a week.

It was his visits I looked forward to the most. He was teaching me so much about the history of this valley and his people.

On one of his visits, he brought me several hand-written stories to read. "These are legends my grandmother handed down to me," he said. "I wrote them down so there would be a record. The old people are dying so fast, and if there is no written record, the stories passed down through the ages will be lost. You will learn much from reading about the people here. Some are true and some are just legend. You will have to sort it out for yourself. And I know you will, because you have a mind for them and you carry their wisdom in your heart."

Handing me the stack of papers, he climbed into his truck and told me he'd be back in a few days.

"Stay inside as much as you can. There's a bad one coming," he told me.

"Oh, I almost forgot," he added. "I brought you something."

He held out his hand with a small leather bundle in it. I took it and unrolled it. It was a small leather pouch only two inches long or so with a rawhide string so it could be worn around the neck.

"This belonged to my grandmother. I think she would like you to have it. We call them medicine pouches. We keep our totems and spirit items next to our hearts where they are safe. You might want to put that ancient dart tip that you found inside and keep it close to your heart," he said.

My eyes widened, "How did you know about that?"

"Don't worry," he said, smiling. "That was a gift just for you to find." Then he drove away.

I sat, watching his truck's dust trail get further and further away, and wondered how he could have possibly known I had found that arrowhead. I looked into the dark blue sky and knew the answer. The Grandfathers. Nothing was a secret from them.

The dogs romped back over to me as I went inside, took my precious tip, and put it in the pouch. It was just the right size for it. I put it around my neck and went out to do the chores.

"Come on fellas, let's enjoy this calm weather while we can."

I fed the horses, cooked up some chili for dinner, did the dishes, and snuggled in for the night, reading the stories the sheriff had left for me.

Soon, I was fast asleep and once again riding my Indian horse across the desert.

❧

I am riding Poppin' along a desert trail at the foot of the mountains. We are heading north of the pack station and the sun is bright overhead. It is winter, yet there hasn't been a storm in days. It's just the right kind of riding weather. We are trotting along when we start to pass a small canyon I have not yet explored. I turn him back and guide him into the canyon as we make our way up through the overgrown brush about a half mile or so.

We come to a small clearing that opens up with cottonwood trees. I get off to look around, and Poppin' walks quietly behind me. Further into the trees I see a flat stone. "Can it be?" I ask myself. I walk over to it and see that it is indeed a grinding stone. It is only about a quarter of the size of the one at the pack station, and the holes certainly aren't as deep, but it's a grinding stone nonetheless.

As I inch toward it I see a small bundle in the grass. I pick it up and it's a small pouch made out of rabbit fur. I turn it over in my hands and it seems very old. I feel something inside. I untie the sinewy cord and open it. Inside is a stone tool of some sort. It is about the size of a clamshell. It's not obsidian. It seems much older than that. As I stare at the object my eyes are quickly drawn to a small path beyond the rock. I carefully put the tool back inside the pouch that seems to have been protecting it for so long, place it in my saddlebags, grab Poppin's reins, and start up the small path. It is so overgrown that I question the wisdom of bringing Poppin' along, but when I turn and look at him he is just plodding along behind me, resigned to the fact that his mistress is off on another of her adventures. Another two hundred feet or so and the trail stops. And there, surrounded by thick brush and trees, is a huge, solitary rock. I walk around it, not exactly sure what it is. It is about five feet tall, six feet wide, and a couple of feet thick.

As I walk around the back of it, I'm startled to find drawings all over its east side. Not drawings like paint or inks, but actually carvings in the stone itself. Dozens of images and characters that are unfamiliar to me. Dropping the reins, I am frozen in time. I reach up, put my hand on the rock, and feel as though a bolt of lightning is striking me. My mind is whirling. My body is shaking uncontrollably. My eyes can't focus. My mouth won't let any sound come out. The rock and the entire world around it start to swirl into a kaleidoscope of colors and shapes, spinning faster and faster. Suddenly, I am not alone. I'm surrounded by a presence I cannot see. My heart calms. My fear subsides. Calm overtakes me and I feel protected. "Protected from what?" I subconsciously ask myself. There are voices. Not my language. Humming and chanting. Hypnotic. My eyes grow sleepy. My body feels heavy. I sink down to the earth, curl up on the soft ground, and feel so comfortable. The voices are so calming and my mind is slipping into a deep sleep.

Suddenly, the sky explodes above me. Thunder and lightning are partnering to announce the arrival of the desert's long awaited deluge. I jump up, not sure of where I am. Then I see the rock and remember I must have been lulled to sleep by the chanting. I look around for Poppin', who is nowhere in sight. The sky lets loose its ocean of water. It's getting darker by the second. Where is that blasted horse?

"Poppin'!" I yell as loud as I can. I try to whistle through overly chapped lips. I can't seem to make the sound come out right. Nothing. I start to run down the path. I get to the grinding rock and still no sign of my horse. Of all the times for him to take off! I keep running down the trail towards the mouth of the canyon. As I round the bend, I come face-to-face with Poppin' who is standing on his rein and can't move. Luckily he doesn't spook at the constant thunder and lightning. I laugh at him and call him a few choice names, gather up the reins, and swing up into the saddle. He senses my urgency, and I don't have to make a sound to turn him into a full gallop back to the pack station. He runs full out as the downpour soaks us.

The sky is as black as a starless night as we arrive safely back to our home. I stop at the front door and rush to get his tack off, then put it inside so it will dry. I tie him up under the eave by the hayshed to cool off before I turn him back out into the corral. As I rub him down with some towels, I reflect on what has transpired. "Poppin', what was in that canyon?" I ask as I walk him to the gate. "What made you run away from me? You've never done that before. Was it the thunder? Or was it the spirits singing to me?" I hug his neck and turn him loose.

ᔓ

I sat up and realized it was morning. The dogs were yipping to get out and the fire in the stove had died. It was pouring outside and it didn't look like it was going to let up any time soon.

When I slowly stumbled out of bed, the dogs were bouncing all around me and almost knocked me over as I opened the back door to let them out and make my way to the outhouse.

The rain was incredible. I had never, ever seen it pour like this.

On the way back to the cabin I glanced over at the horses.

They were huddled together and looked like drowned rats. Poppin' spotted me and whinnied.

"Give me a minute okay?" I yelled at him. I was irritated for some reason, but didn't know why.

As I got back to the door, the dogs were already there anxious to get out of the cold rain.

"Not fit for man or beast, eh?" They just looked at me and barged into the cabin when I opened the door. I knew I was in for a long day as they started shaking all the "wet" off themselves.

I got my clothes on and went in the other room to the wood stove. I stuffed kindling and paper in the stove, lit it, waited until it was ready, and then put a couple of logs on.

Then I started toward the front door where my rain slicker was on the hook and stopped in my tracks.

There on the floor, with a small drying puddle around it, was my saddle.

"How?" my mind raced. "But it was a dream, wasn't it?"

I put on my slicker and reluctantly went out to feed. I threw hay in the driest places I could find; even letting the horses come in under the eaves by the tack room. They were so cold and wet they didn't fight for position. They just waited for me to throw it to them.

While I watched, I wondered how long this weather would last, thinking that I might have to find some blankets to dry them with. Then I gave them a rare treat of grain to help them generate some heat and energy. They must have thought they'd died and gone to heaven.

I looked at Poppin' to determine if he had been ridden lately. But he was so wet there was no telltale saddle mark on him.

Pulling up my hood, I ran back to the cabin, jumping over the fast-moving water that was now running down the sides of the road.

When I got back inside, the fire was starting to warm the place up and the dogs were curled up on the rug in front of the stove. I hung up my slicker and watched the water pool on the floor below it. I walked over to my saddle. It was still damp in places. I absolutely did not recall placing it there.

Then I remembered the dream and my eyes went to the saddlebags still attached to it. I untied them, carried them over to the table, and sat down. My hands were shaking as I opened one side and found it empty. I opened the other side, peered inside, and saw the furry pouch. I reached in, pulled it out, and saw the same sinew tying it closed that had been in the dream. I undid it, opened it, and there was the stone tool.

I sat there revisiting the dream over and over again. It was the same tool, the same pouch. The saddle was wet. How did this happen?

Almost in a trance, I got up and stoked the fire.

I put the pouch away. There were too many questions running through my mind. I needed calm and decided to read more of Sheriff Wright's stories.

Wrapped in my quilt, I cozied up in the easy chair and read for the rest of the day.

❧

"The Paiute Indians of the desert hills have a story about the bright star usually seen low in the eastern sky of summer at about sunrise. It is in the constellation Canis Major and is commonly referred to as the Dog Star, or Sirius. A long time ago a young man from a Paiute village tried to run down a deer. The entire village watched as they both ran across the desert, far away over the edge of the earth and into the sky. There, the runner and the deer were changed into a star. Ever since that time, the People say that the very best deer hunting is when the "deer star" is in the sky.

The Legend of the Deer Star
By Mary Austin

Hear now a tale of the deer-star,
Tale of the days a gone,
When a youth rose up for hunting
In the bluish light of dawn.

Rose up for the red deer hunting
And what should a hunter do
Who has never an arrow feathered?
Nor a bow strung taut and true?

The women laughed from the doorways,
The maidens mocked at the spring;
For thus to be slack at the hunting
Is ever a shameful thing.

The old men nodded and muttered,
But the youth spoke up with a frown:
If I have no gear for hunting,
I will run the red deer down.

He is off by the hills of the morning,
By the dim, untrodden ways;
In the clean, wet, windy marshes
He has the startled deer agraze.

And a buck of the branching antlers
Streams out from the fleeing herd,
And the youth is apt to the running
As the tongue to the spoken word.

They have gone by the broken ridges,
By mesa and hill and swale,
Not once did the red deer falter,
Nor the feet of the runner fail.

So lightly they trod on the lupines
That scarce was the flower stalks bent,
And over the tops of the dusky sage
The wind of their running went.

They have gone by the painted desert,
Where the dawn mists lie uncurled,
And over the purple barrows
On the outer rim of the world.

The People shout from the village,
The sun gets up to spy
The royal deer and the runner,
Clear shining in the sky.

And ever the hunter watches
For the rising of that star
When he comes by the summer mountains
Where the haunts of the red deer are;

When he comes by the morning meadows
Where the young of the red deer hide;

He fares them forth to the hunting
While the deer and the runner bide.

ᔕ

As I finished the story, once again I thought about my saddle, the tool, and the dream.

I picked up another of the Sheriff's books and read through until something caught my eye.

It talked about how the shaman and other spiritual leaders sometimes were able to travel between the spirit world and their physical world at will. There were several stories about this ability. Some did it with the help of peyote and other natural hallucinogens. And some seemed to do it with only their open minds. I wondered how that could be.

Is that what was happening to me? I mean, I was only dreaming, wasn't I? Yet, how could I my wet saddle and the stone tool be explained?

There were a few times last summer when Jim and I would take some peyote and I would get the sense of being in another time. But I was having those experiences without drugs as well. It was just such a mystery.

I finally decided it didn't matter *how* these things were happening to me. What mattered was that they *were* happening.

Somehow, there seemed to be things I needed to learn in my time here on this desert. So I decided to pay better attention from here on out.

Chapter Nineteen

Snakebite

"Grandma, what did you do at Christmas time?" asked Kenny.

"Well, John came up the day before and brought me a few presents from my mom. Then on Christmas day I went to town and had a nice dinner with Don Lutz and his wife. Their family wasn't home so they spoiled me rotten. I couldn't have been happier."

"So was the whole time wet and cold while you were here, Grandma?" Lindsey inquired.

"Well, no. In fact, that year spring came very early. Even though the winter was cold, it was short."

I eased down on the log and continued my story.

ᔓ

Early spring was a beautiful time in this desert. The bright green colors from the unusually wet winter sometimes left me breathless. It was such a stark contrast from the usual dry arid landscape. The lushness of it all would probably only last a few short weeks before the hot summer-like sun once again reigned supreme over this dry wilderness. The wildflowers danced in the gentle breezes and the stream ran high for such a short time that if I hadn't lived there at that time, I might have missed it.

I loved going for walks up the canyon, and every time it seemed that Mother Nature brought out new foliage for me to see.

The cactus flowers with their bright pink hats atop their flat, green paddles that one would never dare touch for fear of those inch long needles sticking out. The rose hips looked plump, luscious, and ripe for the picking. And the wild grapes looked to take over the entire canyon with their long spindly vines.

The whole canyon was ablaze with life, sounds, and color. I would sit at the first stream crossing and just soak it all up. Life here was wonderful.

After one such walk I returned from my stream visit and decided it was such a nice warm day I would spend it cleaning out the water trough.

"It has a buildup of gunk that probably dates back to the day it was placed in that corral," I said to myself.

I got a bucket, knife, and some steel wool from the shed, then headed out to the corral. The dogs were chasing rabbits and the horses were napping.

The trough was really just an old bathtub; its opening for the drain had been permanently sealed, so I had to bail out half of the ice-cold water before I went to work scrubbing the sides of it. Years of algae build-up came off easily as I scrubbed it. This was easier than I had anticipated.

An ancient pipeline that came from the stream a short way up the canyon fed the tub. It continually ran so the tub was never empty. As a consequence of this, water always ran out on the ground around the tub. So it was usually a muddy mess.

I was kneeling next to it trying my best to stay out of the mud when Poppin' came over to see what I was up to. Soon there were two more horses next to me. Then two more. I decided to get playful and started splashing them. That cleared them out in a hurry.

All except Poppin' that is. He liked to get wet. I splashed him one more time. "Now scram," I told him. He went and joined the others who were now rolling in the dirt trying to get that nasty wet stuff off.

"There, that looks fairly clean," I said to myself, pleased with the job I had done.

The day was warming up quite a bit and I headed inside to have some lunch and read my book. The dogs were waiting at the door, anxious to go in and have their afternoon siesta.

After lunch, the dogs and I drifted off for a nap. When I woke up the dogs were still running in their dreams, so I decided to work on my macramé reins. I had learned how to make them from one of the girls at the stable, and I was determined to finish them before John came back. I wanted to give them to him for his new bridle. I must have worked on them for an hour or so before the dogs roused, stretched, and wanted out.

As I let them out the door, I noticed Poncho jerk his head up, squeal, and trot away from the trough where he had been standing.

"Hmm," I said to myself, remembering that I had seen a few bees starting to return to the water trough. "Something sting ya?"

I went back to my knots for another fifteen minutes or so until the dogs were raising such a ruckus I couldn't ignore them any longer. Irritated, I got up and ran out calling them. They were going crazy circling around the water trough and barking furiously. They refused to listen to me, so I knew they had something cornered under the rocks by that trough.

Most of the time, I didn't interfere with their "seek and destroy" missions because I usually didn't have to watch. Those things almost always took place out of my line of sight. I liked it that way. But they were becoming more and more frantic, so I decided to put a stop to it.

I ducked under the rail and yelled at them. Not so much as a pricked ear in response. So I grabbed Frosty by the tail, pulled his muddy little body to me and took him down to the cabin.

Laddie hadn't even noticed his buddy was gone. When I got back to the trough, he was still going crazy circling it. He was now a muddy mess as well.

As I was about to grab his collar, I heard the sound that scared me more than any sound in that desert. The rattlesnake was under a rock next to the trough. I had seen lots of lizards come near the trough and its mud to cool off on really hot summer days, but I had never seen a snake. I thought the horses kept them away

"LADDIE! STOP!" I yelled.

He ignored me. I backed away some, found a small rock, picked it up, and threw it at my stupid dog. It hit him in the side. He lost his concentration long enough for me to grab him and take him to the cabin.

I had killed several snakes at the stables and the canyon down south, but something was different here. Was it that I was alone? What if I messed up and got bit? Whatever the reason, I decided to let it be and soon I saw it slither out of the corral and into the sagebrush.

The dogs were still barking in the cabin and I was about to go in and yell at them when I glanced at the horses.

They were all standing at the far side of the corral and seemed a little spooked by all the excitement. So I went and talked to them.

One by one they sensed things were back to normal and moved away from the corner.

All except for Poncho.

Poncho was standing with his head hanging almost to the ground. Alarm bells sounded in my head.

I crawled under the fence rail and ran over to him. His nose was swollen grotesquely and he was drooling. On the tip of his nose I saw two perfect little puncture marks.

"Oh great. This is just perfect!" I was angry, but had no one to yell at.

"Poncho fella, you're gonna be okay," I told him, sure that I was lying.

"What do I do?" I yelled to the quiet desert? Once again there was no one to answer me. I was stuck, all alone, with a horse emergency and no one to help.

I said a silent prayer to the Grandfathers. They hadn't let me down so far.

I stroked his face and could feel the swelling getting worse under my hand. I said another prayer and sent it up to the ancestors.

Poncho's breathing brought me back to the reality of the situation. He was now taking deep wheezing breaths. As I held his head in my arms, he struggled more and more to breathe. Then I remembered. Horses couldn't breathe through their mouths. It was physically impossible for them to do so.

"He's suffocating!" I yelled. "No, don't let him die!"

Suddenly, he fell to the ground still struggling for breath through nostrils that were almost swollen shut.

I had to *do* something. I wasn't sure what, but I couldn't just stand there and watch him die. All at once an idea came to me.

Running to the tack room, I searched for the piece of rubber hose that John sometimes used to siphon gas from one vehicle to the other. I spotted it, got out my knife, cut a short piece about six inches long, and ran back out to the nearly unconscious horse.

I jammed the piece of hose up one nostril as far as it would go. As he struggled to breathe, suddenly a whoosh of air moved into his lungs. And another. And yet another. Long, deep breaths. A minute or two passed and my thudding heart started to slow down a little. His eyes opened and he abruptly sat up on his chest and snorted through the hose.

I could hear the movement of air as he took in each breath and exhaled. His strength was returning and, after another few minutes, he stood up. A little shaky at first, but soon, he was standing normally.

The hose stayed in place because of the swelling. I would have to figure out a way to keep it there. By that time, the other nostril was swollen completely shut. He was only breathing through the piece of hose. He would have been dead if that hose had not been in the tack room.

As I took a deep breath, I whispered yet another "thank you" to the heavens.

I went back into the tack room and saw a leather punch. I grabbed it and the tackle box, then went back out thinking about what I was going to do. I punched a hole in the end of the hose and grabbed some fishing line from the box. There was a small needle there and I strung some line on it.

"Okay, Poncho, you're gonna have to stay very still for me and hopefully it will only hurt a *little* bit."

As fast as I could, I pushed the needle through the flared edge of his nostril and pulled the line through. He only flinched slightly. Then I tied it off through the hole I had punched in the end of the hose. I tightened it until it felt solid and I was sure it would stay put for however long it was needed.

"So what happens now, Poncho? I've never been through a snakebite before. Have you?" I asked him.

I put him in the small corral so the others wouldn't pick on him. His muzzle was swollen at least three times its normal size.

"So is this bite going to kill you anyway? Or are you gonna be okay?"

My mind was spinning with images of all those old westerns where horses got snake bit and had to be shot. I'd never heard of one in real life being killed by a snake, and of course I'd never known any horse that had been in this situation.

I was pretty sure he wouldn't be eating his dinner, but put some hay in his feeder anyway. I filled his water bucket from the trough, then fed the rest of the horses.

I went and let the thankfully calm dogs out as they put their noses to the ground looking for that long gone snake.

"You'd better not find it!" I yelled to them.

I grabbed another bucket of cold water from trough and found some old towels in the tack room. I decided cold might be good for the swelling, so I soaked them in cold water and wrapped them around Poncho's muzzle, leaving the hose sticking out. It must have felt good because he didn't fight it at all. I kept drizzling cool water over it and we must have stood there for almost an hour. After a while, Poncho lay back down and dozed while I did end-of-the-day chores.

The temperature was warm for a spring evening, so I decided to sleep outside and keep an eye on him during the night. The corral he was in was right next to the old "bunkhouse" and had a wooden walkway under the overhang by the hitching post. It would be a perfect place to sleep off of the ground, and away from snakes.

I went over to the cabin, gathered up some food, my lantern, flashlight, and sleeping bag, and headed back to where Poncho was and settled in for the night.

He got up an ambled over to his water bucket. He seemed thirsty, but just splashed his nose in it. It must have had a soothing effect on the tight swollen skin. After playing in the water a few more minutes, he sucked down a few gulps, then went and lay back down.

I had made up my bed on the wooden walkway just outside of his corral. I lit the lantern, munched on some chips, and listened to the other horses bedding down for the night. I read for a bit and checked on Poncho with the flashlight every ten minutes or so.

The dogs were locked up, so I wouldn't be listening to them chasing things all night.

I loved hearing the sounds of the nighttime desert. The crickets, toads, and frogs were all trying to outdo each other. It must have been close to midnight when the peaceful sounds finally lulled me off to sleep.

I slept soundly for several hours and then woke to the sounds of soft nickering from Poncho, who was lying down on the other side of the hitching post right next to me.

"How ya doing boy?" I asked. He softly nickered again.

I shined the light over at him and assured myself that the hose was still in place. I got out of my bag, ducked under the fence, and sat patting him for a while. He seemed fairly comfortable. He was still breathing well through the hose, and it seemed the swelling had finally slowed.

"Let's try and get some more sleep, fella," I said as I crawled back into my sleeping bag. I slept through the rest of the night.

The sound of nickering woke me once again, as the sun peaked over the hills. This time it was coming from several horses in the big corral.

"Get up! We're hungry!" was the translation I heard.

"Okay, okay. Hold your horses!! Ha-ha!" I answered back. I jumped up out of my sleeping bag and started throwing hay out.

Poncho looked interested and actually trotted over to his pile. He slowly took a few bites. It looked uncomfortable and so bizarre to see that humongous muzzle chewing up his hay. But he managed to eat half of it before he went and drank his fill of water, then he laid back down for a nap.

I thought at that point that maybe, just maybe, we were out of the woods.

Later that day, Don came up for a visit. I showed Poncho to him and he told me I had done a great job!

"I did that to one of my horses about ten years ago. That's the only way you save them when they get bit on the muzzle. They just can't breathe through their mouths like dogs and cats. You gotta open their nostrils! You did exactly the right thing. Real proud of you, girl!"

"I guess I just thought it was common sense to jam something up there to open it up. I'm glad that hose was there, because I don't think there is anything else around that would have worked." I told him.

"You're gonna have to watch for infection and the possibility of the skin all sloughing off," he warned me. "That's real common with snakebites. All the tissue around the bite dies and peels off. He should be on antibiotics for a while. I'm going into Lone Pine today, so I'll pick some up."

"Thank you so much. I hope he'll be okay," I said.

I'm sure he will. We'll get him some penicillin and he'll be fine. He just may not be very pretty for a while. I'll be back in the morning!" he said as he got into his truck.

"Oh, I almost forgot. Sheriff sent this book up for ya!" he said as he backed his truck up to where I was standing. "Said he would see you day after tomorrow!" and he drove off.

The dogs and I went into the cabin. They rested as I read and napped for the rest of the afternoon. I was exhausted.

That evening when I fed them, I did a quick check over all of the horses. I just wanted to make sure no one else was hurt. I intended to get a full night's sleep.

Poncho was looking good. The swelling had stabilized. I decided to leave the hose in until morning.

The next morning when I went to feed, Poncho was lying down. He nickered at me as I approached him. His face was still grotesquely swollen and he didn't get up right away, but his attitude seemed bright and alert, so I finished feeding everyone else. By the time I got back to him, he slowly rose to his feet and shook the dust off. I threw his hay down and he ambled over to it. I felt his nose. It still felt so tight and painful and seemed almost cold to the touch. I checked the hose and it was still firmly in place, so I decided to leave it in until the swelling subsided.

Don returned later that afternoon with a bottle of penicillin, syringes, and needles. I was grateful John had shown me how to give shots or I would have been unprepared to do that to Poncho. Don watched me give the first one, assuring himself that I did indeed know how.

"Well, girl, I think he'll be fine with your nursing care. Seems he's in good hands," he said as he got into his truck. "I'll be back in a few days. Keep him on that for a week. You should have enough. See ya!"

He drove off, leaving me holding a bag full of supplies.

I went around and finished the evening chores, anxious to get to the book that the Sheriff had sent up for me.

After I got dinner and the dishes out of the way, the dogs had settled down for the night, so I plopped down in the easy chair and flipped through the pages. It was another book on the stories and legends of the people of this valley.

This was just what I had wanted to read. More about the Spirit people who were appearing more and more frequently in my dreams, as well as my reality.

Chapter Twenty

The Train

The lonely days sometimes ran one into another. My boredom often gave way to foolishness. I would saddle up and go exploring the vast expanse of desert before me, and occasionally I would do something stupid.

One day on a ride down to the highway, I decided to explore the land on the other side. There were no fences at the time to keep trespassers out. It was all Bureau of Land Management land and used for range cattle. On many occasions we would encounter cows as we were roaming the countryside.

I was riding Hellzapoppin' at a pretty good clip and heading for the reservoir, since I had never gone there before. About halfway between the water and the highway were the train tracks. In those days the trains were long, sometimes one hundred cars or more.

As we got closer to the tracks, I heard a faint whistle coming from the south. I urged Poppin' on to get closer to the tracks. As the train approached he was getting very excited. I don't know what made me do it. I was not in my right mind. But as the train started to pass in front of me and the engineer waved, something snapped in my mind and I was transported back a century to the old west. I clucked at Poppin' to get going and we were off, racing alongside that speeding train. I even drew out my rifle and started waving it in the air. The wind in my face, Poppin's racing hooves over the desert sage, and the train speeding next to me all seemed out of a movie.

I don't know how far we ran like that. It seemed like forever. Poppin's labored breathing and slowing gait brought me back to my senses. What in the world was I doing? Was I crazy? I could have been hurt. But worse than that was the fact that Poppin' could have been hurt. Seriously. The way we were running without me even looking where we were going could have been disastrous if he had stepped in a snake hole or tripped on a rock. Thank goodness there weren't any people on that train watching this spaced-out, stupid girl chasing their train on the back of a charging steed, waving her rifle with a wild-eyed look in her eyes!

I stopped Poppin' and we just stood there for a while. I finally got off and loosened his saddle so he could rest and catch his breath. I sat down on a rock and started to shake.

"That was probably the stupidest thing I had ever done," I told him. I vowed then and there that I would never endanger my horse like that again.

I cinched him back up and mounted him for the five-mile ride back home. We took the rest of the afternoon to just mosey back up that long, winding dirt road.

All the horses nickered a welcome when we reached the corrals. I unsaddled and rubbed Poppin' down good before letting him in to roll and eat. He walked to the feeder as I started throwing hay out, took a few bites, then went over to a corner and lay down. I felt bad for him. I had exhausted him. Hopefully, he wouldn't colic and present me with an emergency I was not equipped to deal with.

As nighttime fell, I went out and checked on him one last time. He was up and drinking. I went over and patted his nose. "I'm so sorry I pushed you like that," I told him. "It won't ever happen again. You're the very best horse in the whole world and I love you so much."

After that day, I never pushed him beyond the limits he was capable of. But, as our relationship grew over the years, there wasn't much he wouldn't do for me. If I needed to take a shortcut off the mountainside, he was always willing. I would just point him and he would go. I learned to always let him do things at his own pace. When he needed to stop and rest, I let him. He was a much better horse in the mountains once we established the rules.

There were a few times when his rules and my rules clashed a bit, though.

One time I was riding in the high country alone, heading back from the Deer Mountain cabin, when he put me in a dangerous situation.

We were up in the trees before it opened up to meadowland behind the pastures at Dutch John Flats. As we were easing down the switchbacks, I was more or less off in another world and not paying attention to things around me. All of a sudden, Poppin' lurched forward, catching me off balance and unable to regain control and stay in the saddle. As I was slipping off the side of him, he was speeding up. "Poppin' stop!" I yelled, but he was saying "No way." I finally had to let go and fell to the ground as he kept racing off toward the cabins. I didn't know what had startled him until I heard a crashing sound off to my right. There, running down the hill towards me, was a bear cub. "Oh no, it's acting like it wants to play," I thought to myself. "Its mother won't think very highly of it picking me."

There was no hope of getting Poppin' back, so I got up and just took off running after my scared horse. As I got further down the trail, not daring to look back, I swear I heard that mama bear flying down the trail after me. It could've been all in my head, but I never turned around to look. I ran faster than my feet have ever carried me, all the way back to the cabin.

When I got to the hitching rail, there was Poppin' standing there, looking at me as if to say, "What took you so long?"

"You *stupid* horse!" I yelled at him. I unsaddled him and turned him out with his friends. Then I sat down to catch my breath.

ᔓ

A few weeks after the "great train robbery," I found myself heading across the highway once more. I had packed a lunch and locked the dogs inside knowing I'd be gone all day. The reservoir and hills behind the highway intrigued me and I wanted to explore them. As we neared the train tracks, I reassured Poppin' that there would be no funny business today. Just walking and exploring.

We rested a time by the water and he had a drink. Then we moved off towards the Coso Mountains to the east. From the reservoir there was a very faint deer trail that we followed. The terrain was so much different on that side of the valley. The hills were more rolling than steep, covered with sagebrush and manzanita, but not very many trees.

We continued to follow the deer trail, which took us into a canyon that had denser vegetation than the face of the mountains. It seemed so dry on this side, and so different from the Sierra side. Poppin' plodded on as I played sightseer. Deeper into the canyon we went. Every now and then there would be a stream crossing that was really just a trickle in places. Even though it was early spring, the water wasn't rushing like in the canyon by the pack station. Here, it even disappeared underground, only to reappear several hundred feet away.

As we got much farther into the canyon, I noticed a slight rise to the trail. It didn't climb steeply, just a gentle rise. The sides of the canyon seemed to be getting narrower. We rounded a corner, and suddenly it opened up to a small meadow with a pool of water.

There was a thin line of water from a spring coming from a rock fissure trickling into it. I laughed to myself, "Now that's what I call a waterfall here in the desert."

The small meadow formed around the pond with wildflowers starting to bloom; bright colorful lupines, white poppies, and red Indian paintbrushes. The only sounds were from the birds flittering about, surprised by my intrusion, and the sounds of the trickling water into the pond, then trickling out and down the canyon. Trickle in, trickle out. "Trickle, trickle little stream. How I wonder where you've beeeen," I sang as I dismounted, proud of myself for making a rhyme.

"Where are we and what have you done with my rider?" Poppin' seemed to say as he cocked his ears at me with a bored look. Then he bent down and grabbed a bite of grass.

We walked over to the water and discovered it was crystal clear. He drank thirstily while I took off his saddle and bridle. I put his halter on him and let him loose to graze. With the lead rope dragging, he would never run off and leave me. Yes, I remember the bear incident, but we had much more trust with each other now.

I wandered around the small body of water and suddenly my heart was filled with joy. There, on the other side, was a small flat rock with deep holes in it. It was much smaller than the millstone at the pack station, but its holes were just as deep. I walked over and sat down next to it. Rubbing my hand over it brought the same feelings I had when touching the one across the way.

I closed my eyes with my hand on the stone and drifted off to that place where my friends were. They welcomed me. Only this time an older Paiute woman greeted me rather than the young girl I was so familiar with.

ஐ

She smiles and beckons me to sit with her. There are several women sitting near us weaving baskets. There are men nearby working on flint tips. One young man looks up and smiles at me, then goes back to chipping away at the smooth, shiny, black rock in his hands. They are all hard at work, turning the obsidian into their weapons and tools. My hand reaches for my pouch and feels the treasure within, wondering if it was made by one of them. The man's eyes look at my pouch and he smiles bigger.

The woman tells me the young girl that I've been visiting is her granddaughter. The girl told her I have a curious soul and that I'm not afraid to learn the old ways. She says "I will be your teacher for a time. You are seeking answers and I will try to give them to you. You have had a difficult life thus far, yes? Not knowing a direction or peace?"

"Well yes, until I came here. I still don't understand how I'm here with you. I know it must be a dream," I say as I look around at the camp and how everyone else is ignoring me. Like I'm supposed to be there.

"We have been watching after you since the very first time you came to this place. We saw a girl with so much hurt in her heart that she cried to the ancestors seeking their help without even knowing it. Now you just need to open your mind and your heart and you will learn all that you have been seeking. But the shadows grow long now daughter..."

ᔕ

When I woke, the canyon was shaded and I hadn't even eaten my lunch. I sat up trying to clear my head and looked around for Poppin'. He was napping, too. I whistled to him and he popped right up. I think he sensed it was late as well. He trotted over. I saddled him up, put his bridle back on, and swung up on the saddle. As I was mounting him, my eyes were drawn to a small dark opening in the hillside about a hundred feet up above the "waterfall." It appeared to be a small cave.

"Wow, I wonder where that goes," I said. "Let's go explore. Just a little ways." Poppin' seemed uninterested.

"Fine! I'll go alone!" I said as I hopped off. "Stay put for a few minutes." He went back to eating.

I found a small overgrown path that zigzagged up the side of the hill. It was steep and full of loose rocks. It was overgrown with sage and manzanita, so I had to pick my steps carefully through the brush. As I reached the opening, it was much larger than it appeared from below. The brush almost covered the entrance and it must have been by pure chance that I spotted it. I pushed aside the bushes and stared into the dark cavern. Then I took a few steps in and let my eyes adjust to the dim light. The sun was giving off just enough light to let me see what appeared to be ancient drawings on the walls of the cave.

I stepped in closer and a feeling came over me that I had been here before.

"That's silly. You've never even been past the train tracks before," I said to myself. A sense of absolute calm touched me as I walked further inside. There were drawings on both sides of the walls. I reached out my hand and lightly touched a crude etching of a bighorn sheep. I felt an instant bond with the creator of this masterpiece.

I scanned the interior of the cave and it became clear to me that somehow, by some miracle, this cave had been hidden enough so as not to have been vandalized like almost every other ancient "find" in the Owens Valley.

There was a spot on the floor where a dark area was ringed with dark grey rocks. Was it an old fire pit? A few feet away from that was a small pile of what looked like bones. I reached out, picked one up and saw that it was a tool of some sort made from bone. It was very light in weight and felt brittle. I turned it over in my hand, but it didn't break like I expected.

Could this cave have belonged to the ancient Martis people the Sheriff had told me about? I wanted to stay and explore much longer but the fading light reminded me that I was a couple hours away from the pack station and I'd better get going. I took my bandana out of my pocket, and gently wrapped the bone up to show the Sheriff. I took one last look around and left the cave.

Vowing to return when I had more time, I made my way down the trail whistling to Poppin' as I went. He met me at the bottom with a "Hurry up, let's get back," kind of look. His stomach always was his number one priority. I put my little bundle in my saddlebag and checked Poppin's cinch before mounting up. I looked up the hill and could barely see the opening. Turning around we broke into a slow lope down the trail.

By the time we reached the highway it was dusk. It would be dark long before we reached the corrals. Poppin' didn't seem to mind the steady trot he was maintaining. As we made the power line road, the almost full moon was peaking over the tops of the Cosos. Poppin' once again broke into a slow lope and before we knew it, the horses were hollering their silly heads off at us. They were hungry and we were out foolin' around and shirking our responsibilities. Poppin' answered each whinny with several of his own. No doubt telling them about all the things I forced him to do. Yeah, right!

As we got to the corrals, there were a bunch of hungry horses standing very impatiently. "Okay, Okay, you're just going to have to wait while I take care of Poppin'," I told them. I unsaddled him and tied him to the hitching post. Then I ran to the cabin and let the dogs out. I didn't even want to go inside and see what *they* had done all day! They raced out and off they went in different directions to have some freedom for a while.

I went to the haystack and started throwing feed out to the grateful horses, then went back and rubbed Poppin' down real good. He had barely broken a sweat loping up that three-mile long road. "You're absolutely amazing!" I told him.

I turned him out with his buddies. He went right over and chased Blaze away from a feeder and dug in. I laughed as I walked across to the cabin. I grabbed some firewood as I went in, lit the lantern, and surveyed the damage from the dogs. It wasn't as bad as it could have been. I cleaned up a chewed up pillow and put some water on for tea, then settled in for the night. The dogs let me know they were ready to come in and I fed them, and settled down with my tea and my journal. I needed to record the events of today while they were still fresh in my mind.

Tabby jumped up on the bed and started purring and my eyes got heavy, so out went the light and off to dreamland I went. Funny though, I slept like a rock that night with no dreams at all.

Chapter Twenty-One

The Sweat Lodge

Once in a while, during my guardianship of the pack station and the horses, John would show up and tell me he had a group coming for an "off season" trip. Early spring was common for such trips to occur, especially if the snow pack was light.

Since there were no phones, I never knew when he might show up until I would hear the familiar roar of the Big Rig chugging up the road and watch its slow familiar dust cloud.

While I waited, my mind would try to guess what he had in store for me. Often, he'd hop out and say, "Got a small group showing up first thing in the morning. You'd best go check the tack and make sure all is ready."

I tried to ride all the horses during the winter to keep them in shape. I would look over the saddles and bridles every couple of days to be sure they weren't damp or getting mildewed. I'd clean them with Neatsfoot Oil once a month or so. Mostly, it was a dry cold, not a damp cold. That was much better for the leather.

The dogs were napping in the middle of the road by the cabin, and I was out lunging horses, when I noticed their ears prick up. I looked in the direction they zoned in on and, sure enough, I saw the truck coming up the road.

It was a beautiful, crisp, early spring day and I had worked my way through about half of the horses. There were also several of them out roaming around the cabin and grazing on the early green shoots poking through the loose sandy soil under all the sagebrush.

When John got a little closer, all heads popped up and several horses whinnied a welcome to him. I tied up the horse I was working and gave a whistle to the others.

As his truck pulled up a couple of his older horses gathered next to him and trotted alongside until he came to a stop by the corral. It was funny to watch his horses with him. They were like kids whose parents have been away for a long time. I was just the babysitter. They showed their true colors of how much they loved him every time he came.

"Got some stuff here for you," he called.

He'd brought more feed for the critters, a letter from my mom, and some books I had asked for. We unloaded the hay and feed sacks, fed the horses, then pulled the truck down to the cabin and unloaded the rest of the goodies. He also brought more wood, thank goodness. My stack was getting low.

"So are you just here overnight?" I asked as we carried boxes into the cabin.

"Nope, we got a couple of dads bringing their sons tomorrow for a few days of fishing. The river ought to be pretty high right now. Should be good fishing. You'll take them in tomorrow morning and stay a few days. Don't look like there's much snow on the pass, so you should be okay," John said as he carried the last load in. "Have you been in at all to check out the trail?"

"I rode as far as the summit last week. There are a few patches of snow here and there, but it's been sunny and a bit warmer, so it shouldn't be a problem," I said as I put away the food he'd brought. "So how come you aren't going in?"

"I've got some work to do on the truck. Think I'll take it to Don and see if he can help me figure it out. It's just not acting right," he said.

"So, since when did a vehicle of yours act right?" I asked as I ducked to avoid the box of crackers he threw at me. We both laughed and finished putting everything away.

"Here's the box of supplies you asked for. Hope I got everything." He set the box on the table.

I started unloading it, and it felt like Christmas as I pulled out a new bottle of shampoo, a new stick of deodorant, toothpaste, a new hair brush, some new socks, Band Aids, a box of tampons, a couple of bars of soap, several boxes of strike anywhere matches (a must have!), and a spool of nylon cord for the macramé halters and reins I was making. Also in the box were a couple of cartons of cigarettes and several packs of gum. A whole month's supply of essentials. I was so excited. It was amazing what you do without to live in this desert. And, equally amazing, were the things you absolutely could *not* live without. Just those few things made my life a bit easier in this wilderness.

I started looking through some of the books he brought and my heart sang for joy. I had asked for books about the Paiute people and Indian history in the Great Basin to read. Maybe these books would help me better understand all the things Sheriff Wright was trying to relate to me with his grandmother's stories.

John and I lit the lantern, ate a can of chili, and then played cards until he turned in for the night.

I grabbed the books, took the lantern into my room, and crawled into bed to read.

The book I was reading talked about the importance of the tribe's medicine men, and the shaman. I was fascinated reading about their vision quests. It went into great detail about some of the rock carvings found around the desert. They were very, very old.

They were called petroglyphs and were all over the Owens Valley, as well as many other places in the U.S. and the world. No one really understood what they meant. There were dozens of theories. Some thought they signaled a successful hunt. Others thought the shaman entered the supernatural world through his art on the rocks.

Often they would enter this state to use their powers to cure the sick, gain control over animals, look into the future, and curse their enemies.

They also believed they could control the weather. As the natural cycles of the earth brought this area into the dry years, they would trek to their spirit rocks to beg the ancestors to send them rain.

Suddenly, I remembered my dream and how I felt when I touched that stone in the canyon. The feelings I had experienced became crystal clear. I knew what those stones were for. I knew what the carvings meant. There was definitely a connection between those rocks and the spirit world! I had been there! Only briefly, but I'd been there.

The next part of the book talked about sweat lodges and their healing properties.

Most civilizations practiced some form of bathing or sweats. Oddly, in the dark ages, the Europeans thought bathing was bad. The Native Americans routinely had some form of sweat lodge. Most of the Plains Indians built small lodges and used hot stones, but some tribes back east had long houses where they used fire inside for those ceremonies. The Paiute and Shoshone built sweat lodges for a variety of ceremonies. The sweat lodge allowed the body as well as the mind to be cleansed. Many problems could be avoided and solved in the sweat. Prayers would be said and all was in tune with the Great Spirit.

The next book I picked up was called "Legends – Told by the Old People" by Adolf Hungry Wolf. It had many stories about Creation as passed down from the Elders of different tribes. I came to a story about the origin of the Sweat Lodge. I was intrigued.

Origin of the Sweat Lodge
A Nez Perce Story

Long ago, in the days of the Animal People, Sweat Lodge was a man. He foresaw the coming of Human Beings, the real inhabitants of the Earth. So one day he called all the Animal People together to give each one a name and to tell him his duties.

In the council, Sweat Lodge stood up and made a speech: "We have lived on Earth for a long while, but we shall not be in our present condition much longer. A different People are coming to live here. We must part from each other and go to different places. Each of you must decide whether you wish to belong to the animal beings that walk, fly, or creep or those that swim. You will now make your choice."

Then Sweat Lodge turned to Elk. "You will first come this way. What do you wish to be?"

"I wish to be what I am, an Elk."

"Let us see you run or gallop," said Sweat Lodge.

So Elk galloped off in a graceful manner, and then returned.

"You are right," decided Sweat Lodge. "You are an Elk."

Sweat Lodge called Eagle to him and asked, "What do you wish to be, Eagle?"

"I wish to be just what I am, an Eagle."

"Let us see you fly," replied Sweat Lodge.

Eagle flew, rising higher and higher and with hardly a ripple on his outstretched wings.

Sweat Lodge called him back and said to him. "You are an Eagle. You will be king over all the Birds of the Air. You will soar in the Sky. You will live in the crags and peaks of the highest Mountains. The Human Beings will admire you."

Happy with that decision, Eagle flew away. Everybody watched him until he disappeared in the Sky.

"I wish to be like Eagle," Bluejay told Sweat Lodge.

Wanting to give everyone a chance, Sweat Lodge said again, "Let us see you fly."

Bluejay flew into the air, trying to imitate the easy, graceful flight of the eagle. But he failed to keep himself balanced and was soon flapping his wings.

Noticing his awkwardness, Sweat Lodge called Bluejay back to him and said, "A Jay is a Jay. You will have to be contented as you are."

When Bear came forward, Sweat Lodge said to him, "You will be known among Human Beings as a very fierce Animal. You will kill and eat People, and they will fear you."

Bear went off into the woods and has since been known as a fierce animal.

Then to all walking creatures, except Coyote, and all the flying creatures, to all the Animals and Birds, all the Snakes and Frogs and Turtles and Fish, Sweat Lodge gave names and the creatures scattered.

After they had gone, Sweat Lodge called Coyote to him and said, "You have been wise and cunning. A man to be feared you have been. This Earth shall become like the air, empty and void, yet your name shall last forever. The new Human Beings who are to come will hear your name and say, 'Yes, Coyote was great in his time.' Now, what do you wish to be?"

"I have long lived as Coyote," he replied. "I want to be noble like Eagle or Elk or Cougar."

Sweat Lodge let him show what he could do. First, Coyote tried his best to fly like Eagle, but he could only jump around, this way and that way. He could not fly, poor fellow. Then he tried to imitate the Elk in his graceful gallop. For a short distance he succeeded, but soon returned to his own gait. He ran a little way, stopped short, and looked around.

"You look exactly like yourself, Coyote," laughed Sweat Lodge. "You will be a Coyote."

Poor Coyote ran off, howling, to some unknown place. Before he got out of sight, he stopped, turned his head, and stood, just like a coyote.

Sweat Lodge, left alone, spoke to himself: "All now are gone, and the new People will be coming soon. When they arrive, they should find something that will give them strength and power. "I will place myself on the ground, for the use of the Human Beings who are to come. Whoever will visit me now and then, to him I will give power. He will become great in war and great in peace. He will have success in Fishing and Hunting. To all who come to me for protection I will give strength and power."

Sweat Lodge spoke with earnestness. Then he lay down on his hands and knees and waited for the first People. He has lain that way ever since and has given power to all who have sought it from him.

ல

At this point my eyes were getting very heavy, so I decided to turn the lantern out before I fell asleep with it on. I was always careful to make sure I put the lantern out before I fell asleep. Didn't want to start a fire.

I snuggled down into my nice, warm sleeping bag with Frosty curled up at my feet and Laddie snoring on the floor beside me. I said some prayers of thanks and drifted off to sleep.

ல

I am sitting with a group of Native women. They are talking excitedly about the ceremony that is about to take place. It is strange because I feel perfectly at ease as they include me in their conversation.

"What is happening?" I ask, surprised at the sound of my voice that is not speaking my own language.

"The men are getting ready to enter the Temescal. It is important for them to be purified and clean as they pray to the Great Spirit for a successful hunt tomorrow." The old Paiute woman next to me replies. "We will have a women's sweat when the men are done. Your eyes will be opened, child, and you will see the grandfathers who have been watching out for you during your time in this place."

I look around at all of the activity that is taking place. It is dusk and the sun has sunk past the peaks of the tall rugged mountains across the valley. The sky is streaked with pinks and purples as the night approaches.

In front of me is the sweat lodge. I see the frame of the structure, made of soft willow boughs bent to form a dome and tied together with withes. In the center I see a slight depression in the ground. There are piles of skins folded and sitting nearby. There is a large fire that is being fed by several men and in the center of that fire are many large stones. While the fire is heating the stones, the men take the folded skins and start to cover the skeletal form. After they are done there is a perfect little domed hut sitting in front of me.

The shaman comes forward and lights his sage bundle. The old woman explains to me that he smudges himself to rid his body and mind of any bad medicine he may be carrying around. He then enters the sweat lodge to purify it and drive out any negative energy. I hear the rhythmic sounds of chanting inside the lodge. He stays inside for about five minutes or so, then comes out and continues his song.

The old woman tells me there is much for me to learn about the custom of the sweat.

"The sweat lodge represents the womb of Mother Earth. It is dark inside to show us our ignorance. The hot stones represent the coming of

life and the hissing steam is the creative force of the universe being activated. The entrance always faces east, the source of all life and power, the dawn of wisdom. The fire heating the rocks is the ever-living light of the world, eternity. The People have been cleansed in the sweat lodge since before time itself."

I watch as about ten men form a line to be smudged as they wait to enter the lodge.

One by one they enter, until they are all sitting in a circle around the depression in the middle of the floor. The shaman enters last and calls for the vessel full of water. He marks a circle with the deer antlers he is holding. The water is brought in and placed on the circle. Then he calls for the rocks to be brought in. One of the hunters uses antlers to lift the stones one by one from the fire and hands them to the Medicine Man inside. He then reverently places the rock in its special place in the pit. There are now five rocks in the pit and then he calls for the flap of the lodge to be closed.

Soon, I hear the melodic sounds of singing and prayers being offered. The sounds are beautiful to me. I can understand them perfectly.

The old woman who is still sitting next to me explains, "As the medicine man sprinkles water on the hot stones, the steam from the rocks gets very hot. With nowhere for it to escape, the bodies of those seated around the pit absorb it. Very soon, they are sweating and their bodies are being cleansed. As they sit, feeling the intense heat increase, they begin to pray. One by one around the circle, they pray for whatever it is they are seeking. When they are done, the shaman gives a final blessing, and the door is opened up. Sometimes they come out in the cool air before the next round, and sometimes they don't."

"How many rounds do they do?" I ask as three or four of the men come out so wet they look like they just got out of a pool. Their bodies are dripping, shiny, and radiant. They look so at peace.

"They will usually do five rounds adding more rocks each time," she replies.

I stare at the proud men standing in front of the lodge, lost in their own spiritual thoughts.

One young man stands to the side of them with his head bowed. His body is glistening in the rosy light, and sweat drips and pools at his feet. He is younger than the rest who came out. His body is strong and sinewy, lean and shiny. I blush as I think to myself how handsome he is.

Shaken from my thoughts, I hear the medicine man call the men back in. As the young hunter turns to go back inside I see him briefly glance toward me. It is so brief that he is back inside before I can process his look.

"His name is Little Bear," the old woman says with a knowing look in her eye.

I blush even deeper as my eyes follow the last of them into the lodge. Once more the rocks are lifted into place. Fifteen rocks this time. Singing and prayers are heard as before. And, as before, after fifteen minutes or so, they reemerge. This time as they exit the lodge, a few of them run for the river a short distance away. They plunge their overheated bodies into the icy water, turn around and run back to the lodge. Little Bear is trotting back and this time his look is longer. He pauses in front of me. His eyes search mine. Something stirs inside of me. He disappears inside the lodge.

I want to know more about him, but the woman nudges me and says we have to get ready.

"Ready for what?" I ask.

"For your cleansing sweat. The women sweat as the men do, only for different reasons. Many girls and women sweat during their moon time to take away the cramping in the womb. New mothers sweat to rid themselves of the sore muscles used to bring forth new life. Old women sweat to ease the pain in our old bones. It is healthy for the whole body and mind. The men do it for good fortune at the hunt, spiritual power, strength against their enemies, and for guidance from the Great Spirit. The sweat is also used to cure fevers and sickness."

She leads me away to her small hut. Inside, she undresses me (I am not aware of what I had been wearing) and wraps a rabbit skin blanket around my waist. She leaves my small leather pouch around my neck, which contains the perfect arrowhead I found. As she begins softly singing, she circles around me with her eagle feather, brushing my skin with it as if she is flicking away flies in the same manner I had seen the medicine man do to the men. Then she asks me to drink as she offers me a gourd filled with dark liquid. It has a bitter, sour taste.

"Drink it all," she says. "Your body will need the energy from this tea." I drink it down without asking what it is. She is circling around me again with a small, lit bundle of sage. The aroma is intoxicating. It fills my senses. She says to breathe it deep. I do and want more, much more. My mind is at peace. I feel in perfect harmony with my Mother the Earth. She is still singing and I close my eyes and feel my mind being taken away by the voices in my head singing with her. Suddenly, she stops. All is quiet.

She leads me out of her shelter and I see a group of women standing in front of the sweat lodge. Each dressed as I am. Each being cleansed as I had been.

She puts a small piece of bark in my mouth and tells me to leave it there, that it will keep my mouth from getting dry.

As we file into the lodge, I look off to the side and see Little Bear staring at me with a smile in his eyes. I am sure I am blushing again, but have no time to think about it as I am ushered inside and the old woman motions for me to sit.

I am at the center, in the back of the lodge.

There are seven women and the medicine man. The water is refilled and returned to its circle. He motions for the rocks to be brought in. There are five to start.

I can feel their heat radiating into the air as they are placed in the pit in front of me.

I am nervous and excited at the same time.

He sprinkles sage and cedar on the rocks and they sparkle and burn. The aroma is wonderful. He takes his eagle wing and waves it over the rocks so the smoke comes our way.

"For you!" he says as he is waving the smoke to each of us in turn.

The medicine man then signals for the flap to close. It is dark.

He starts to sing. My eyes are closed to allow my senses to absorb everything that is going to happen here. I hear him sprinkle the first water on the rocks. The hissing gets louder as he adds more water.

Suddenly, the heat overtakes me. It fills my nose and mouth. It is hot, but not unbearably so. As the healer sings and puts more water on the rocks, the sweat starts to pour forth from my body. He stops singing and asks us all to pray, one by one, around the circle. As the prayers are offered up, at the end of each, we all say "Ho." I don't even think about what I am going to say. It just comes out.

"Father, please help me learn what I am supposed to learn here. I am confused and ask for guidance and protection. That is all." I hear everyone say, "Ho."

The prayers continue until everyone has had a turn. Then the shaman prays once more and suddenly the cover is lifted and fresh cool air comes rushing in.

None of us leave the lodge after this first round. After about five minutes, the medicine man asks for ten more rocks.

He looks at me and says, "This will be very hot for you since you have not experienced it before. Are you sure you want to stay?"

I nervously nod my head.

"Good. Then, I will ask you to leave the lodge after this round. Too much too soon is not good for you. You will do well to stay through this one," he states.

I nod again.

The rocks are brought in and he carefully places them with his forked antlers. There is now a tall pile of rocks so hot that some are glowing red. They look as though they have just come from the molten center of the

Earth. The flap is closed and he starts his song and goes through all the same motions as in the first round.

The aroma of the sage and cedar fill my senses once again. It is nirvana to my mind. Then, he sprinkles the first water on the rocks.

Oh my Lord! I have never, EVER felt fire in my lungs before. That is what it feels like, lungs on fire. I can't inhale through my mouth or nose. I find I am taking short gulps of air that is all on fire. I hold my breath. Then I have to inhale more fire. How am I going to live through this? He sprinkles more water.

Just as panic starts to overtake me, his melodic singing begins. I try to concentrate on what he is singing to distract me from my urge to flee. As my mind relaxes, soon my body calms as well. I am drenched with sweat. I rub my arms and legs and feel them coated with liquid. How can all of that moisture come out of all those little pores so fast?

As I start to settle into the rhythm of his song, he asks for the prayers to begin. He puts more water on the stones. A furnace blast rushes into my nostrils. I try to breathe and cannot.

Again panic sets in. It's my turn to pray. What do I say? I don't want them to know how scared I am becoming.

Out comes, "Help me endure, Great Spirit. Help me understand." That is all I can manage. They all say "Ho."

My pounding heart now slows, and I feel the leather pouch in my tightly squeezed fist. My breathing is starting to slow a bit. He sprinkles more water and I brace for the onslaught of super-heated air. But it is more manageable this time. My head feels light and my mind is drifting. A voice in my head tells me to open myself. Open my senses to the Earth. All the knowledge I need is already inside of me. I just have to listen with my heart. The prayers are finished and he sings a final prayer himself.

The flap is opened and cold air that must have been sent from heaven pours into that lodge.

My eyes are blurry. I think they have been sweating, too. Everywhere, my body drips a seemingly endless amount of sweat. My long hair is stuck to my back. I look down and my amulet pouch is dripping between my wet breasts. Everything is dripping! How can there be so much liquid inside of one body?

The shaman helps me to my feet and the old woman is there to take my arm.

My whole body feels like it belongs to another person.

As she leads me out, I notice Little Bear sitting by the fire. He looks up as we pass, nods at me, and smiles. I manage a slight smile, and then begin to feel faint. I can barely move my legs.

He jumps up to help the old woman walk me back to her small hut. As we get inside she motions for him to guide me to her pallet. He gently sets me down, all the while looking deep into my eyes. His eyes hypnotize me. I know them.

She begins to massage my skin, rubbing all the sweat back into my arms and legs and shoulders. I feel so exhausted and so clean.

"Does it always feel like this?" I ask.

She smiles, but he answers, "Yes, if you allow it to." He gets up to leave, turns, and says to me, "You will prepare my meal tonight!" and walks out.

I look at the woman, "What does he mean?"

"He is impressed with you. It is an honor for a hunter to ask a woman to prepare his meal the night before a hunt. You are fortunate indeed. Little Bear will become the next medicine man when his father, Running Bear, crosses to the spirit world. He will need a strong woman at his side. You sleep now. Your body needs to replenish. It has done well this first sweat."

She covers me with a light fur and I am soon dreaming of Little Bear and what all of this means.

ᔕ

Voices outside nudged me from my extraordinary dream.

John was talking to people outside and I realized that the group had arrived from the city that we were packing in that day.

I needed to get up. But my mind wanted to continue the dream about Little Bear.

"Roni! Get your butt outta bed and get out here. What are ya gonna do? Sleep all day and let these horses pack themselves up the mountain?" John yelled.

With that I was up, dressed, and out the door before he was finished yelling at me.

"Sorry, John, I was coming. Honest!" And I headed to the corral and started catching horses.

The group I took in that day consisted of several teenage boys and their fathers. They were going to fish and ride and enjoy nature, they said.

I knew it was going to be a long three days when I saw they had no respect for the "Nature" they were supposedly going in to enjoy. They were loud and boisterous on the trail and complained because they didn't see any wildlife.

I tried to explain to them that they weren't likely to see any unless they could be a bit quieter. I picked up candy and gum wrappers dropped by them the whole way up the trail. They had no desire to learn about this place, how to treat the horses, where to find the best fishing hole, or how to take care of their food so the critters would stay out of it. I couldn't tell them anything because they knew everything. They just wanted to be macho and loud.

"So, I'll just shut myself up, keep to myself, keep picking up after them, and take care of the horses," I said to myself. "Thankfully, they're staying in the smaller cabin and I have the big one all to myself, so I don't have to listen to them all night."

The second night, around midnight, I heard screaming coming from outside.

I bounced out of my bed, got my boots on, grabbed the flashlight, went out the door, and shined the light up to their cabin.

"Oh, my!" I giggled. "Lions and Tigers and *bears*. Oh my!"

The screams were all coming from inside the cabin while a medium-sized bear was pounding on the outside of their cabin door, which had been previously ripped off by bears and repaired many times. I could barely contain my laughter. Those macho men in there were crying like babies.

I went back inside and grabbed my rifle, put a round in the chamber, went back out and fired into the air.

"Get outta here!" I yelled, and the bear scampered off. I went over to the cabin, opened the door and found a group of scared men and boys all huddled together in their skivvies.

"You've got food in here, don't ya?" I asked. "I told you to put away it or the bears would find it. Believe me now? This is their world. You aren't in the big city, safe from wild animals. This is the real world. You have GOT to respect that."

"Dad, I want to go home," one scared boy said.

"I suggest you get any food you may have in here, take it outside, and put it in the lock box now, so we can all finish our beauty sleep, and then we'll talk in the morning," I scolded them as I headed back to my cabin.

It didn't matter what I said to them. I wouldn't change their outlook on life. How come some people just didn't get it?

Turned out they didn't care much for nature after all. I packed them out the next day.

After they left, I sat on the rocks above the pack station and felt the gentle breezes swirl around me and hug my soul.

My friends were here with me. I hadn't felt them while I was with those city people. It wasn't only the animals that shied away from the loudness; it was the spirits as well. I spent the rest of the day enjoying their presence and wondering how some people could be so disrespectful of Mother Earth.

Chapter Twenty-Two

Blood Red Moon

Jim often came to the pack station to get away from the city, school, and job responsibilities. He came to meditate and commune with the mountains and the spirits.

I loved it when he came because, more than anyone else, he understood me. There was a connection with us that went beyond friends. It was almost a spiritual connection of our souls, like they had been entwined for eons. Ours was a deeply personal relationship, sharing our innermost thoughts, dreams, ideas and, at times, other things. But more than anything else, he just "got" me. I could be myself with him. I could share my deepest feelings about anything and everything, and I knew he wouldn't make light of anything I said.

We shared many amazing experiences at the pack station. During the busy summer seasons with so many people coming and going, we would ride up to the cabin at Deer Mountain for a chance to be alone with each other. There, he taught me how a man is supposed to treat a woman. And often, along with our physical journey, we would share peyote or mescaline and stay for hours basking in the visions and spiritual journeys we would share there. We would lay in the meadow and see faces in the clouds racing overhead, etched with nameless faces that seemed older than the Earth itself. We would sit on rocks overlooking the meadow and see visions of native Paiute people going about their lives. Then suddenly, screaming, dust and panic would interrupt the calm, peaceful visions as we saw soldiers riding towards their small encampment. We saw these things happening right in front of us, yet we were powerless to do anything but sit and cry for those innocents that were murdered before our very eyes.

We shared these things with few others.

One night on the desert after taking mescaline, Jim and I were walking around exploring the desert in our heightened state of awareness. Everything was so vivid and the stars shone so bright. We sat by the grinding stone for a while feeling the ancients around us.

"Let's walk a little ways up the canyon," Jim suggested after a time. We had the sensation of being escorted by our invisible friends. There was no moon out, yet the trail was brightly lit for us. We had a feeling of belonging to this place, and we were welcomed into a world not of this time, but of ages past.

As we returned down the trail, we took a detour up to the big rocks on the hill behind the cabin. The night was warm but dark, and we were soaking up the magnificence of our universe. That was not hard to do on that desert at night with the bright, starlit sky. We sat on the rocks not speaking, but communicating our thoughts to the heavens just the same. It was a magical night. The darkness wrapped itself around us and we sat for hours trying to count the stars.

While we were staring into the heavens, we became aware of a change creeping over the landscape. We sat in stunned silence as a red glow started to peek over the top of the eastern hills. It got brighter and brighter until the whole desert seemed awash in red. Then we watched the biggest, fullest moon rise up over the mountain to greet us. It was blood red in color. The whole sky and desert was a blood red hue.

ꝏ

Jim and I looked at each other in amazement. We didn't know what to say. We just silently watched as it rose, slowly sending its eerie color to the heavens and snuffing out the stars one by one.

As it got higher, the palette changed to a lighter red, and the landscape changed with it. Then the color changed to light orange as it got higher still in the sky. By the time it was high above us it had turned bright white. The desert was as brightly lit as we had ever seen it. Everything was as crystal clear as if it were daylight. We could see the grinding stone; the horses, many of who were lying down; and the buildings. We could even follow the dirt road all the way to the highway.

I think the most beautiful thing I saw that night was the water at the reservoir and the rippling changes of iridescent shades as the moon rose higher. At first a sea of red, then orange, then twinkling white as it shouted its thanks to sister moon for this magical night.

We sat there half the night not wanting to break whatever spell had been cast over our universe.

Finally, we climbed down and slipped into the sleeping bags we had laid out away from the cabin. But we couldn't sleep and kept asking each other if we had really seen what we thought we had seen. At last we drifted off to sleep holding each other with visions of that moon etched in our dreams

The next morning when we walked into the cabin everyone asked at once, "Did you see it?"

"It was awesome!"

"You saw it right?"

Jim and I looked at each other and smiled. Our secret wasn't so secret after all. It had really happened and there were several "sober" people to testify to it.

The next night stayed dark. Jim and I fell asleep together staring off into the heavens hoping for a repeat of the night before.

But all that came to me that night was another incredible dream.

∽

It is a chilly, star-filled, fall evening. I am sitting next to Little Bear around the main campfire. We sit close enough for me to feel the heat radiating from his body. We have grown close during my visits and he seems to know my thoughts without me having to speak. He reminds me of another who seems to always see into my soul.

Somehow, I understand their language. It is all so strange, but I stopped trying to figure it out long ago. I just go with the dreams as they come to me. They are dreams, are they not?

Running Bear and the other Paiute elders are telling stories and we laugh as they act them out with great theatrics.

As we sit listening, I become aware of a change in the dark night sky. The sky is slowly turning a crimson red.

It is getting brighter and brighter, and the color deepens.

All voices are now silent as we gaze to the eastern hills and watch a fine red crescent line appear on the horizon.

Slowly it rises from its slumber behind the mountain, growing bigger and deeper red.

A quarter ways up, now half the color of blood, the moon rises and the whole universe takes on her blood red color.

We all stand at the same time facing this magnificent full orb, so close we want to reach out and touch it. Her beauty mesmerizes us, yet we are fearful of the unknown.

The elders begin whispering to each other. I can't hear what they are saying.

The moon rises higher, becoming a brighter red. The landscape changes with her. Colors change from red to light orange, and finally as she reaches the top of the sky, a brilliant, pure white streams out from her in every direction. The desert is as brightly lit as it would be at dawn.

Now the assembled clan members start to wander off, one by one, to their sleeping furs. There is no privacy, but it seems no one cares.

Little Bear takes my hand and leads me to his furs and we sit. I am still dazed by the beauty of the full moon this night. I ask him what all the whispering was about.

"They are worried. A blood moon usually is a bad omen," he answers as he strokes my arm and takes my hand in his. "But I believe it is a good omen that you are here this night to see it with me."

He searches deep into my eyes and I return his stare. His light eyes are so familiar to me and so very different from the others.

"Do I know you from another time?" I ask.

"We have known each other forever," he replies as he takes me in his arms to kiss me.

We lay down together, and the hunger we have been trying to ignore all evening explodes and then is blissfully satisfied. I drift off to sleep with Little Bear still caressing me.

ᔕ

As the sun poked up from behind the eastern hills, like daggers its rays pierced my eyelids. I opened my eyes and saw Jim staring at me from just inches away.

"Good morning, Sunshine!" he said. "How'd you sleep?"

I was startled to see those same eyes from my dream staring back at me.

"I had the most unbelievable dream," I told him.

"Do tell," he said, as he kissed me, got up, and walked away toward the horses.

I sat in my sleeping bag watching him feed and tried to sort out what was real, what was not, and became more confused than ever. Finally, I decided to just let things be. I felt so much peace in my heart.

I had Little Bear in my head, Jim in my present, and I had seen a blood red moon. Twice!

Unlike most things experienced with drugs, it remained crystal clear in our minds. And even years later we could dig that picture of the Blood Red Moon out of our memory files and see it all over again.

What an incredible experience it was.

Chapter Twenty-Three

The Cave

The grandchildren were eager for another story, and of course I loved sharing the stories with their smiling faces. I was hopeful that they would remember these stories enough to tell their own children and grandchildren someday. I desperately wanted them to sense the importance of the history in this place and how it helped shape me. I wish they could have experienced what I did firsthand. But perhaps my stories would be enough to stir a small sense in them of belonging to the land. Even little Alli and the younger ones seemed anxious for the stories, yet I wondered just how much they understood at their young age. Then I noticed Alli holding a piece of obsidian, rubbing it between her fingers subconsciously, her twinkling eyes turned up to me waiting for me to begin.

"It was a hot spring day when I decided to ride down to the cave again," I began.

"The Sheriff had been telling me so many tales about the people who once lived here and I felt I knew them personally through my dreams. I hadn't told him about the cave and the tools I found there. I felt it still needed to be my secret."

ᔓ

I eagerly threw out extra helpings of hay for the horses in case I was gone through dinner. I let Poppin' eat while I prepared snacks to take along. Then, I locked the dogs inside and saddled up Poppin' and off we went.

The ride down the road was brisk. Poppin' seemed to know we were off on another adventure. I'm not sure how he sensed these things, but he did. On those excursions, he was a different kind of horse. Animated and interested. When we headed *up* the trail to the high country, he was all business. He knew he had work to do. But going *down* the road, he knew there was a difference! He knew he was going on an adventure!

We made the reservoir in record time. I soon found the little trail we had taken before and we made our way up the small canyon to the meadow. I dismounted, took his bridle off so he could graze, and sat and wolfed down my sandwich before setting out on foot to explore the cave.

As I climbed the trail towards the opening of the cave, I noticed the trail was steeper and more crumbly than I remembered. My smooth-soled boots felt slippery on the rocks and loose dirt. When I stepped over a large rock where the trail had disappeared, I was surprised by the familiar but unwelcome sound of a rattlesnake. It was pure reflex to jump back and that's just what I did. Unfortunately, when I jumped back, my foot caught on a rock and I went tumbling down the hillside. I don't remember stopping. I must have been knocked out for a bit.

I don't know how long before I came to, but when I did, I was still part way up the hill, and had an enormous headache. I also had a badly injured ankle. I couldn't put any weight on it.

"Oh no. Please don't let it be broken!" I whispered to the Grandfathers. "Please!"

I couldn't stand on it. I was afraid that if I took my boot off to look at it, I wouldn't get it back on.

"Crap, what am I going to do now?"

In the minutes that I sat there, the pain got worse and worse.

Then it dawned on me that I didn't want to be on that hillside where, somewhere, there was the rattlesnake that caused this whole fiasco.

So, I whistled to Poppin'. His head popped up looking at me.

"Come get me, boy. I'm hurt."

I whistled again and he started trotting towards me.

I didn't know if he would actually climb this crumbling trail or not, but he picked his way up as I kept calling to him. He didn't even slow down when some of the rocks slid out behind him. His ears were pricked up and he was focused on my voice as I kept telling him to go easy. He never, ever wavered from his course. Straight up that trail to me. Oh, how I loved that horse!

He stopped in front of me and snorted. It was clear that he was miffed at me for interrupting his grassy snack. I think he was starting to sense the late hour as well. He was fidgeting a bit as I tried to reach up for a stirrup. My head and my ankle hurt so badly. He kept moving.

"HELL! Hold still!" I yelled, calling him by his bad name. He stopped and stood still. He knew what that tone of voice meant.

Once he was still I was able to grab onto the stirrup, but I wasn't able to get on him. So I just grabbed the saddle horn.

"Take me down to the water, boy."

He slowly turned around, dragging me at his side, and picked his way ever so gently back down to the meadow.

I let go and flopped down onto the meadow's soft grass.

Poppin' stood guard as I slipped away to sleep.

My dreams pulled me through the past to ancient times.

ᔓ

I wake to the sounds of voices. The language is not familiar. It is dark, yet there is a glow from a fire. My blurry vision clears and I see shadows, flames dancing.

Then suddenly, an ancient, old woman is kneeling beside me offering me a drink of water. She is much older than the old Paiute woman in my previous dreams.

I don't understand what she is saying but I know she wants me to drink. I take the gourd from her hand and sip the ice-cold water. Looking around I see other women staring at me. The old woman smiles and sees the confusion in my eyes. She points to my ankle, which is wrapped in leather skins, and I remember falling. I remember Poppin' dragging me to the meadow, then nothing after that.

When I start to stand, I wince and she reaches for me to stop. She makes a gesture indicating that I should stay off of my foot, so I settle back down on the furs and take a look around.

We are in the cave.

There are groups of people; men, women, and children sitting around the fire.

The old woman says something and they all look my way and nod.

She smiles, looks back at me, and I can't help but smile at her. She seems pleased and gets up, walks over to the fire, and says something to a man.

He looks my way and nods.

She grabs a stick with a piece of meat on it, walks back and offers it to me. As I eat, my eyes wander from person to person, wondering what they are thinking.

They all seem at ease at my presence in this cave. I, on the other hand, am slightly uncomfortable. Things seem a bit different here than from my other dreams. A bit older perhaps.

The ancient-looking woman comes back and sits next to me. She again offers me water, which I greedily gulp down.

She speaks to me, I look up and once again she is smiling. I can't understand her language. It is a different dialect than the young girl from the previous dreams.

As I look around at them their dress appears different as well. There is much less of it. The cave is enormous. The fire pit and cooking area are at the front of the cave. There are drawings on the walls, and along the walls are several sleeping areas. It appears that several families live here.

The men and boys appear to be getting ready for something. There is much excitement.

Suddenly the old woman rises and motions for me to go with her. As I tentatively stand up, I realize my ankle no longer hurts. I am amazed as I rush to keep up with her.

The women are preparing food and provisions for the men, who look as though they are going on a hunt.

The old woman gives me a leather bag, motions for me to follow her and do as she does.

Several baskets are laid out with food in them that I am unfamiliar with. We put some of this and a little of that in the pouches. Once they are full, we tie them shut with a thin strip of rawhide.

Suddenly, the man who had been talking to the old woman is standing in front of me.

He holds out his hand. I'm unsure of what he wants.

The old woman says, "He wants the pouch you have prepared for him." I am dumbfounded that I understand her. I hold the bag up to him and he takes it from me with a smile. I look at his weapons. He sees my curiosity and hands me one of his long darts to examine. I touch the feathers on the shaft and then run my fingers over the smooth black obsidian tip.

In the back recesses of my mind I remember what Sheriff Wright told me about the archeological digs in this area that uncovered points like this that were estimated to be at least seven thousand years old. I realize I am holding one of them in my hand. I am numb. And the man who likely made that beautiful point is standing right next to me. I hand it back to him and he puts it in the quiver on his back. He motions for me to follow him out of the cave. I watch as the other women also follow their men out.

Suddenly, they all let out a big whoop, waving weapons in the air.

And just as suddenly, it is quiet and the men are trotting down the hill to the valley floor to search for deer.

The weather is brisk and the sun is just about to peak over the horizon. One woman touches my arm and points behind me into the sky. Then, I see it for the first time, the Deer Star. Although I am sure these people don't know the story of the Deer Star, this must be the star that creates the story in future times. Or maybe these are the storytellers.

I must remember the location of this star so I will be able to find it wherever I may be.

It is brighter than any other star I have ever seen, and now I understand how it can be taken as a sign for a good hunt.

As I turn back toward the cave, the old woman comes alongside and says, "Look." She points down at the desert floor. I don't recognize what I am seeing. It is teeming with life. There are streams lined with abundant foliage. There is a large pond a bit further down. And finally, a fertile valley that looks nothing like the dry arid wasteland of my time.

The woman picks up a basket and motions for me to follow. I pick up a basket and run to catch up. We hike down to the pond. All the women are checking traps set the night before. There are fish in several of them.

We gather some of the kutsavi along the side of the pond. I learn this is fly pupae. We head back to the cave to prepare the pupae and fish for the evening meal.

"The hunters will be hungry, and it is our job to have food ready for our providers," the old woman says to me.

We stop by a tree near the cave. She reaches into her basket and pulls out two stone knives. One is a scraper and one has a cutting edge. She hands them to me and then laughs when she realizes I have no idea what to do with them.

"Do you not know how to prepare fish?"

"Not really," I answer, still not sure why we can understand each other.

"Your time is so different from mine. I will show you," she says as she takes the fish out of her basket and begins to clean them. "I want you to think of the bright light in the sky. Why do you think we are given the sign?"

I pick out a fish from my basket and she hands me the knife. "So you know when the hunt will be successful?" I answer.

"Yes, but why? You know the outcome, but not the why. Our Earth gives us a sign when she knows we have been without for a long time. Do you think these few fish can feed our large clan very long? It is time for a feast. Earth ensures our survival by giving us what we need when we need it. She gives us no more, and no less. Is it different in your time?"

She stops gutting the fish and seeks an answer from me.

I ignore her mention of another time and ask, "You mean the Earth tracks your existence to know when you need things?"

"Yes. She tells us when to move, when to hunt, how to live and survive. She gives us herbs for medicine and willows for baskets. She gives us everything, and tonight if the hunt is good, as it will be, we will celebrate our Earth and give back to her. Have you never done that?" she asks.

"No, I have never celebrated a good hunt or given back to the Earth. But how do you know that? And how do you know I am from another time?"

The woman looks deep into my eyes and says. "Because you were sent to this place to learn. I am to teach you. Do you think that we have not been watching you and taking care of you during your alone time here? We have heard your pleas to the sky, and seen your tears. You are very similar to us in many ways, and yet you don't live as we do. But I can sense a longing to belong to the Earth and to The People deep down inside of you. In your heart you yearn for the things of your world to be different."

"Oh, it is much, much different. If only we were as thoughtful as your people. In my time man takes it all, whenever he wants, regardless of whether he needs it or not. The waste. It disgusts me. But I never thought about how it could be different." My mind is racing trying to take this all in.

"I am here to show you that you do belong to the Earth, and you will always have a people who are your people, whether in the future or in the past. It is important to learn how Earth takes care of her own." She smiles at me. "Finish your fish; you are killing it more than is necessary."

I look down at my mutilated fish and lay it next to her perfectly cleaned fish. I am embarrassed because I have destroyed a fish that could have fed one of the hunters on their return.

"Do not look so sad. I can fix it." She takes the fish from me and says, "Watch closely. When I do my next fish you do each step with me. Then you will know."

I watch and study intently. By the time she does the next one, I am ready. She lays a fish in front of me and as she starts to clean hers, I copy her movements exactly. I am impressed with her teaching abilities and by the time we are finished I am an expert.

We carry our baskets back up to the cave and give the waiting women the pupae we collected from the edge of the pond. They will prepare it for the meal with the fish. I am not too sure about eating fly pupae.

I sit down by the fire and watch the women going about their chores, and suddenly realize that the Sheriff had said these people probably didn't have fire. The old woman comes and sits next to me with herbs and sage to wrap the fish in.

"I did not think you had fire. It is commonly thought that you did not," I say to her as we work to prepare the fish.

"It is true that it is not common that we build a fire. And we don't usually have one this close to where we sleep. But we do have fire as you can see. Why do they think we don't have fire?" she asks.

"I can't remember the exact explanation, but it has something to do with never finding any burnt areas like cooking pits." I reply.

"Look at the fire. Tell me why they will never find what they seek," the old woman instructed.

I look for several minutes trying to figure out the woman's puzzle. "Your fire does not touch the ground. It is built up over the ground. Why?"

"Would you burn your provider? We protect her. She gives us rocks to build up a place to put fire," the woman says reverently.

I stare at the rocks and say, "But they have never found any of these burnt rocks either. They are looking for things like this."

"And they won't find them until the Earth decides to share them. She does not divulge all of her secrets at once. We place these rocks where she tells us, and they are not usually close to our sleeping areas. In due time your seekers may find what they are searching for. Or maybe it shall be hidden forever," the old woman says as she places the fish under the rock formation holding the fire.

"What do I do now?" I ask.

"Baskets. You must learn how to weave baskets. By the time girls reach your age they know how to make several kinds of baskets and traps. Of course, girls your age would also normally be married. So, come, and I will teach you how to make a simple basket," she says as she leads me to a thicket of small willows. I watch as she cuts many branches of different lengths. She dips the reeds in the stream to soften them so they will bend and not break. I sit next to her. "Just do exactly as I do," she says to me. After a couple of hours, I have a basket that looks just like, well almost like, the old woman's new basket. "Keep that with you always," she says to me. "Your basket is very important to you. It can carry things, store things, and be an extra arm when you need one."

Suddenly, there was the sound of excited voices and shouting.

"It's time to return to the cave. The hunters are back," the woman said. "We will have much work to do to get ready for the celebration tonight. We must prepare the deer for the feast."

"But I thought the fish…" I start to say.

"The fish are for the hunters who have not eaten all day. I know, we packed pouches for them, but they don't take the time to eat when they are looking for food for the clan. The clan always comes first to them. They return from their hunt starving and anxious to tell their tales," she says as she leads the way back.

When we reach the cave, the hunter who took the pouch from me that morning seems to be searching for something. His back is to us as we enter.

"He looks for you," the woman says and giggles as she shouts at him. He turns around and his eyes lock with mine. Those familiar eyes. If only I could remember where I have seen them before.

A smile comes to his face as he walks toward me. Forcefully, he grabs my arm and starts pulling me down a trail that goes around to the other side of the cave. At first I am fearful, but I look back to see the old woman, carrying our baskets, running after us as fast as she is able. She doesn't look worried, so I relax. I can see other women giggling as he drags me past them. He finally stops and we are standing in front of the carcasses of three deer.

He sees the questions in my eyes. He says, "You will clean the deer for the celebration tonight. Because of your good hunt bundle, your interest in my darts, and with thanks to the Earth, I have been lucky at the hunt. You have brought me luck," as he hands me his knife.

I look at the knife in my hand.

"I have to clean all of these deer?" I ask. "I'm not sure how…"

"I will help," says the old woman. She turns to the hunter and tells him to lay the deer across the big, flat boulders for us. He does as he is told and leaves us to this chore.

"Well, now you will learn this most basic necessity. How to clean deer properly and respectfully is a very important job in the clan. The deer and the bighorn sheep are our most revered animals. They sustain us through long cold winters when food is scarce. You will need your basket to hold the hearts of these animals for The People," she says to me as I reach to take my basket from her.

"The what?" I ask.

"Just do what I tell you and save your questions for later," she relates.

"First, you must bleed the deer," she instructs, as she places her tightly woven basket underneath the first deer's neck and pierces it with her knife. With the head hanging lower than the rest, the blood flows freely into her basket.

"This blood is precious to us. We will use it in the ceremony tonight."

She then tells me how to make the incision into the belly to remove the organs. She has placed a large basket near me for this. I make the cut from the throat to the gut. The knife blade is so sharp, yet it is made of stone. I stare at it amazed. I reach inside and pull out the still warm organs. I remember seeing hunters do this, and it is no different here. I am covered in the deer's blood, but it doesn't bother me.

"Put those into this basket. Except for the hearts," she says. "Those go into your basket for tonight."

I just nod and keep at my work. She tells me how to separate the hide from the meat.

"It is important to keep it all in one piece if you can. Large hides become clothing and protection." I nod as I make the necessary cuts down the legs. She shows me how to strip the hide from the legs and pull it off whole. It comes away from the meat freely.

"That is good," she says. "You have done well for your first time. Save the tails for the hunter. He will wear them or give them as gifts."

I go to the next deer and repeat what I did to the first. Only this time, without instruction from the old woman.

There are now several other women watching me as well. They are whispering and giggling among themselves and I begin to feel self-conscious.

"Do they need to be here?" I ask the woman.

"It's all right, child, they are only saying kind things about you," she answers.

"Sorry. I guess I'm just feeling insecure. Those feelings crop back up every now and then," I say as I start in on the third deer.

"You have come a long way in the years since bad things were done to you. You were punishing yourself when it was another who should have been punished. You are not to blame for any of the behaviors you went through between your young years and the time you arrived here. We have watched over you all this time, and find you to be an honest, sincere person seeking the knowledge of the Ancients in order to understand the world you live in a little better. We are trying to give you what you seek," she tells me.

I continue working to remove the hide of the deer when tears start to fall down my face. I can't hold them back. I finish with the deer hide, then sit and continue to cry. She comes and sits next to me, encircling me with her arms. I feel more than her arms around me. There are many unseen beings with us. I can't seem to get the tears to stop.

"You've never cried about the loss of your innocence have you? It's been building in you and you have pushed it to the very back of your memories. You need to cry and cleanse your soul of this, child. Cry it all out," she tells me.

"I never could cry about these things when I was young. I didn't tell anyone about it. I was so ashamed," I sob. "After several, years I told my mom. She was divorcing him anyway, so she used that to her advantage. She never spoke of it again after I told her. I never got any help, and had no one to talk to." The tears keep falling. "I always used to wonder what my life would have been like if I had grown up with my father."

She nods to indicate she understands.

"So to compensate for what was lacking in my life as well as to cover up the pain of my stepfather's deeds, I found that if I could give a boy what he wanted, I would be liked. Simple as that. And I have never, ever felt loved or even liked. That is, until I came to this place. John changed everything for me. I owe him so much. And now it seems I owe you as well."

"Dear child, he didn't change you. He gave you the opportunity to change the way you see yourself. He gave you his trust and his love. Because of that, you are finding the true person that is YOU starting to immerge. You will be a beautiful, wise mother of many someday. True love waits for you. Someone who will cherish you forever," she says as she hugs me close.

My tears dry up as I look at her. There is a sparkle of wisdom in her cloudy gray eyes.

"Yeah, right. Who would want me forever?" I ask, as I stand and gather up the basket. "So what am I supposed to do with this stuff now?"

"We will place all of the organs under the fire to roast. The hearts will be used tonight." she answers.

She whistles and right away the young hunter trots down to us. "She is done with the butchering, Red Wolf. You may take the meat to the fires."

He looks over the neatly quartered carcasses and then looks at me. He nods his approval and hollers for several other hunters to come and help carry the meat to the site of the celebration.

"Where do you have this celebration?" I ask

"The top of the hill above the cave. It's the closest we can get to the Great Spirit without crossing over. Come. We must get back to the cave and rest before tonight's celebration. Bring the basket with you and I will show you what to do," the old woman says as she rises and leads me back toward the cave.

"But I need to clean up," I tell her as I look down and see myself covered in blood.

"Why do you need to clean yourself?" she asks.

"Well, I'm filthy and bloody." I say embarrassed.

"Why are you filthy? You are wearing the reward of the Earth. She has given us food, and we will celebrate. She has provided for us. Why would you think of it as dirt?"

"It's just that…well how can I explain…"

"You are not in your time now. Here in ours, we celebrate the life's blood of the animals, which the Earth gives to us. Can you understand that?" she asks.

I nod, while trying to see her point of view. The stains of blood are like badges and finery given to them by the Earth and should not be discarded as frivolous.

We walk past the cave entrance and proceed to the stream to clean the knives. I pay special attention to Red Wolf's knife. My hands are now clean from washing the knives, but I still have blood on my arms and down the front of the fur apron I am wearing. So I am sure there must be blood on my face as well. I run my fingers through my matted, tangled, bloodstained, blonde hair.

"Ick!" I mutter to myself as we head back toward the cave.

It is quiet in the cave. Everyone is napping or doing quiet activities.

"Why are they all so quiet?" I ask.

"Tonight's celebration will go on into the dawn. Everyone rests the day of such celebrating. You should too!" she orders as she takes my basket and places it next to hers.

She motions for me to lie down on her furs and rest. I do as I am told and drift off to sleep.

∽

I was shoved awake by Poppin' who was tired of standing around waiting for me. He was hungry and wanted to get back to his buddies.

He kept nudging me with his muzzle, and as I came out of my stupor, my mind was slightly confused. Where was I? I looked around and saw that I was lying by the small pond where I had stopped Poppin' and let go of the stirrup.

As I tried to stand, I remembered exactly what had happened.

"Oh, the snake," I said. "Now I remember." I grabbed the stirrup and pulled myself to stand. He just stood there. I could steady myself on it, but couldn't put full weight on my ankle. I grabbed his bridle off of the saddle horn and he dropped his head to take the bit.

"Okay, boy, you need to stand real still while I try to get up on ya," I said, as I tightened the cinch.

I put my good foot in the stirrup and hoisted myself onto his back. My throbbing ankle came to rest on the other side. I tried to put it in the stirrup, but it hurt too much. "Guess I'll have to ride lop-sided, Poppin' old friend. You better be good and not spook or anything like that." Boy was I glad I wasn't on Brownie right then. I never would have made it back.

The ride up the road took longer this time because I had to make him walk. He wanted to go faster, but it was too painful for me. So we fought and argued all the way home. I was exhausted by the time we reached the cabin. I gingerly stepped down from the saddle, took it off of him, and hopped as I led him to the corral.

All the horses were excited to see us. I was glad I had thrown out extra hay for them.

I put Poppin' in the small corral, threw him some hay, and hobbled down to the cabin. I could tell the horses were not happy about me ignoring them, but it was all I could do to get Poppin' taken care of.

The dogs flew by me as I opened the door. They hadn't wreaked too much havoc inside while I was gone. I closed the door, dropped my saddlebag on the table, and collapsed on the couch. It was dark outside by this time as I struggled to stay awake until I could let the dogs back in. But after being cooped up all day I was in for a wait, and I drifted off to sleep.

Their barking woke me. I started to jump up, remembering my ankle just in time. I hopped to the door, let them in, put some food in their dish and went to my bed.

I lay down without even taking off my boots, but my ankle was throbbing and I sat up thinking I should take it off because of the swelling. After I took off the good one, I started pulling off the injured one. The pain went straight to my head. As I pulled on it, I was seeing stars and circles and soon nothing but darkness.

The dogs barking brought me out of the darkness. It was light out. In fact, it looked like it was noon or later. "Oh crap," I said as I sat up. The dogs continued to bark.

Then I heard him.

"Roni? You in there?" the Sheriff asked.

"Yeah, come on in," I told him as I looked at my ankle and saw it was wrapped with a thin piece of leather. I was staring at it when Sheriff Wright came through the door to my room and saw it too.

"What happened?"

"Uh, a little mishap," I grinned.

Then I told him the story of my day looking for the cave, climbing the rock, and slipping when the snake appeared. I told him how Poppin' had come to my rescue and took me down the hill to the pond, and how I fell asleep. I didn't mention the dream.

"Then how'd your ankle get wrapped like that?" he asked.

"Um, I'm not sure. I don't know where that came from. I slept for a long time in the meadow below the cave. But I never took off my boots. I was afraid to," I told him as he examined my ankle closer.

"Well, I don't think it's broke. You're lucky. You need to stick closer to home here, girl. What would have happened if you had gotten hurt worse than this? What if Poppin' had run off? What if

I had come here today and just found Poppin' with a saddle on and no you? I didn't know you were riding down across the highway. I would have never looked down there. You could have died there! No one goes there!" His voice was getting angrier.

"I'm okay though. None of that happened. Really, I'm fine." I responded.

"You just can't go gallivanting all over this desert like that. You are a young girl. There are people out there looking for young girls just like you. Girls who are anxious to put their miserable lives behind them and join forces with people who pretend to care. That Charles Manson and his gang are somewhere in this desert right now. Did you know that?" he stopped his rant and looked at me.

"I'm sorry," I said. "I didn't know." And I started to cry.

"Oh, Roni, it's okay. I didn't mean to upset you. It's just that when I saw the horses milling around unfed, the dogs still locked up, and called for you and got no answer, I got real worried. We've been tracking those folks for a few days now. I was worried that they had found their way here. I'm sorry I scared you. But you really do need to be careful. They are bad, bad people. Now let's get some coffee going and I'll go feed the horses for you."

He helped me stand up and led me out to the couch and then went out to feed the horses. After he returned, he brewed up a pot of coffee for us. Then we talked some more about the dangers of me riding anywhere alone right now.

"At least until we catch them. Okay?" he asked.

"Okay," I answered. "But you'd better catch them quick! I've still got exploring to do!"

"What am I going to do with you? Your curiosity is going to get you in trouble!" he said

"I'm not worried," I told him. "I've got many Grandfathers looking after me. You said so yourself!"

"That I did, girl, that I did. Now, let me take a closer look at that ankle."

I held up my leg as he examined the leather strap wrapped around it sort of like an ace bandage.

"And you have no idea where this came from?" he asked.

"Nope."

"Have you been traveling between the worlds again? That is the only explanation for this type of wrap. It is of the old ways. It's even older than my Grandmother's mother's ways. You have been to see the Ancients haven't you?"

I just smiled slightly at him.

"Ah, I can see it in your eyes. You don't have to tell me. I can see. I've journeyed to them before. It's okay for me to know," he said as he stood to go. "Keep the strap on until it feels loose. Then your ankle will be better. Stay off of it as much as you can. I'll be back tomorrow. And lock the doors!"

The dogs raced back in as I watched him go throw extra hay into the corral so I didn't have to go out. He got in his truck and started down the dirt road as I counted myself very lucky to have him for my friend.

Maybe next time I will tell him of my dreams, I thought.

I settled back on the couch with my book and read for the rest of the day and into the evening.

I managed to hobble to the door, let the dogs out for a few minutes, whistled for them to come in, and stoked the fire one last time before going to bed.

No dreams entered the blackness; I slept soundly the whole night long.

Chapter Twenty-Four

Last Days Alone

Finally, it was the first of May, 1969. I had survived late fall, winter, and early spring alone.

As I got things ready for John to bring the rest of the horses up and return to regular operations, I was able to reflect on what my time alone had meant to me.

All of the many things that I'd experienced made me grow up and realize I could do much more for myself than I had ever thought possible. I could keep a cool head in an emergency. I could hold out hope of finding someone to love me. I could have a friendly relationship with Jim and not expect too much in return. (I had finally figured out he was indeed a free spirit.) I could stand up for myself to adult men. And, I could be in charge of the operations and have things run as smoothly as when John was here.

Over the winter I had gained the respect of several townsfolk as well as the Sheriff. They went from treating me as an outsider to making me one of their own. An adopted Olanchan! Life just didn't seem like it could get any better.

I exercised all the horses every day so they would be ready to work when John arrived. That meant riding from sun up to sun down. They were happy to be back to work. I would ride one and pony two alongside. We'd go out for a couple of hours, and then I would come back, switch and take out three more. It went like that for two solid weeks.

On the day before John was to arrive, I wanted to take one more ride to the cave. I knew it would be my last for a while. Soon, all the teenagers who came for the summer would be there, and once people started coming to the pack station there wouldn't be time for me to ride down across the highway. I didn't want to share that ride with anybody, and it was very hard to go anywhere alone once they all arrived.

I still had not told the Sheriff about the experience from that first visit. I felt I needed to keep that secret to myself. He knew that something had gone on though, because he had seen my stone and obsidian tools. He had seen my ankle wrapped in leather by the old woman. He had seen the changes in me as well. Without having to ask that wise man knew I had crossed into their world. I finally understood that he was a Medicine Man among his people. That is why he could read so much into things without me uttering a single word. It was so clear to me now.

Excitedly, I planned one more visit to the cave. I saddled Poppin' for this last ride across the highway. I threw out extra hay and locked up the dogs. They weren't going to be very happy.

It felt like it was going to be a very warm day, so I packed an extra canteen of water. Then I grabbed a few apples for Poppin', some snacks for me, and we headed off down the road.

After all the work I had been doing with the other horses, he seemed excited to be getting out without dragging them along. His walk was bouncy, his ears were alert, and he was very animated. I could tell it was going to be a good day. Warm, but good.

By the time we crossed the highway, it was more than just warm. It was hot! Unusually hot for this early in the spring. I thought about turning around and going back, but I reasoned to myself that it would be better to keep going and rest all day at the pond hidden in that cool canyon.

We continued our trek across the desert. By the time we reached the reservoir the heat was heavy on the land. There was little movement of wildlife and no chirping of birds or insects. We stopped to take a drink from the cool water and, as I looked back toward the pack station, I was struck by how bleached out everything looked. The heat took the color out of everything and caused ripples in the landscape.

Poppin' seemed to be handling the heat okay, so on we went.

Soon we were climbing that trail into the hills and, within a short time, we were on the shady side of the canyon. A few more bends in the trail, and we were at that lovely, little meadow. The grasses were slowly dying from lack of rain and the sudden onslaught of heated air, but there was still enough for Poppin' to forage on while I made my visit to the cave.

This time I took off all of Poppin's tack; bridle and saddle. I was betting I would be more careful this time and wouldn't need the saddle to pull me anywhere. Poppin' was only sweaty under his saddle. He had stayed in such great shape all winter because of our excursions. Most real, some imagined. Though to this day I think they were *all* real!

He trotted off to drink his fill from the pond. I sat down and ate my sandwich and he came back over to me snooping around my saddlebags for the apples he was sure were in there. He tried to pick my saddle bag up and I yelled at him. He dropped it and shook his head at me.

"Okay, okay, I'll get them out for you. Then, you can just go explore yourself. You can go as far as the hobbles will take you!" I told him as I got up to pull out the apples.

Poppin' watched me warily as I untied the leather hobbles from my saddle and put them around his front legs. He was immediately unhappy with me, and I laughed as he attempted to raise first one foot and then the other. He remembered what they were.

With a resigned snort, he gave me one last nasty look before leaning back on his hind feet and taking a little jump forward with both front feet at once. He repeated the action until he was happy with where he was, then started grazing.

"I'm sorry!" I told him, but he wouldn't even look at me! Boy, could he hold a grudge!

"Okay, I'm leaving now! Don't go running off!" He looked at me and yawned.

I walked over to the base of the hill where the cave was and scouted carefully this time for any snakes that might be sunbathing. As I made my way up the trail, I looked over and around rocks, determined that I would not be taken by surprise again.

The trail was a bit firmer this time. The loose rock must have washed away with the heavy rains the first of April. It was fast becoming baked hard from the heat.

While I climbed steadily up toward the cave, the sun grew hotter and hotter. I looked back down at Poppin' who was still munching away. The meadow was now shaded so I wasn't worried about him getting overheated.

When I reached the cave, I saw it had a nice new growth of sagebrush growing right in front of the entrance. The brush would soon conceal the opening from below. Maybe this cave would remain forever hidden after all. I stepped around the bush into a blast of coolness inside the cave. The bright noontime sun shed enough light into the cave for me to make out everything clearly.

Nothing had changed from my last visit. The dark rocks of a fire pit were still near the opening. The small pile of stone tools were still scattered near it. I walked over to one wall and reached up to touch a drawing. As I traced the etching with my finger, I remembered the experience from when I touched that other rock. Real or dream, the feeling was fresh in my mind. This time there was no charge of energy. Just the cold stone wall and her many images.

Slowly, almost reverently, I continued around the cave, examining each drawing. There were so many different images. I remembered the book I had read describing what scientists felt some of them meant. I touched each and every one of those images and finally reached the back of the cave where I saw some old furs and the sleeping area of the old woman from my last dream. I looked around and saw markings on the ground from several sleeping areas.

It was obvious after all the reading I had done that this cave was much, much older than the Paiute people.

Then I saw the basket I had made in my dream. My heart soared. It was true. I HAD traveled between the times. I sat down on the ancient woman's fur and tried to contemplate what it all meant.

Almost in a trance, I reached for the basket and once again the energy of the spirits overtook me. My head started spinning; the voices came again, louder and louder. I felt dizzy, almost nauseous. I lay down on the furs and as I was thinking of how musty they smelled I was taken once more to that ancient place…

☙

…The old woman is shaking me awake. I sit up on the furs and notice a bustle of activity.

"We have rested long enough. We have to get ready for the celebration," she says to me.

I blink trying to clear my head.

"What do we need to do?" I ask her.

She is busy putting things into baskets and wrapping the organ meats in wet leaves. She stands and says, "Come, it is time to go."

She leads me up a small hidden trail behind the cave that leads to the top of the hill. As we get closer, I see the fires burning, and hear the sounds of drums filling the air.

A small flicker of fear must have crossed my face, because she tells me, "You have no need to be afraid child. Tonight is a great celebration for our bounty. Red Wolf believes that YOU had a part in that good luck. So he will include you in our Ceremony. Don't be afraid and just look at me if you don't understand something."

The old woman places the meat she prepared on the stones below the fire to roast in the wet leaves. There are many other bundles as well. The aromas coming from them make my stomach rumble. I can't remember when I last ate.

The rest of the clan is already gathered. We are high on a hill looking out on a beautiful scene. The verdant valley below is teeming with life. There is a river flowing through rich vegetation. I see herds of deer and in the foothills there are several bighorn sheep. I can't believe this can be the same desert I came from.

The sun gives way to the moon rising in the east, and soon it is full and bright overhead. It is light as day on this mountaintop. The people are dancing to the drumbeats, and every man, woman, and child seem lost in the rapture of the pounding drums.

The old woman sits and pulls me beside her. Those who are not dancing are seated in a circle around those who are. It is a rather large circle.

Suddenly the drums stop. The woman squeezes my hand.

"It begins," she says.

All the dancers make their way to the outside of the circle and sit down.

The only one still standing is Red Wolf. He comes and stands in front of me. He reaches for my hand and pulls me up next to him. I look down at my teacher. She nods with a smile.

He holds out his hand. I don't understand.

"The knife," she says.

Understanding, I hand him his knife. He inspects it thoroughly, looks at me, and smiles. He motions for the basket with the blood and hearts to be brought forward. A young maiden steps forward carrying my basket, now tinged dark brown from the blood inside, and places it at my feet.

I don't know what I am supposed to do, and once again I look to my teacher.

"Pick up the largest heart and offer it to him," she whispers.

I reach inside the basket and feel for the largest heart. They are cool and slimy from the clotted blood and I resist the urge to pull my hand away. I lift the heart out, holding it with both hands, and slowly rise up facing him. I hold my arms up so the heart is right in front of him. I'm not sure what he will do. I try not to shake.

He then raises his arms and turns in both directions, motioning to the gathered clan. They start to cheer. He then gestures toward me and they cheer again. Then he leans over and takes a bite out of the heart. It is all I can do not to drop it because I am shaking so hard.

The clan quiets once more. He looks at me with his bloodstained chin, still chewing the raw meat, and he takes the heart from my hands. He is looking deep into my eyes and I see those familiar eyes again. Then he holds the heart up and offers it to me.

I wonder to myself what am I supposed to do? He raises it to my mouth and I see I am to do as he did. I lean in and take a bite as he steadies it. It is tough and hard to bite off. Once my piece is free and I am chewing the clan erupts in cheers.

He then starts moving around the circle offering each clan member a bite of the heart. The old woman whispers for me to pick up the basket and follow him. As the first one is consumed he asks for the second, then the third. There is exactly one bite for all members.

As we make our way around the circle, it becomes apparent that I am one of them. They smile at me and touch my arm as we pass. I am still covered in the lifeblood of the three deer. I would look hideous to anyone from my time. But these people make me feel beautiful. He makes me feel beautiful.

When we arrive back at where we started, Red Wolf leans down and offers a bite to my teacher. It is obvious he respects her very much. She takes a bite and takes the basket from me.

I start to sit back down, but he grabs my hand and leads me to the center of the circle once more. All is quiet but for the chirping of the crickets and the croaking of the toads. I can hear my heart pounding. He holds his knife aloft. Turning so all can see it. Then he takes my hand and turns the palm up. My teacher sees the fear in my eyes. She smiles at me and nods that all is okay. My heart calms a bit.

Red Wolf takes the knife tip, pierces the center of my palm, and draws the knife across it. He waits for the blood to flow. It hurts slightly, but he holds my hand tightly and I don't try to withdraw it. I sense it would be a sign of weakness. He looks into my eyes and smiles. Then he places the knife on his palm and does the same.

Once his blood is flowing, he grasps my hand tightly in his and squeezes them together. Still grasping my hand, he turns to the clan and says, "I present to you my sister from afar. She is clan now."

As he is finishes speaking, the drums start up again. All the people jump up and start dancing once more. Red Wolf leads me around, dancing and singing. I join in and it seems as natural as if I have been doing it all my life.

When the pink and orange colors of dawn start to take over the sky, the celebration begins to wind down. The fires have died and the People are wandering off to their beds. Red Wolf brings me back to my teacher. He then nods to me, smiles at the old woman, and walks away.

She and I walk down the trail to the cave.

"You are part of the clan now. You will always belong here in this world. Earth has given you a place to belong. You must always treat her with respect and know that everything you receive comes from her, whether you are with us or not."

"I will remember," I say as we reach the entrance to the cave.

Red Wolf is waiting for us. He takes my hand and examines it. He draws his finger down the cut. It doesn't hurt at all. Then he takes his knife from his waist and hands it to me. "This is for you to remember me. You will make someone very happy someday. You will be a good wife and clan member. You are forever my sister, and I am proud of that. I will always be here when you need me." He smiles once more, and walks away.

"Come child. It is time for sleep. You have a long journey tomorrow," she says wearily.

As we sit down on her furs, I noticed a beautiful, rolled-up deer hide and my now clean basket.

"You will take these things when you leave here. You will need them in your world. I, also, will be here when you are in need. Just call for the Grandfathers and we will be near. Now sleep, it has been a long day."

Exhausted, I lay down by my teacher and soon she is breathing rhythmically in deep sleep, and I am reliving the night's events in my head. I look at my hand and a feeling of peace comes over me. I feel so protected.

The sounds of children laughing wake me, and as I sit up I notice the old woman is gone from her bed. I look around for her and see her by the cook fire. She sees me sit up and motions for me to come.

The whole clan is waking from their rest after the all night celebration. The women nod and smile at me as I make my way from the rear of the cave to the front and stand near the fire. One of them offers me a warm drink in a gourd. The tea is bitter tasting, but warming to me.

"You slept restlessly last night," she states. "Were there dreams that kept you from your rest?"

Surprised at her uncanny ability to read my mind, I answer, "I'm not sure. I am just so overwhelmed by all that is happening to me in this place. I guess I just don't want it to end. I have never, ever felt such a sense of family before. It's all I have ever dreamed of, to have a real family like this. How can I thank you for teaching me these things?"

"I have already told you, by living your life respectful of the land. And always carry the knowledge of what you have learned in here," she says as she puts her hand over my heart.

I feel tears welling up in my eyes.

"I don't want to go back," I tell her.

"You must," she says.

"I know," I answer with tears welling up in my eyes as she leads me to the mouth of the cave. She hands me the bundle and says to keep it close.

Red Wolf is waiting for me. Once more he takes my hand in his. He squeezes it firmly and says, "Always remember! Safe Journey." Then he lets go and leads me to the trail down to the meadow.

I stop and turn around. The old woman smiles and walks into the cave.

❧

I turned around and saw Poppin' still in the meadow grazing. I looked down and saw my own worn Levis. Not the blood-smeared apron I had gone to sleep in. It seemed like time had stood still. Poppin' was as I had left him, but I felt I had been gone for more than twenty-four hours.

The horse merely glanced at me as I clambered down the hill. I hollered at him. He went back to eating.

"Oh, still upset are we?" I asked as I got near him. He ignored me while I took his hobbles off and we walked over to where the saddle was. I took out my canteen and drank long and hard. I was so thirsty. The day was still very warm.

I sat and realized I had a bundle tied around my waist. I looked inside and found the deerskin with the basket I had made. Also inside was an obsidian dart tip, very much like the one I had found near the grinding stone. But this one was shiny and new and perfect in every way. I slipped my leather pouch out from beneath my shirt and took out the old one. They were almost identical. So was Red Wolf the creator of both?

My mind was spinning so fast putting it all together. I *had* traveled back in time. I had proof of it right here with me. But did I need proof? Who would I tell? Why would I tell? And, who would believe me if I did tell? Only one person I could think of.

I got up and started putting Poppin's tack on him so we could start the long ride home. He was still pouting, but I knew he would perk up once we were back on the trail. I led him to the pond for a drink. As he drank, I bent down to wet my hair and almost jumped back when I noticed it was matted with dirt and blood.

My heart started to pound. I took a deep breath.

"Just breathe, girl, just breathe," I told myself.

Then, I dunked my whole head in the water and got it as clean as possible. It would feel good to have wet hair on what I knew would be a hot ride.

I stood, tightened the cinch, and secured my saddle bags. Then I tied my special bundle to the saddle and mounted up. Poppin' immediately became his old self, his irritation at me forgotten in his excitement at the prospect of going home.

As we headed away from the meadow, I turned around and looked up toward the cave. Nothing could be seen. I had the distinct feeling I would never be here again.

We walked along at a pretty good clip, and coming out of that small canyon by the reservoir I could tell it was late afternoon. The landscape still rippled and had no color. It was probably ninety-five degrees. Poppin' was antsy to get going, but I wouldn't let him do more than walk. It would be too easy for him to get overheated on a day like today.

The heat and steady clip clop of his hoof beats on the hard ground lulled me into an almost trance-like state as we moved past the shimmering water in the reservoir. In my mind I started hearing the stirrings of many voices, and became aware of a change in the landscape.

Almost miraculously, things were turning from dry and brown to lush and green. I slowly looked on both sides of me and I saw the beautiful, verdant valley teeming with life that I had seen before with the old woman.

The clan members arrived to wave at me as I slowly rode past them. The Ancients. The Martis People. All of them were smiling and yelling their goodbyes. I waved back and saw Red Wolf with my teacher. Once again, tears stung my eyes as I continued my ride. "Remember!" they said together. "Remember!"

A little farther up the road the landscape changed again. This time it was a bit dryer, yet still different and much lusher than present day. There were rivers, streams, and ponds, with trees lining them.

With a start, I saw the sweat lodge by the river just as it had been in my dream.

Then, I saw the People on both sides of me. The Paiute. They were smiling and cheering me home. I felt so much love from them. Running Bear was standing there so proud. Naked children were running beside us trying to pet Poppin'. So I stopped for a moment to let them. He enjoyed the attention so much; he must have felt he was in heaven. The old women of the tribe smiled at me and nodded. The young girl, who was my first contact with these people, came forward and gave me the rabbit skin we had worked on together. She smiled at me and I knew we would be friends forever.

Then I saw him.

The one I was hoping above all else to see. Little Bear.

I stopped and got off the horse as he approached. I was trembling as he embraced me. I started to cry. He stood back and wiped my tears away.

"Do not cry for me. I will be fine. And do not cry for you. Someone waits for you who will cherish you forever. He is a good man and you will have the family you hope for. I will be watching out for you. Remember what you have learned on this journey."

He reached up and removed the eagle feather from his ebony hair. "Keep this feather as a token of my affection for you and a sign I will always be with you." He tied the eagle feather in my hair, kissed my forehead, and turned me back around toward Poppin'.

I mounted up, took one last look at him through my tears, reluctantly turned away from him, and continued up the road to the pack station.

Next, I noticed the desert getting more like it was supposed to be. Dry and arid. I saw workers digging tunnels and ditches. The Aqueduct.

From my reading I knew that the Aqueduct was the deathblow to the Owens Valley as it took all the water away from the desert and sent it to Los Angeles. Dust clouds spun up from the ground and punctuated my thoughts about how desolate the area became after that and what it meant to the remaining Paiute on the reservations in the Owens Valley. These once peaceful people who farmed this land with natural crops could no longer get anything to grow with no water. Their way of life simply withered away and died.

The scene changed again as I neared the power line road. I saw it then in Sam Lewis' time.

His pack station was a flurry of activity. People loved to come here and pack with Sam. He had a great respect for the land as well. Sam and his wranglers were saddling horses. I could see his family helping him make provisions ready. As I rode by, Sam waved. His wife and children smiled at me. He said, "Remember what you learn here, girl. These lessons will stay with you your whole life. It was a pleasure ridin' with ya!"

The vision faded as I approached the pack station.

It was dusk and all the horses were at the rail whinnying at us as we got nearer to the corrals. Poppin' broke into a trot and started answering his buddies. He seemed anxious to tell them how much I abused him by hobbling him, and how humiliating that was.

"Tell them what you want, ya old nag, I was playing it safe!" I said to him.

Then I saw the Sheriff's truck. I noticed he had fed the horses. He was sitting in his truck taking a nap with his hat down over his face.

"Waiting for anyone special?" I said as we rode by.

His hat fell off as he woke with a start.

"Where the heck have you been? I've been here for hours!" he said as he got out of the truck, seeming more than a little irritated.

"I left early this morning for a long ride before all those people get here tomorrow. I just needed some time alone to sort stuff out," I said as I unsaddled Poppin'.

I could see him looking at the assortment of things I had collected on this trip. His eyes scanned the basket and bundle. Then, he reached to touch the eagle feather in my hair.

"You have been far, little sister," he said with a gleam in his eye. "Someday you must tell me about it."

"Someday I will!" I told him as we headed to the cabin where the dogs were going crazy. "Come in for coffee?"

"No, I'd better get back. I just wanted to make sure you were okay. Thank goodness John is coming back tomorrow. You have given me way too many gray hairs! Here is a special book of poems my grandmother liked. Thought you might like it too. I'll see you next week," he said as he got in his truck and drove off.

The dogs didn't want to be cooped up for a while so I decided to go to the grinding stone for a few quiet moments before dark. The sky was a dark pink and purple and it was so quiet and calm. A gentle breeze was blowing and it was still pleasant out after such a hot day.

We walked down along the rim of the canyon until we came to the rock. The dogs went scampering off looking for anything that moved.

As I approached the stone, I saw a shadow on it. I wasn't sure what it was until I got closer to it.

My heart stopped.

Laying on the rock was a beautiful eagle feather, and I knew it had been placed there for me. I picked it up and turned it over in my hand.

Then I took the one out of my hair and held them next to each other. One was ancient, one was young. Gifts for me from afar. Treasured keepsakes of my time there.

I clipped them both in my hair and returned to the cabin.

I gathered all of my treasures together on the table; the bone tools found on earlier "dream" trips; the basket faintly stained with blood, but beautiful just the same; the deerskin, soft and supple; the knife with the sharp black blade attached to a deer antler handle; the dart tips in my pouch both given and found; and, the most treasured things of all, the eagle feathers. It is said that it was on Eagle's wings the Grandfathers flew to the Spirit world. The feathers were sacred.

Yes, this last ride was important. It would set the tone for the remainder of my life. I was forever changed.

I went out and threw some more hay to the horses, called the dogs, returned to the cabin, and got things settled in for the night.

When the sun went down, the spring chill returned, so I built a nice fire to keep the cabin comfy during the night. I was tired from my long ride and turned in early with the new book from the Sheriff.

After I settled down into my cozy covers, I examined the book. It was called "Many Winters" by Nancy Wood.

I opened it and was mesmerized by the sketches of old Indian faces; wise, wrinkled, sad, faces. Beautiful faces. And the poems were hauntingly beautiful as well. I could not believe how the book spoke to my time with the Ancients and how the Sheriff could be so in tune with those spirits who were with me on that longest trail.

I quickly read through them all and reached the next to the last page where I came upon a poem called "Old Woman."

As I read it, I was reliving my time in the cave with the Old Woman, my teacher.

This poem must have been written about her!

My soul could have written it for her.

Old Woman,
It is you.
It was you even when
I did not see you except
In the eyes of my spirit.
Old Woman,
With you I saw
The dead log giving life
And the mid-winter stream
Rippling up for the spring and
The mountains a long way off
Telling us of beginnings.
Old Woman,
With you I knew
The peace of high places
And the meaning of a flower
Curled up against the wind
Or leaning toward the sun.
Old Woman, In small things always
There was you as if
All nature contained your thoughts and so
I learned from rocks and rainbows

Tall trees and butterflies.
Old Woman,
There was you in the eagle
Flying free and lonely
And in the eyes of a deer
I saw once in an untamed place.
Old Woman,
There is you in all good things
That awaken me and say
My life was richer, fuller
Because you lived with me.

Chapter Twenty-Five

Lazy Days on the Desert

I went back home a few times that spring after my time alone.

I was more and more out of tune with my mother. I no longer had any friends who weren't connected to the stables, so the pack station became my permanent home for the most part. Trips home became few and far between. As the seasons ran into one another I kept busy with packing and horses.

By the spring of 1971, the experiences of my "alone" days were fading. Sure I still had moments when the Ancients would whisper to me and I occasionally still found treasures left for me on the desert. But mainly I was just too busy with the hustle and bustle of John's booming business to have time to think about those things. For whatever reasons, my heart seemed to know my "learning" time was over.

Late that spring on a trip home, I found myself jumpy and ill at ease and longed for the quiet of the pack station. Being away from the constant, droning city noise had such a calming effect on the soul. The natural sounds of the desert were so much more pleasant than at home. Back in the city, the honking horns, blaring sirens, and squealing brakes drowned out the wind whispering to me through the trees, the songs of the robins and, on most nights, the chirping crickets. And of course, I longed for the voices of my spirit friends that stood no chance at all of being heard in the city. It seemed my whole being longed for the peace and solitude that the pack station brought me.

Then I met a new group of kids at the stable and I seemed to "fit in" with them perfectly. The newcomers couldn't wait to go to the pack station and see what it was all about. And of course, once they experienced it there was no keeping them away. Sorta like me when I first went. If your heart and soul were open to what the desert had to tell you, you were hooked forever.

The summer of 1971 was a turning point in many of our young lives.

Jim and I had settled into a special platonic relationship as he went off to college. He would always be important in my journey to learn about myself.

There was a group of us who were at the pack station pretty much all summer long, and the majority of the time we were without adult supervision. After all, I was nineteen and had already lived there alone for many months at a time over the course of three years, and my buddy, Jerry, was twenty-three. How much supervision did we need? We were adults and in charge of teenagers and horses. Life was as good as it could be.

Hippie hair and hippie clothes were still in and Jerry had the hippie bus! Thankfully, it wasn't painted in psychedelic colors.

We all lived the "hippie" way of life. We took such joy in celebrating nature, love, and togetherness. We were high on life and all it had in store. We were free from the constraints of city life, and could ride a horse across the desert pretending it was two hundred years ago. There was no better feeling in the whole world.

The core of our group that summer consisted of: Tracy, Clark, Katie, Pam, Cary, Cheryl, Julie, Emily, Sandy, Jerry, and his cousins, Jim, Terri, Sheryl, and Mark. Not all of those people were always there at the same time, but I was almost always there to ride herd on them.

Occasionally, Mrs. S. (Tracy's and Clark's mom) would appear and have the kitchen smelling like Grandma's house with all of her home cooking. Whenever she was there, she was in front of that ancient stove humming and singing as if she hadn't a care in the world. We were in heaven eating her cooking after subsisting mainly on chili, mac and cheese, and hot dogs. "I think I'm going to adopt you!" I told her munching on one of her yummy shortbread cookies. When not cooking or reading books, she was directing games. She was always looking for someone to challenge to a match at whatever game she happened to have with her at the time.

Another form of entertainment we had were the water trough baths during the heat of those summer days. The old bathtub trough always stayed cool with the piped water from the stream up the canyon. Most of those baths were voluntary. But there was one person in the group who was forever getting dumped in the trough for his smart mouth and silly antics. Clark never seemed to know when to shut up and would keep it up until the person he was antagonizing had had enough. Then, you would see Clark being drug, carried, or herded to the trough. It seemed he spent half the summer submerged in it.

On one occasion it was near dusk, and there was a cool breeze blowing down from the mountain. He had just gotten dunked for the umpteenth time and was shivering very violently when he got out. All of us took pity on him and got the hot shower going for him. It was an outside shower, enclosed with a tarp wrapped around a few posts and open on the top and bottom. Since he seemed to always be in the doghouse, he didn't really trust any of us to leave him alone, but we all promised that we wouldn't do anything to him and he could strip off his wet clothes and get warmed up. Just when he got all of his clothes off and was getting rid of his goose bumps in the shower, along came Tracy, his sister, with a bucket of ice cold water from the trough. We all pleaded with her, telling her how we promised him we would be good. She got the biggest smile on her face and said, "Well, I didn't!" and poured the bucket out over the top of the open shower stall. The ear-splitting cries that came from that poor cold boy echoed across the desert and back again!

There has been a special spot in my heart for Clark ever since that day. He grew up that summer in ways known only to him and one other. And no, he didn't stop pestering people, and yes, he kept right on getting dunked.

Almost all of us "kids" smoked cigarettes in those days.

One particularly hot day we had run out of cigarettes and were down to smoking butts. We were literally foraging around on the ground looking for butts. We had scraped together just enough money to be able to buy one pack.

The next hour was spent discussing what kind should be purchased, Marlboro or Kool. Half of us smoked one kind and half the other. Marlboro won out because that was the brand that I smoked. Jerry and Tracy collected our sad supply of coins and headed off to town to buy a pack.

It was one of those hundred-degree days and I am not sure whose idea it was to get naked, but that is exactly what we did.

"Come on, let's do it," I agreed. "Let's all be naked when Jerry and Tracy get back from town, just to see the look on their faces." Sometimes you just had to improvise to avoid boredom.

It was almost an hour later when we heard the VW bus straining up the road. We were giggling so hard we were afraid they would know something was up. But as they pulled alongside the cabin we all quieted down and were gathered at the table playing cards, albeit sans clothing. When they walked through the door, their mouths dropped open as they looked around at all of us acting perfectly normal as if nothing was amiss, as if we were always buck naked in the afternoon. They looked at us, and then looked at each other asking, without words, if they were really seeing what they thought they were seeing.

About that time, we looked out the window past them to see Jerry's VW rolling backwards. We yelled that the bus was leaving and they both ran out to stop it. We started laughing so hard we were crying. The look on their faces coupled with the panic of the VW rolling away was priceless. Once they had it stopped and the brake properly set, they asked each other out loud if we were all really naked inside. After agreeing it was true, they came through the door and ripped off all their clothes and joined us.

We all laughed and played cards for hours. Our small group spent the rest of the afternoon in our birthday suits, running outside with a certain unfettered freedom, watching out of the corner of our eyes for any signs of visitors driving up the road who probably wouldn't quite understand.

I remember standing naked in the moonlight at the grinding stone that evening and being taken back in time by the spirits hovering around that canyon. With the billions of stars overhead and the vast open nothingness of the desert, I was living a thousand years ago. A magical, mystical place with every living thing on Earth living in harmony with the land.

I sensed that my time in the desert was short. I couldn't put my finger on *why* I felt that way. Maybe it was a message from the Spirits themselves, and at that moment I think I knew there would never be another ride to the cave. I was saddened.

A kaleidoscope of images began to fill my mind as I stared off into the heavens. The people I saw were all going about their routines and were not aware of my prying eyes. There were naked children playing under the watchful eyes of their mothers as they gathered plants and herbs and headed for the grinding stone on the edge of the canyon. There were the men and young boys sitting outside of thatched huts chipping away at the arrows and points they were making, with much laughter and singing. Soon, adolescent boys returned with rabbits that had been killed for this day's meal. The young girl from my dream took them to skin. There was the old woman, my teacher, leaning over and guiding the hands of a young maiden. All was in harmony, as it had been for the millennia. Peaceful, living off the land, only taking what was necessary for survival. I was living my dreams all over again.

This peaceful canyon and desert that I loved so much had been home to such a special people for thousands of years. My dreams had taught me so much about them. As the vision faded and the stars once again twinkled brightly, I sat down alone under the now moonless sky.

"I want you to know that I vow that I will try to live my life to make you proud," I said out loud. "I want you to know I have listened and learned those things you thought were important to impart to me."

The stars were then so numerous that I couldn't find an empty space in the sky. I felt very, very small and insignificant. My presence in this place didn't really matter.

But theirs had.

Chapter Twenty-Six

Love Comes Calling

The summers at the pack station were always the best, mainly because there wasn't a lot of work. On those long, hot, lazy days after chores were done, we usually had nothing to do but explore the desert and mountains around us. Not many teenagers had the taste of freedom we enjoyed and would never have known in the city. On most occasions, there was no adult around.

The summer I was nineteen, I spent the spring and summer as the chief wrangler and "boss lady." John had given me a free rein to run the place when he was in the city. Of course, we all pretty much ran it when he was at the pack station too. He liked it that way!

As I said earlier, that was the year the "new" people joined our group at the stables. People who made me feel like part of a family for the first time. As if I had known them my whole life.

Jimmy M's kids started coming around to ride and hang out with their friends and soon there was a whole parcel full of new young blood infusing itself into the old, tired, musty cobwebs of the old barn. Life at the stable was starting to be exciting again.

His oldest daughter, Terri, had already leased a gorgeous Appaloosa named "Moneta." She was a beautiful mare and of course I loved her very much just because she was spotted!

His second daughter, Sheryl, was a little imp in glasses who fell in love with a great big Tennessee Walker mare we had named "Calamity."

"Watching that little spec of a girl crawl all over the back of the big horse is a marvel to behold," I told John on one of the occasions when he was there. "She will stretch out lengthwise on her side, perched atop that big ol' horse. The two of them have something really special!"

His son Mark, the youngest, took a liking to my little horse "Sparol." I was so wrapped up in my life at the pack station with Poppin' and Brownie that little ol' Sparol had just sort of fallen into being one of the stable string horses. He didn't have anyone using him and I was glad that Mark took a liking to him. He deserved to be loved by someone and I felt guilty about riding him anymore. So he became Mark's horse.

Rounding out Jimmy's "gang" were his cousins, Johnny and Jerry. Johnny was going through a divorce and took refuge at his cousin's house, while Jerry had just gotten out of the Navy where he was on a sub in Vietnam, and needed a place to crash.

Jerry was your typical (at that time) long-haired hippie dude wearing tie-dyed shirts and driving a Volkswagen bus. He was (and still is) one of the most easygoing, huggable people I have ever met. He was always there to help with anything that needed to be done at the stable. John grew to depend on him and me to make sure horses were fed and hay was bought. He became a great friend of mine. He was just plain old fun, could make anyone laugh, and was always willing to pull a person out of their funk and put a smile on their face.

Johnny wasn't seen much around the stable or even Jimmy's house, because he always seemed to be at work, but the rest of them became part of the stable family. We would ride horses all day and then go jump into Jim's pool to rinse off all that grit and dirt from the stable.

Along with the new energy this family brought to us came their neighbors. There was Mrs. S, soon to be the matriarch of our group. As I mentioned before, she could do amazing things in the kitchen. It seemed she was always in there whipping up "vittles" for all her kids, humming all the while she was doing it. She was a woman of amazing strength and character, and became an important part of those last two years at the pack station. She was always there with a Band Aid, a book, or a game. Whatever was needed would magically appear when Mrs. S. was around.

Her daughter was Tracy. She was a fun, exuberant, bespectacled blonde with her own horse named Cindy. She fit right in and became one of my favorite cohorts. Her younger brother, Clark, was the gangly, smart aleck kid who constantly dug his own grave every time he opened his mouth, and begged for another bath in the trough.

Tagging along with Clark came his best friends Cary and "Bear."

"Bear" was a big strong kid who could heave bales of hay like no one I had ever met before. And Cary was the handsomest teenage boy I had ever laid eyes on. His eyes could set a girl to swooning with barely a glance.

Cary and Clark soon became my little slaves. They were about fifteen and would follow me around with their big puppy-dog eyes and fall all over themselves trying to do things for me. They often would start fighting trying to be "the one" who did the chore. They were totally in "lust" with me, the older woman. I had never had someone "worship" me before, so I ate it up. I never had to saddle my own horse or get my own tack if they were on scene.

The spring of 1971 found us always congregating up at Jimmy's house in the evenings. The main reason? A POOL!

Johnny and Jim would come home from work and have a scotch together, but I would stay out by the pool with Jerry and the kids. Jerry was so entertaining and life was just so much fun now with this new group of people. Everything that revolved around the stables now included these two families and their friends. I think they all thought that I would hook up with Jerry since it seemed that we were always together.

But my eye had been drawn to that quiet guy, his older brother. He stayed back out of the fray when we were all playing around the pool. I would try flirting with him, but wouldn't get much of a response. A definite deflation of the growing confidence I had gained as a vixen with teenage boys lusting after her. I really didn't think he was interested in me. He had a four-year-old daughter, Kim, and being newly divorced most likely wasn't looking for a relationship so soon. I found myself spending more and more time at that house so I could see him, even though he virtually ignored me most of the time. Or so I thought.

One Sunday afternoon that spring, I was at the house with the whole gang, probably flirting horribly with Cary and Clark, when Johnny came out to the den where we always lounged about when not swimming. He stood in front of me and said, "So do you want to take a ride with me to take Kim home?"

I gulped, as I looked around at all the big smiley faces in the room, and said, "Love to."

I floated out the front door, got into his gold, 1965 fastback Mustang with him and his little girl, and drove off to Heaven.

I fell in love with him not long after. We were together just about every second he was home. He worked forty-five minutes away and had to get up early to beat L.A.'s infamous rush hour traffic. But that didn't stop us from lying on Jimmy's front room floor making out while listening to the Rolling Stones on Jerry's stereo with the blinking speaker lights until the wee hours of the morning.

We were such opposites. I was loud and outspoken; he was quiet and kept his thoughts to himself. I wore Levis, t-shirts, and boots; he was used to girls who dressed up and wore makeup. I was a tomboy and he liked more feminine-acting girls. As we got to know each other, we were so attracted to each other that soon those differences meant nothing. Plus, I had long fingernails that gave him goose bumps when I scratched his back. Simply said, that was all it took!

As spring turned to summer, my life at the pack station returned. That summer, though, I was in love and the pack station certainly put a crimp in MY newfound love life.

One Friday night on the desert, we were all getting ready to call it a night. We had a group to pack in early the next morning.

We'd been telling many ghost stories and holding séances (a favorite thing to do). As we were walking down from the "tin shed," we spotted a pair of headlights coming up the road. There was much speculation over who it could be. Some thought it was John, others thought the Sheriff.

It usually took seven or eight minutes for cars to get up the road. But this one seemed to be flying. We couldn't tell until that car pulled up in front of the cabin. It was Johnny in Jim's little Triumph TR6.

We were all standing there outside the cabin as the car came screeching to a halt in a cloud of dust, and he jumped out, flew around the car, grabbed me, and kissed me like I had never been kissed.

My man had come to see me. I was in heaven being kissed by the first man to really truly love me. All the bystanders were snickering and laughing at us, but I was oblivious to them all. Cary and Clark nicknamed us Snickers and Snookums after that evening!

"What are you doing here?" I asked him.

"I got home from work, had a beer with Jim, and suddenly I just knew I had to be here, so I stood up, told Jim, 'I've gotta go!'"

Jim was taken by surprise. "Where?"

"Pack Station," Johnny told him. "He just tossed me the keys to the TR and I drove up to spend the weekend with you."

And that's how it was the rest of the summer. If he could, he would drive up almost every weekend, sometimes even bringing Kim along.

On one such visit I put Kim up on Flash, the calmest, easiest horse of the string. She and Flash were just moseying around behind Sandy. I had been giving Kim lessons and she was getting comfortable on those big horses. She was the youngest child I had ever taught. Johnny and I were in the cabin relaxing and watching her.

All of a sudden something spooked Flash, and he took off across the desert below the corrals. We could see Kim slide off of his side and then drop to the ground.

"Oh crap!" yelled Johnny. He jumped up and sprinted out of the cabin barefoot, leaping over sagebrush and rocks to "save" his little girl. She was uninjured, but scared. He came back with her in his arms, sat down, and looked at his bloodied feet and said, "Next time I think I'll put my boots on first!"

There were no phones, so I never knew if he was coming or not. But most of the time he did, and that summer was simply the best one I had ever spent at the pack station. We would ride together all over the desert and high country. I showed him all of my favorite spots. I showed him my quiet places and even some of my Spiritual places. But I never took him across the highway. That would remain my secret place forever.

I was so in love that I rarely thought about the dreams I had before I met him. It was HIS image that now filled my head at night. He was the first man who seemed to sincerely care about my feelings. He respected me. It felt different with him than with any other boy/man I had ever been with.

Maybe Little Bear was right. Maybe there finally WAS someone who would love and cherish me forever.

After that summer passed, the true "summer of love" for me, I went on several hunting trips for John. But it just wasn't the same for me anymore. At the pack station, I felt empty if Johnny wasn't there. I could now tolerate the city if I was with him, and I always had my horses to escape on when I felt closed in.

My life was changing, shifting, maturing. I loved him so. I now had focus, and saw a future that had meaning. It was so different from all those years ago when I had no dreams. Those days when I was a scared, abused girl who wasn't worth anything to anybody. Until John took me under his care and changed the course of my life.

Johnny proposed to me that fall.

One night while we were lying on the floor in Jim's front room listening to the Stones, he was quieter than normal.

"What's wrong?" I asked him. He seemed preoccupied and nervous. I didn't know what to think. I was afraid there was something seriously wrong.

Finally he blurted out "So, do you think you could make a home for us?"

I laughed and said, "What do you mean?"

He hesitated then answered, "You know, take care of Kim and me?"

"Are you asking me to marry you, Johnny McFadden?"

"Yes, I guess that's what I am doing. Will you?" he said in his usual quiet voice.

"Well, seeing as how I haven't had many other offers, I guess maybe I should!" I kidded him. "I love you John McFadden! And I love your daughter. I'll do my best to make a home for you both!"

That November, Jimmy's gang all piled into Jim's station wagon and headed to Albuquerque for a family vacation. I was helping John close the pack station for the season when that station wagon came flying up that dirt road and they kidnapped me and took me with them. We had four adults and three teens in a cramped station wagon.

We stopped and saw the Grand Canyon and had a blast, then on to Albuquerque. A real family vacation! This was a new experience for me.

In Albuquerque we decided we wanted to get married in January. Only six weeks away. He wanted to get married on New Year's Day so he would always remember his anniversary.

I said to him, "Johnny, do you have any idea what goes on in Pasadena on New Year's Day? There's this little thing called the Rose Parade that pretty much closes off the whole town. No one would be able to get here, much less want to miss football just for our wedding."

"Oh, I guess you're right. Okay then, the next Saturday, the eighth. Is that okay? That way it will always be one week after New Year's," he replied.

"Okay with me. Let's call Mom and tell her she has a rush wedding to plan." I started to giggle.

"What?" he asked.

"She'll think I'm pregnant! This could be fun!"

My Mom loved Johnny. After bringing home so many dreadful guys, finally she was happy with my choice. She was so happy that she wanted to do something special. She gave Johnny the diamond from her engagement ring from my dad, whom I had never known, and he had it set in a ring for me.

We got married that January 8th, 1972, in front of friends and family and all our cohorts from the stables! The minister who had known me from childhood actually looked to see if I had my boots on under that long dress! My Uncle Dick gave me away and my new life began.

We honeymooned in New Mexico and lived for the first three months of our marriage at Jimmy's house. I soon became "mom" to

Terri, Sheryl, and Mark, a position not without its difficulties, but we all survived it.

During those first months, we moved the horses to a new stable at the top of Fair Oaks Avenue in Altadena. There was a little tiny house right next to the barn and that became our first home! It was my castle. It was also a popular hangout place for all the stable kids. I continued to work for John, feeding, cleaning, and riding.

We got the contract for supplying horses to one of the Girl Scout camps that spring. We went to the auction every Friday and bought a truckload of horses and brought them to the stable. I spent the next week riding them to see if they were suitable for kids. Some of them were really, really rank. I'm lucky I wasn't killed by some of those wigged out horses, which had obviously been drugged at the auction.

And there was still the Pack Station. We went every couple of weeks. I couldn't stay there anymore without Johnny. It just wasn't the same for me. He had a job and had to work, so our trips became fewer and fewer.

I went on several hunting trips that fall, though, including that infamous twenty-first birthday bash with Vic. The strangest thing happened on that trip. When we arrived at the pack station late that night, for some reason, instead of going into the cabin and sleeping, we all slept in the trucks. About three in the morning a loud roaring noise woke us up. All of us sat up in the back of the truck to see the cabin completely engulfed in flames. Just like that, it burned to the ground in minutes.

We were so confused by what happened. We counted heads and couldn't find Jim Slaughter. After several frantic moments, he came out from under the big rig. We were all present and accounted for. None of us had been inside that cabin. Since it hadn't been used in a couple of weeks, what had started that fire? We will never know.

In reality it was the beginning of the end for John and the pack station. The Forest Service had revoked all the leases and was making plans to turn that whole National Forest area back into wilderness. I felt so bad for John. His whole way of life in those mountains was coming to an end. John, the man who turned my life around. The man who meant everything to me.

Unbeknownst to us, the Forest Service was planning on burning down all of the cabins up in the high country. There would no longer be shelter for hikers, campers, or riders to take refuge in if bad weather stranded them. Gone forever would be all of the history engraved on those cabin walls. There were names and dates of hundreds of visitors spanning over seventy-five years. Grand, sturdy log cabins built by Sam Lewis and others in that wild country, gone. They didn't care. I couldn't imagine it.

There was one more trip after that to take in a last group of hunters and pack up all of our belongings. With an immense sense of sadness, I relished every moment of what I was sure was my very last pack trip. If only I had known then that they were going to burn all the cabins down, I would have taken many more pictures, but on that last trip, I didn't even have my camera with me. So I had to make sure the images were imprinted forever in my mind.

I rode to all of my favorite places. I spent time in the high cabin at Deer Mountain thinking about all of my secret times there with Jim and later with my husband.

I rode all of the secret trails where I had heard spirits sing to me. Their voices still sang to me. They were happy for me, wished me well, and whispered that my life now had meaning and not to be sad about leaving this place. It would always be deep inside my heart. This way of life I cherished would fade from my memories, but never completely be extinguished.

I rode back to the cabin that last evening, unsure of what the future held, but knowing it would be wonderful. I had been told it would be by all of my friends in the spirit world. They had all been part of my growth during those seven years.

The Ancients, the Sierra Lady Pack Station, and a man named John Slaughter.

Epilogue

After the pack station closed down, my time with John became less and less. Babies started coming and life changed so much.

I got rid of all but two of my horses. Life with children took over and there just wasn't the time to devote to them. Brownie and Poppin' would remain with me until they died of old age. They were the two best horses that ever lived, and are buried next to each other on our property.

Johnny and I raised our four children together. We had Kim often as well. And all of that love and success with our children I owe, in part, to my time at the pack station. I went from being an outcast, confused young girl heading down a dangerous road to being a confident, self-assured leader who was in tune with Mother Earth, hoping to instill some of the ancient's wisdom into her life and the lives of her children.

This reunion was meant to show my children and grandchildren how I got from A to Z, so to speak. How I became the person they know. I'm not sure I have succeeded in sharing my deepest thoughts and feelings.

As I finish my story I look around at the fire-lit faces. The boys look at me and grin.

"That was good Gramma. Do you have any more stories to tell? You made those up right?" asks Terry.

"Of course she did." replies Kenny. I look around at the adult faces and see amusement in their eyes.

"Yeah, Gramma, those weren't REAL stories were they?" says Kacee as she gets up and brushes off her backside.

"Okay everyone, enough campfire stories, off to bed," my oldest daughter says as she heads for her tent. "Maybe Grandma will make up some others to tell tomorrow night."

I stare after her, wishing that she could sense the beings here in this place. I just sigh, content that I can remember how I felt all those years ago, living in this place with them.

As the rest get up to leave, I notice Lindsey still sitting on her rock. She is staring at me with a twinkling look in her eye. It is a look that says she understands, and I can tell that she wants to know more.

I look at her and smile.

She slowly looks to the stars, then back at me with wonder.

And then, suddenly, my soul leaps for joy as I realize that she can feel them too!

"If you talk to the animals they will talk with you and you will know each other. If you do not talk to them you will not know them and what you do not know, you will fear. What one fears, one destroys."

~Chief Dan George~

Addendum

June 2015

Sadly, John's wife of over sixty years, Normalee, passed away in 2007. It was his wish to take her ashes to the pack station.

Once again we gathered at the place we loved to support John and say goodbye to Normalee. Several people who had not been able to come to the previous gatherings came to this one, including John and Normalee's daughter, Sharon.

We laughed and cried as more stories of the past were shared. Jim and I shared with each other some of the 'spiritual' experiences we had each had in the ensuing years after our years together in the high country and desert. We will always be connected to each other because of those times.

In the years after that gathering in 2007, I was busy working and writing and time just seemed to fly by. John and I would talk on the phone occasionally, and he would always ask "When ya comin' down?"

"Soon," would always be my answer.

Before I knew it 2014 was here and John's ninety-sixth birthday was approaching.

He called me and asked if I was coming to his party? I thought, geez ninety-six… how could I *not* go?

Altadena is ten hours from my home. This was going to be a whirlwind weekend trip!

I arraigned with his caretaker to keep it a surprise. I didn't want to disappoint him if plans fell through.

June 9, 2014, his birthday, he was sitting on his little scooter (his iron horse) in his front yard waiting for a friend to show up. We drove up and I got out of the car. It took him a second to realize it was me. Then he said in classic John Slaughter tone, "Well it's about damned time you got here!"

We hugged and reminisced for a couple of hours. We took pictures of us with the book, which he carries everywhere! He made me promise that when he passed, I would take his ashes to the pack station. I told him I would.

Too soon it was time to get back on the road for the ten hour trip home. I hugged him so hard trying to hold back my tears. I knew in my heart that it would be that last time I saw John, the man who took a chance on this confused young girl and turned my life around.

John S. Slaughter passed away peacefully in his sleep November 23, 2014 at the age of ninety-six years and five months. I'm told that all he talked about those last few months were my visit and "his" book.

I will keep my promise and take him as soon as I can to his beloved desert where the spirits there will welcome him home.

Photos

Roni with her first horse Sparol

John Slaughter on his mustang Zorro

Sam Lewis Pack Station, 1970

Cabin on the desert across from corrals

Corrals on the desert

Deer Point—the "quarter way" mark—in the center of the photo

Trailhead-Haiwee Canyon

Looking back down the steep, narrow trail

Packing in a group of kids

John "tailing" a horse on the climb to the summit

John's horse haulin' Big Rig

Cabin on the desert 1930s

Sam Lewis pack string making their way up the switchbacks

Sam Lewis and one of his pack horses c. 1930

Sam Lewis bringing his horses in from grazing the desert

Sam Lewis, his wife Olive, and their children

Sam Lewis crossing the south fork of the Kern River

Sam Lewis packing a horse

Meadow at Deer Mountain where horses went missing

Roni's beloved Hellzapoppin'

Roni's horse Brownie

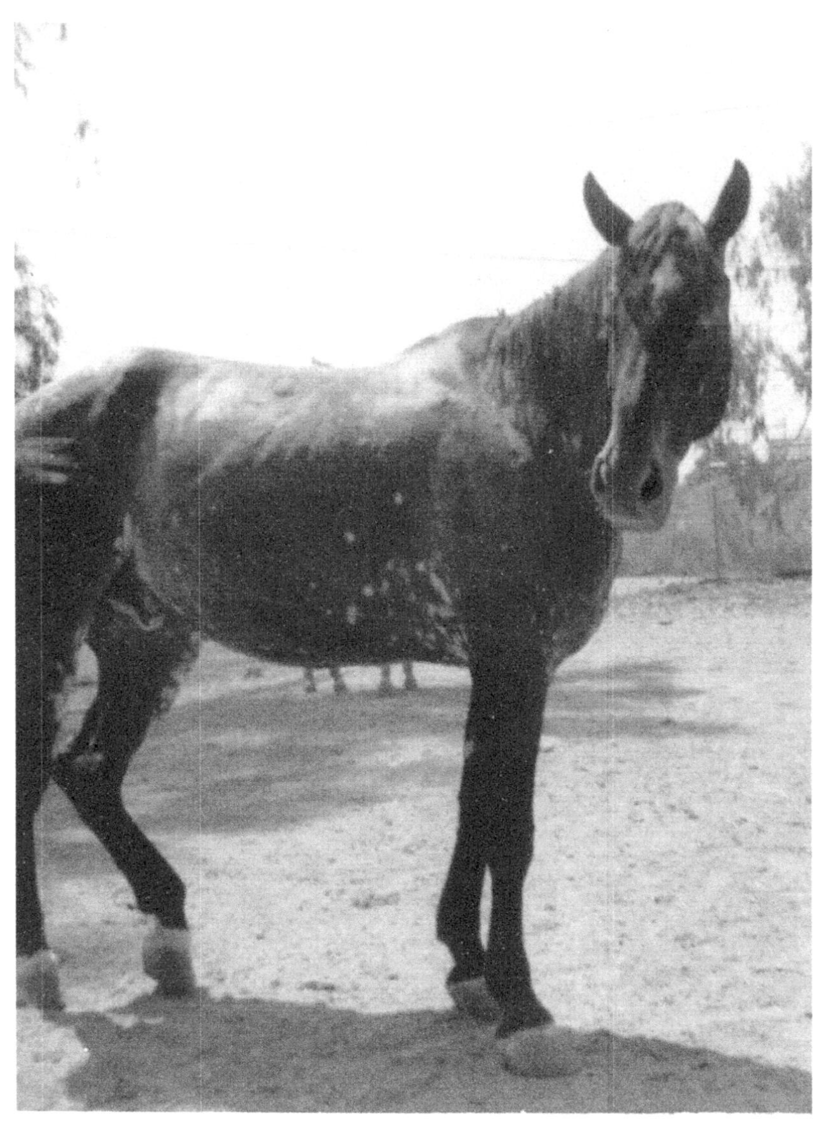

Big Daddy 1970

Little Oats – Every mountain lion's friend

Mustang stallion Jade

Roni riding herd on a group of kids

Main cabin at Dutch John Flats, 1968

Old stove inside the high cabin at Deer Mountain

Smaller cabin at Dutch John after a bear ripped off the door

Frosty going after rats

Roni and Hellzapoppin' in the high country

Roni's pard, Tonette – A better deer hunter than most men

Vic doing dishes

Roni's 21st birthday cake packed in as a surprise from Vic

Frosty sitting in the road always waiting for who?

Laddie

Roni on Jade's son Chamois with Hobi and Frosty

The small cabin after we repaired the door

Our best pack horse Sandpiper

Four year old Kim on Flash right before he took off with her

Roni on Hellzapoppin' out scouting for deer

Hellzapoppin' and friends resting in corral on the desert

Hunters getting ready at the hitching rail

Hellzapoppin' in the pasture behind the cabins at Dutch John Flat

The very steep trail up from Deer Point

A small trailside grinding stone at Deer Point

The breathtaking view at the summit looking down at Haiwee Reservoir

The desert grinding stone looking north toward Olancha

My eagle feathers on the stone

The massive grinding stone on the desert – the place of Roni's spiritual awakening

Roni on Hellzapoppin' on the desert

Johnny on Hellzapoppin' with Laddie

The pack station with everything gone except our campers in 2003

All that remains as a sentinel to the past

John Slaughter in 2004

John Slaughter June 9, 2014

Permissions

"The Legend of the Deer Star" by Mary Austin, used by permission from Edward Gaynor, Small Special Collections Library, University of Virginia

"Origin of the Sweat Lodge ~ A Nez Pierce Story" from Good Medicine Book, by Adolf Hungry Wolf. Used by permission.

"Old Woman" by Nancy Wood, copyrighted by Nancy Wood, from Many Winters, Doubleday and Co. All rights reserved. Used by permission.

Photos of Sam Lewis and his family courtesy of his daughter, Helen Coolidge.

Acknowledgments

The idea for this book began in 2003 when I organized a reunion at the Pack Station with John Slaughter and about thirty other people who had not been together in over forty years. From the stories told around the campfire that weekend memories came flooding back to me. As the stories rose from the ashes, I started writing them down. A sort of journal, if you will, to remind me of the special things that had happened to me in that incredible place. As we were gathered around the fire on our last night, someone mentioned that there should be a book about this special place. All eyes turned to me. Why? I'm not a writer! But the seed was planted that night.

I started researching the pack station, looking for anyone who may have known Sam Lewis and the history of the place. I wanted to write the story of the place itself. The time of the Native Americans, then Sam, and finally us. I found most of the Paiute information that is in the book online. The search for Sam Lewis was a bit more difficult, but I was led to a woman in Lone Pine who knew his daughter Helen. It turns out Helen lives just twenty minutes away from me in Potter Valley, CA. How coincidental is that? I met with Helen and received Sam's "diary," as well as many, many pictures of him and his family at the Pack Station as well as his "High Lonesome Ranch" in the 1920s and 1930s. I am so grateful to Helen and Merle Coolidge for sharing her father with me.

We met Sam's granddaughter, Cherie, the very next year when we had a second reunion at the pack station. She drives to Lone Pine every Memorial Day to put flowers on Sam's and Olive's graves. As she was driving back home, she noticed the glint of many vehicles at the base of the canyon where the pack station once stood. So she turned up that three-mile-long dirt road and introduced herself. We were shocked and so surprised. We visited for several hours and it was she who told us where the "High Lonesome" was as well as the petroglyph rock we had heard so much about.

After she left, several of us loaded up and headed for the "High Lonesome." The same strong pull to the past grabbed us as we walked around the deserted old ranch. We came away from there with a newfound appreciation for the man who had built the place that we loved so much. We felt we had a personal relationship with the man who had built the cabins we spent so much time in. And our connection to the spirits of that desert was cemented after that visit.

As I tried to write the story about the PLACE, my thoughts kept turning back to John and the story of how he saved me. Soon, all those journal pages came to life as the stories of MY time there came to the forefront. My dreams were full of my own experiences during the seven years I spent there. I realized that each one of us has our own story of the pack station and those years. It was clear to me that I needed to tell mine.

In the eight years it has taken to write this book, it has gone through many, many changes, including the title. I have come close to giving up so many times, only to be goaded on by good friends. As I presented draft after draft of the manuscript that, for a long time, was called "Sierra Lady," I was sure I would never see some of those friends again. But they all "seemed" to like it and I coveted their suggestions and critiques.

First, I want to thank the co-author of my first book, "Josephine~A Tale of Hope and Happy Endings," Gail "Bunny" McLeod. We met via email through a sad circumstance and became fast friends. I could not have written this without her help in developing a little dialog for my characters. Even though she is 3000 miles away, she was always there with an idea or a comment. (Sadly, Bunny passed away in March 2013.)

Please check out her other books: "Who Says Kids Can't Fight Global Warming," written with Patrick Harrison, "Christmas in Distress," written with A. L. Niflhaim, and a science fiction book, "Probed by Aliens," written with Van Strickland. She has also written over seventy books for a Korean publishing company, GlenndomanKorea, and is one of the most popular children's authors in Korea.

Very special thanks to my dear friend Sterling Wright for his guidance in Native American lore. I can't thank him enough for allowing me to participate in a **real** Sweat Lodge Ceremony. It is something I will never, ever forget. I hope my telling of it provides some insight into how special and spiritual it is for the participants.

My heartfelt thanks go to my dearest friends in the "Willits Birthday Club and Terrorists Society," of which I am one of the founding members. I am also the youngest! Those precious ladies have seen this manuscript through from the beginning and I promised I would name them here. Thank you, Bev Roach, Polly McKibben, Wilma Sweazey, JoMarie Tripp, Clare Curry, Nancy Trumble, Dotty Newell, Kitty Owens, Kathy Neff, Charlotte Butler, Bettye Bays and, last but not least, Diane Collins who did the final proof editing for me. She gets a gold star! I could not have done this without the love, laughs, and support of all of you! Come on February!

I also want to thank my online "book club" friends. All of you girls on the "Friends of Gladys" Yahoo list have been so helpful to me during this journey!

I am so grateful to my author friend, Doris Eraldi, for letting me pester her unmercifully for her advice! I love your books Doris, and you inspired me to press on!

Thank you to my wonderful friends at the Ridgewood Ranch for allowing me the use of the Ranch logo for my publishing company! I feel forever connected to Seabiscuit through you!

Many, *many* thanks to my editor, Jon D'Amore. You helped me more than you will ever know! I'm so grateful you were there to hold my hand and guide me through this maze we call self-publishing. Your book "The Boss *Always* Sits in the Back" ROCKS!!!!!!!!! I can't wait to see the movie!

Thank you to my sister, Jonnie Geber, and her husband, Terry, who read a first copy of the manuscript. She gave me constant encouragement and wouldn't let me give up!

And, lastly, a giant THANK YOU and I LOVE YOU to my family; Johnny, Kim, Randi, Jaime, Shane, and Corey. YOU are the reason I had to tell this story.

About the Author

Roni McFadden is the mother of four and grandmother of fifteen. She lives in Willits, California with her husband of forty years, John.

Little did they know when moving to Northern California that the property they bought and built a house on was once part of the Ridgewood Ranch, home of the famous racehorse Seabiscuit. Roni began a career with the equine vets that have cared for the horses at the ranch for over twenty years, and through that connection was able to write and publish her first book. "Josephine~A Tale of Hope and Happy Endings" is a children's book about a great granddaughter of the legendary Seabiscuit who becomes orphaned at four days of age and follows the filly as she is accepted by a surrogate mare. All proceeds from the sale of "Josephine" go to the Howard Hospital Foundation and the T.R.A.I.L. therapeutic riding program at the Ridgewood Ranch in Willits, CA.

Roni's association with Josephine and the Ridgewood Ranch enabled her to start her own small publishing company, which she named "The Biscuit Press." Are there more books planned?

Yes!

Made in the USA
Coppell, TX
15 November 2020